TODAY'S HANDBOOK PLUS

This book is the property of:

Last name:_____   First name: _____

You are soon going to find yourself behind the wheel of a motorized vehicle assuming some very serious responsibilities. Your goal will be to share the roadway with all the other vehicles, cyclists, and pedestrians in such a manner as to acquit yourself both DEFENSIVELY, INTELLIGENTLY and COOPERATIVELY.

This text, presented in a concise, informative and instructional format, synthesizes the improvements that both science and research have made in the strategies needed to safely and intelligently operate a vehicle in this day and age on our modern highways.

Your best teacher will be experience, but it must be based on the professional training you received from a traffic safety education program. Building on this training, you have a solid foundation on which you can continue developing your skills. Your driving will then be a safe, pleasant and rewarding experience.

Charles D. Torreiro

Charles D. Torreiro
AUTHOR / EDITOR

Eric Beaulieu
Charles L.D. Torreiro
ILLUSTRATORS &
GRAPHIC DESIGN

William M. Cole, PhD
Byron Briton
North Shore Driving School
Dan Com Inc
Jason Stolz
CAE Safety Consultants
CONSULTANTS

CINTOR DESIGN
Cindy Torreiro
COVER DESIGN

www.ntsa-drivers-ed.com
info@ntsa-drivers-ed.com
cdtorreiro@yahoo.com

7953 Duranceau
LaSalle, Québec
Canada H8P 3R8

Toll-free: (866) 475-1999
Tel.: (514) 363-2999
Fax: (514) 365-8367

 *TRAFFIC SAFETY PUBLISHERS WISHES TO THANK ALL THE REVIEWERS AND CONSULTANTS WHO HELPED IN THE PRODUCTION OF THIS MANUAL!*

Bob Ouellette and Steve McNeish
AAA Driving School
Allied Group
Connecticut

Dave Zak
Director of Training
a-Adams School of Driving
Illinois

Jack Sousa
President
Academy of Driving
Connecticut

Sharon Postigo
President
D&D Driving School
Ohio

Thomas A. Pecoraro and Paul R. Starks
Directors
I Drive Smart
Maryland

Jack and Sheila Varnado
Directors
Louisiana Driving School
Louisiana

Brad Huspek
School Administrator
Sears Authorized Driving School
Michigan

CONTENTS

MODULE ONE

MODULE TWO

MODULE THREE

CHAPTER 5 - ROAD RAGE

CHAPTER 6 - ALCOHOL & OTHER DRUGS

MODULE FOUR

CHAPTER 7 - PRELIMINARIES

CHAPTER 8 - KNOWING YOUR VEHICLE

CHAPTER 9 - BASIC MANEUVERS

CONTENTS

MODULE FIVE

CHAPTER 10 - DEFENSIVE DRIVING

MODULE SIX

CHAPTER 11 - LAWS OF PHYSICS

CHAPTER 12 - STOPPING DISTANCES

CHAPTER 13 - SAFETY TECHNOLOGY

MODULE SEVEN

CHAPTER 14 - DRIVING TECHNIQUES

MODULE TEN

GLOSSARY

INDEX

The Highway Transportation System

The United States is one of the most mobile societies in the world. A vast network of highways has been built to accommodate the public and private vehicles that provide this mobility. From pedestrians to the largest transport trucks, they all share this system.

Each individual person, whether walking, riding a bicycle or operating a motorized vehicle, is the nucleus of the safe and efficient operation of the Highway Transportation System or HTS.

The responsibility of each individual is to respect the rules of the system as they apply to him or her and cooperate with other road users. You are already familiar with the HTS as it applies to pedestrians and, perhaps, cyclists. Now that you are becoming a driver, you must become more familiar with this role and its responsibilities.

AFTER COMPLETING THIS CHAPTER, THE STUDENT MUST BE ABLE TO UNDERSTAND, IDENTIFY AND RESPOND TO:

- the concept of the Highway Transportation System.
- sharing the HTS with other road users.
- the individual role and responsibilities of road users.

Understanding the HTS

As a passenger, you have more than likely experienced some of the freedom that an automobile provides. Many millions of Americans drive countless miles every day in their automobiles for a wide variety of reasons. Meanwhile, others ride bicycles or motorcycles, drive trucks, vans, or buses to earn their livelihood, or operate emergency or other vehicles to supply essential public services. All of these people (and others) must share the same streets, roads, and highways. This inevitably leads to conflicts.

A multitude of professionals are involved in the proper planning or improvement of this complex system of roadways. From the planning, the design, to the placement of traffic control devices, engineers labor to provide a safe environment. Municipal, state and federal regulations govern all aspects of the use of the HTS. Yet, despite all of these efforts, the safe operation of the HTS depends on the attitude and behavior of each of its users.

With the freedom and mobility that the ability to drive will grant you, you must be prepared to accept the responsibilities as well. It is your duty to know the rules, to abide by them and, further, to be courteous and communicate with other road users. You are responsible for your safety, the safety of your passengers, as well as the safety of other users who share the HTS.

If your vehicle was alone on the road, driving would be a simple task. The fact is that the HTS is becoming more and more crowded every day.

Sharing the Road

In order to be able to anticipate potential hazards, it is important to understand the special needs and characteristics of the others who will be sharing the roadway.

To share the road safely and effectively, you must observe, anticipate the movements of others, and communicate your intentions. Proper management of visibility, time and space (Chapter 10) will minimize the risks that are inherent in driving a vehicle in the HTS.

PEDESTRIANS

Pedestrians are the most vulnerable and least trained of roadway users. Many do not drive and do not understand the characteristics of motorized vehicles. They may not know or obey the traffic rules and signals; nor understand the problems of visibility when driving, especially at night.

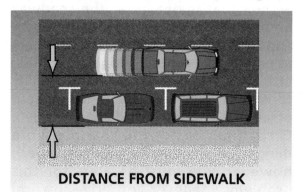

DISTANCE FROM SIDEWALK

Children are unpredictable. They are smaller and more difficult to see. Their poor judgment and understanding of the consequences may lead them to run into the roadway. Watch for them near playgrounds, schools, at the side of the road and, in many areas where they may use the street as their playground.

The elderly and the physically or visually impaired are slower to decide and then to cross the roadway. Avoid honking the horn or revving the engine; these noises are distracting and cover important audible cues used by the blind. Also avoid blocking designated crosswalks. This is an inconvenience for any pedestrian, makes

crossing a street especially difficult for the blind, and violates the rule of always yielding to pedestrians. Be patient, and give them the extra time required.

Adults, who should know better, often jaywalk or dart into the roadway without looking, especially in bad weather, when jogging or when hurrying.

Always yield to pedestrians, even when they enter the roadway improperly. Cooperate and stop when other drivers stop to yield to pedestrians crossing. Reduce your speed and increase your space from the curb in areas where they are present. Communicate, tap your horn from a distance to attract their attention. Make sure they see you. At intersections, always check for pedestrian movement before entering, whether turning or proceeding straight ahead.

SAFETY TIPS

In 2006, 4,784 pedestrians were killed and 61,000 pedestrians were injured in traffic crashes in the United States. On average, a pedestrian is killed every 110 minutes, and a pedestrian is injured every 9 minutes.

Older pedestrians (ages 70+) accounted for 15% of pedestrian fatalities; nearly one-fifth of all traffic fatalities under age 16 were pedestrians.
NHTSA - DOT HS 810 810

ANIMALS

Small animals, whether a dog in the city or a raccoon in the country, may dart into your path. Check traffic, then brake sharply if it can be done safely; never risk a collision or put someone's life in jeopardy to avoid a small animal. Swerve to avoid, only after checking carefully.

Larger animals, like deer, moose, etc., can cause considerable damage to your vehicle and its occupants. At high speed, never swerve to avoid a deer or other large animal. Rather, brake firmly in a straight line until you are stopped or the speed is reduced as much as possible.

If you are unable to stop and a crash is imminent, release the brakes just before impact. Releasing the brakes will cause the front of the vehicle to rise and lessen the likelihood the animal will come onto the hood and crash into the windshield.

Should you maintain braking upon impact, the bumper strikes lower on the legs of the animal which increases the likelihood of it coming onto the hood and into the windshield. Large animals crashing through the windshield will likely cause serious injury and sometimes death.

In either situation, you can minimize the hazard by scanning the road and the sides of the road ahead looking for any animal that might enter the roadway unexpectedly, by reducing your speed, and by leaving as wide a margin of safety as possible. Be especially vigilant at dusk, at night, in fog, and in adverse visibility conditions when signs are posted to warn of animal crossings or "Open Range". Certain periods of the year are more dangerous (June, July and November); however, you must be alert for this problem whenever you drive in rural areas. *Remember, not all of the animals are on the road signs!*

BICYCLES

Cyclists are using the HTS in ever increasing numbers for pleasure, to work, or to commute. They swerve to avoid storm drains, puddles, potholes, and debris on the roadway and may move into your path. Many disregard traffic signs, signals, and rules of right-of-way. Often they ride at excessive speeds for the driving conditions.

Check for cyclists before turning, changing lanes, or opening your door when parked. Make cyclists aware of your

SAFETY TIPS

In 2006, 773 pedalcyclists were killed and 44,000 were injured in traffic crashes in the United States. More than one-seventh of the pedalcyclists killed in traffic crashes in 2006 were between 5 and 15 years old. Alcohol involvement - either by the driver or the cyclist - was reported in more than one-third of these.
NHTSA - DOT HS 810 802

position and your intentions. Tap the horn (from a distance) to communicate. Be sure to give them plenty of space when passing in the city and even more when passing in the country where the higher speed may cause cyclists problems because of air turbulence. Never pass when there is oncoming traffic.

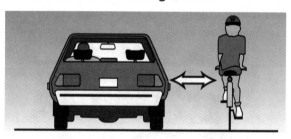

If you ride a bicycle, obey the rules, signs and signals. Ride with the flow of traffic and use hand signals to communicate your intentions. Wear light colored clothing and make sure your bicycle is properly equipped with a headlight and reflectors if you ride at night.

MOTORCYCLES

Motorcyclists are usually better trained and more observant of the HTS rules, signs and signals than cyclists and pedestrians. When properly trained, they are more mobile and can stop more quickly. If inexperienced, they may have

problems swerving, braking and handling curves. Often, they may exceed the limits of their experience.

Because of their size, motorcycles are less visible. Watch for them when changing lanes, turning (especially when turning left across their path), or when opening your door after parking. Increase your following distance when a motorcycle precedes you. Always leave them a full lane of traffic, especially when passing, even though they may only occupy the right or left third of the lane.

SAFETY TIPS

In 2006, 4,810 motorcyclists were killed in traffic crashes in the United States - the ninth straight yearly increase!

40 percent of fatal crashes in 2006 involved automobiles turning left, 51 percent occurred at intersections, and the vast majority (93 percent) on non-interstate roads. NHTSA - DOT HS 810 816

If you ride a motorcycle, learn to ride properly and practice avoidance and emergency braking techniques. Dress properly, **including a helmet**. Enroll yourself in a Motorcycle Safety Foundation approved program and learn the riding strategies and correct lane positions in traffic that will keep you out of trouble.

HEAVY VEHICLES

Vans, trucks, trailer trucks, and buses are usually driven by professionals. They have an excellent view of the road ahead because of the raised position of the driver, but this is offset by their lack of maneuvrability, longer braking distances, much slower acceleration, and extra blind spots (NO ZONES).

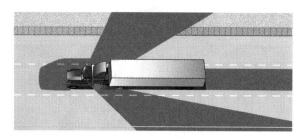

In the city, they stop frequently and may block the flow of traffic. On highways, they climb hills more slowly and tend to increase speed on downhills. Because of their size, they block your field of vision.

When you follow a large vehicle (truck, bus, recreational vehicle, etc.), increase your time interval to diminish this effect. If you increase your following distance to the point that you can see the side-view mirrors, then the driver can see you in the mirror. Your field of vision has also been improved.

When passing, realize the maneuver will take longer. Beware of the air turbulence they produce; leave extra space by moving to the side of your lane away from them. If a heavy vehicle approaches from the rear and follows your vehicle too closely (tailgates), ease off the accelerator or change lanes to encourage it to pass. Cooperate with these vehicles as they have difficulty moving in the HTS.

BUSES

Transit buses transport passengers over fixed routes and do not necessarily stop at every stop. Don't assume that they will.

A decal on the rear of the bus reminds drivers to yield and cooperate with the bus as it moves out of and back into the flow of traffic. Give them space; do not perform any sudden maneuvers in front of them (passengers may be standing), nor turn across their path while they are stopped at an intersection (they may move unexpectedly).

Transit buses are given special turning privileges at certain intersections and are permitted to proceed before other traffic at other locations. Be aware of these special situations and watch for buses that may turn beside your vehicle or move before you. On occasion, you may be required to stop prior to the corner to leave space for them to turn.

OTHER VEHICLES

Emergency vehicles - they are responding to emergencies when lights and/or sirens are operating. The law obliges you to cooperate and clear the way within the limits of safety.

Slow-moving vehicles - be patient. Follow at a safe distance. Look for a safe opportunity to pass.

Recreational vehicles - RVs - they are heavy and usually have poor road handling capabilities. Allow extra space around them and increase your following distance.

All-terrain vehicles and snowmobiles - watch for them at the sides of the road, when approaching and when crossing the road.

Responsibilities of Road Users

Each and every individual who shares the HTS is responsible for knowing the rules and regulations that govern its operation. **IGNORANCE IS NO EXCUSE.** As you progressed from pedestrian to cyclist and now, becoming a driver, your awareness and responsibilities must increase accordingly.

As a driver, you have four basic legal responsibilities: your physical condition, the condition of your vehicle, you must possess a valid driver's license for the class of vehicle that you are driving, and you must be able to satisfy the demands of state financial responsibility laws.

Throughout this text, you will learn how to utilize the HTS properly and safely as the driver of a motorized vehicle. Your legal responsibilities will be discussed in detail. Moreover, you will learn a system to prepare yourself to drive defensively, never taking it for granted that other road users will conduct themselves correctly. **EXPECT THE UNEXPECTED**. You must learn to manage your time, space, and visibility to reduce the element of risk that is inherent in the use of the HTS. Your safety, your passengers' safety, and the safety of the other road users with whom you share the roadway is **YOUR RESPONSIBILITY**.

Review

TERMS TO REMEMBER - WRITE A SHORT DEFINITION FOR THE FOLLOWING :

- HTS
- Pedestrians
- Jaywalk
- Cyclists
- Motorcyclists
- Following distance
- Tailgater
- Emergency vehicles
- Slow-moving vehicles
- Recreational vehicles
- All terrain vehicles
- Driver's responsibilities

SUMMARY

The main goal of the HTS is to facilitate the safe and efficient movement of all road users from place to place. Sharing the road requires every participant to abide by his/her responsibilities. The driver of a motorized vehicle must be aware of all the characteristics of the different individuals who may share the HTS in order to minimize the risks that they may present.

TEST A - COMPLETE THE SENTENCES BY FILLING IN THE BLANKS

1. The goal of the _____ is to enable the safe and efficient movement of all road users.

2. _____, _____ and _____ regulations govern all aspects of the use of the HTS.

3. It is your duty to know the rules, to abide by them and, further, to be _____ and _____ with other road users.

4. Pedestrians are the most _____ of roadway users.

5. Always yield to _____, even when they do not have the right-of-way.

6. _____ are less visible than other road vehicles.

7. When following a motorcycle, you should _____ your following distance.

TODAY'S HANDBOOK PLUS WORKBOOK

*Check your comprehension and mastery of the contents of this chapter by completing the corresponding exercise that is found in the complement to the **TODAY'S HANDBOOK PLUS**:*

TODAY'S HANDBOOK PLUS WORKBOOK

Complete the exercise on Pages 2 and 3. If necessary, review the chapter when uncertain of an answer and refer to your instructor for further guidance.

Traffic Control Devices

Could you imagine using the Highway Transportation System (HTS.) if there were no traffic control devices at all? No lines on the pavement! No signs! No traffic signals!

Road signs and traffic signals are the visual vocabulary of all road users that facilitate the use of the H.T.S. for everyone. It is an evolving language that all road users are required to know. Fortunately, the vocabulary is based on shapes, colors, and symbols and once-learned, permits the understanding of new signs that may not have previously been seen.

Attempts are in progress to achieve world-wide standardization of this vocabulary in our ever-shrinking global community. Until such time, we are responsible for interpreting these traffic control devices correctly, wherever you may drive a motorized vehicle or use the HTS.

AFTER COMPLETING THIS CHAPTER, THE STUDENT MUST BE ABLE TO UNDERSTAND, IDENTIFY AND RESPOND TO:

- **traffic signs, signals and pavement markings.**
- **traffic control persons.**
- **hand signals.**

2

 2-A

Traffic Signs

National standards for road signs have been set up by the National Joint Committee on Uniform Traffic Control Devices. Using shapes, colors, and symbols, as the basis of a clear and accurate language which is easily understood. It is a universal language that even the non-reader can decipher.

Before studying these signs individually, some basic principles are:

- Sign symbols are generally read from the bottom towards the top
- Arrows indicate the direction of the flow of traffic
- A black shield indicates a fixed obstacle.

THERE ARE FOUR CATEGORIES OF ROAD SIGNS

1- REGULATORY SIGNS
- Remind road users of specific rules (obligations, prohibitions, etc.) that apply in each traffic situation where they are posted.
- The background colors are red, white and black.

2- WARNING SIGNS
- Draw the attention to imminent danger or upcoming regulatory signs.
- The background color is yellow and fluorescent yellowgreen.
- The diamond shape indicates the danger is up ahead.

3- GUIDE SIGNS
- Provide information. - route markers, directions, destinations, services, points of interest or recreation, etc.
- The background colors are: BLUE + RED, WHITE + BLACK, GREEN, BLUE, & BROWN.

4- CONSTRUCTION / WORK SITE SIGNS
- Draw the attention of road users to road repairs, detours, special road closing for sports events, etc.
- The background color is orange.
- The diamond shape indicates the danger is up ahead.

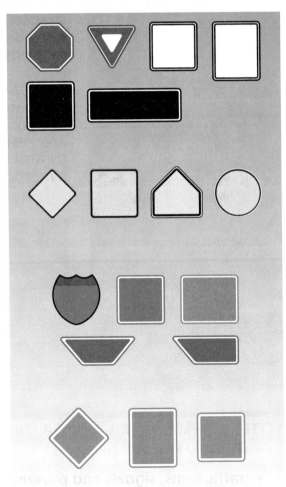

1 - REGULATORY SIGNS

Regulatory signs tell road users what they may or may not do in any specific area of the HTS. These signs are usually square or rectangular with black lettering or symbols on a white background, white lettering or symbols on a black background, or white lettering or symbols on a red background. Some regulatory signs are exceptions; they are :

UNIQUE PURPOSE REGULATORY SIGNS

The **STOP SIGN** is a red octagon with white markings. It requires a mandatory stop at the white line or before the crosswalk if there is no stop line. If there is neither a line or a crosswalk, stop before your vehicle reaches the cross street. Check that you may proceed safely after yielding to all road users that do not have to stop.

The **YIELD SIGN** - a red and white triangle pointing downward - requires that you slow (stop if necessary - when traffic is close enough to present a hazard) and give the right of way to the other traffic. Proceed when you can do so without interfering with the flow of traffic.

The **WRONG WAY SIGN** indicates that traffic is moving in an oncoming direction on this roadway. It prohibits you from entering the roadway. If you are already on the roadway, steer off the traveled portion of the road and change direction as soon as you safely can.

The **DO NOT ENTER SIGN** prohibits you from entering the roadway. Traffic is moving in an oncoming direction on the roadway; it is either a one-way road or an exit ramp for an expressway.

A white rectangle with black lettering - **DO NOT PASS** - posted on the right side of the road indicates a no passing zone. A yellow pennant with similar lettering posted on the left is a highly visible warning of the same regulation. A white rectangle with black lettering - PASS WITH CARE - indicates the end of the no passing zone.

The **RAILROAD CROSSBUCK** posted a few feet from the railroad tracks is a white X with railroad crossing in black lettering. This sign obliges some road users to make a complete stop whether a train is coming or not. Passenger vehicles should slow down and check both ways carefully. Be prepared to stop in case a train is approaching or you are following a vehicle that is required to stop.

2

SPEED LIMIT SIGNS

The **POSTED SPEED LIMIT** is the maximum or minimum speed at which you can legally drive in this particular zone based on road and normal traffic conditions. These speeds are intended for ideal driving conditions.

When road, weather, visibility, or traffic conditions are not ideal, the driver must determine the BASIC SPEED LIMIT; the speed that will be safe for the existing conditions. Normally, minimum speed limits will no longer apply in poor driving conditions.

Many states post NIGHT SPEED LIMIT SIGNS - white lettering on a black square background - because of reduced visibility at night. Like all speed limits, the night speed limit is based on ideal road conditions.

REDUCED SPEED SIGNS inform the driver that a lower speed is posted ahead; the driver should begin to slow in order to be able to comply with the reduced speed when he reaches the zone.

ONE WAY SIGNS

The **ONE-WAY SIGN** designates the direction of the flow of traffic. Signs at intersections, are posted on the near right and the far left corners or above the roadway where they are most visible to traffic from both directions.

Another indicator of a one-way street is the stop line which is painted from curb to curb (all the way across the street).

2

LANE-USE CONTROL SIGNS

LANE-USE CONTROL SIGNS mounted at the side of the roadway - white rectangles with black arrows and lettering oblige the driver in the lane indicated to travel in the direction shown, or restrict the use of the lane to certain vehicles.

Drivers must plan ahead and place their vehicles in the correct lane to maneuver in the intended direction. Do not occupy the restricted lane unless permitted

LANE-USE CONTROL SIGNS

LANE-USE CONTROL SIGNS mounted overhead designate the lane below the sign for a specific purpose. They have similar shapes and colors. They also inform the driver of the same regulations and restrictions as the signs posted at the side of the roadway. Both of these types of signs are usually accompanied by arrows and/or symbols painted on the pavement in the applicable lanes.

TRAFFIC DIRECTION SIGNS

Black lettering or symbols on a white background, these signs oblige drivers to pass on the indicated side of an obstacle or median in the roadway.

2

PROHIBITORY SIGNS

New signs using a red circle and bar with a black symbol on a white square background are gradually replacing white rectangles with black lettering. The red circle and bar means NO.

TURN PROHIBITION SIGNS

When used in conjunction with black arrows it prohibits a left turn, right turn, or U turn.

EXCLUSION SIGNS

When used with a black symbol, it prohibits the vehicle represented from using this roadway.

PARKING + STOPPING CONTROL SIGNS

These signs regulate the zones, times and days where parking or stopping is permitted or prohibited - variations occur from one municipality to another.

- **Red** - No parking, standing or stopping
- **Green** - Time limited parking.

PEDESTRIAN CONTROL SIGNS

PEDESTRIAN CONTROL SIGNS remind pedestrians of the need to walk facing the traffic on rural roads where no sidewalks are provided; limit pedestrian crossing to safe places; and instruct pedestrians on the use of the traffic control lights.

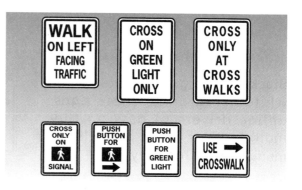

OTHER REGULATORY SIGNS

The **STOP HERE ON RED** sign is posted near some intersections with traffic lights. When the stop line is abnormally far from the corner, it indicates where you must stop your vehicle when the light is red.

The **DIVIDED HIGHWAY SIGNS** advise the driver of an upcoming intersection where the roadway is divided by a median or a separation.

Signs may remind drivers to **OBEY YOUR SIGNAL LIGHT**, or that **ONCOMING TRAFFIC HAS LONGER GREEN** whenever the timing of the traffic lights is not the same for drivers in opposing directions.

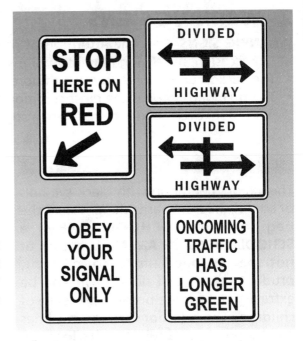

HEAVY VEHICLE SIGNS

Where an extra lane has been provided on an upgrade for slow-moving traffic, these signs direct them to use the lane.

Due to severe weakening of the road surface, condition of the pavement, or bridges, loads may be limited.

This black rectangle with white lettering indicates a weigh station for heavy vehicles, it requires these vehicles to exit and have their load limits verified.

TRUCK ROUTE and **HAZARDOUS CARGO** signs oblige such vehicles to follow the designated roadways.

2 - WARNING SIGNS

WARNING SIGNS draw the attention of road users to imminent or upcoming danger or, on occasion, upcoming regulatory signs.
- The background color is yellow (or fluorescent yellow) with black lettering or symbols.
- The diamond shape is the most common and warns of upcoming danger. The pentagon, circle, and rectangle are also used in specific circumstances.

SCHOOL SIGNS

The yellow pentagon with black symbols of school children warns the driver of the beginning of a **SCHOOL ZONE** or a **SCHOOL CROSSING AHEAD**. Whether or not special speed limits are present, prudent drivers will slow down and be extra vigilant for the possible presence of children. The addition of crossing lines on the pentagon indicates the location of the **SCHOOL CROSSING**. The possible presence of crossing guards or school patrols will help control the traffic.

ADVANCE REGULATORY SIGNS

The **STOP AHEAD, YIELD AHEAD** and **SIGNAL AHEAD** warning signs (whether using the symbols or the word messages) are intended for use on approaches to these regulatory signs. They are posted when the regulatory signs are not clearly visible for a sufficient distance to permit drivers to bring their vehicles to a stop in time under normal driving conditions. The problem may be a curve in the roadway or an overpass that obstructs the approaching driver's view.

A **TAB** indicating the distance to the regulatory sign may be installed below the warning sign.

Drivers should slow and prepare to stop.

ADVANCE TURN OR CURVE SIGNS

These warning signs, posted before turns and curves, are primarily for the benefit of drivers unfamiliar with the road. They do, however, by the symbol inform all drivers what to expect.

The **ADVISORY SPEED PLATE** may accompany a curve sign and recommend the maximum safe speed in ideal conditions.

The **CHEVRON ALIGNMENT** may replace delineators on a curve.

The **LARGE ARROW** (on a yellow rectangle) when posted in a curve warns of an especially dangerous point in the curve.

ADVANCE CROSSING SIGNS

ADVANCE CROSSING SIGNS alert drivers to unexpected entries into the roadway. The type of possible entry is symbolized on the sign.

If such crossings occur at a particular location , a tab or auxiliary distance sign may supplement these signs to indicate the distance to the exact location.

At the particular location a **CROSSING SIGN** may be posted. (The addition of crossing lines to the same sign).

Drivers should reduce their speed in order to be able to stop if necessary.

2

ADVANCE INTERSECTION SIGNS

ADVANCE INTERSECTION SIGNS indicate the presence of obscured junctions ahead. The symbol represents the situation graphically and the relative widths of the lines demonstrate the importance of the intersecting roads. These signs are not usually posted where junction or directional signing is already present.

Drivers should verify the situation ahead, be prepared for unexpected entries into the roadway, and remember that passing maneuvers are illegal when approaching intersections.

LANE REDUCTION SIGNS

LANE REDUCTION signs warn drivers of the loss of one or more traffic lanes on a multi-lane roadway. Drivers should safely enter the continuing lane as soon as possible, and/or facilitate the lane change maneuver for other drivers.

The **NARROW BRIDGE** sign warns the driver to adjust his speed so that he will reach the bridge before or after the oncoming traffic.

DIVIDED HIGHWAY SIGNS

DIVIDED HIGHWAY ENDS warns the driver that the highway ahead will no longer be divided by a physical barrier.

DIVIDED HIGHWAY AHEAD is posted on the approaches to a section of roadway where the traffic will be separated by a physical barrier.

The **TWO-WAY TRAFFIC** sign supplements the message (divided highway ends) and may be posted at intervals to remind drivers that they are no longer on a divided highway.

2

RAILROAD SIGNS

The round, yellow sign, with a black X and two R's, is a warning of a **RAILROAD CROSSING AHEAD**. Slow down, be prepared to stop, and check both ways carefully.

The tab **EXEMPT** under, this sign indicates that drivers normally required to stop, are free from that obligation in this case, **UNLESS A TRAIN IS COMING**.

CONVERGING ROADWAYS

This **MERGE SIGN** warns motorists that possible vehicles on an entrance ahead will attempt to join the flow of traffic. Drivers should be prepared to facilitate the merging maneuvers; if possible, a lane change to the left.

The **ADDED LANE SIGN** is posted in advance of a point where two roadways converge and merging maneuvers are not required - a parallel lane exists for the entering traffic. Drivers should still exercise caution as some vehicles might try to enter their lane.

WARNING - NO PASSING ZONE - SIGN

The yellow pennant posted on the left side of the roadway indicates the beginning of the **NO-PASSING ZONE**. The high visibility of this sign in passing maneuvers warns drivers from an adequate distance of the no-passing zone.

OBSTACLES IN THE ROADWAY

Signs posted on obstacles within or at the side of the road to warn and to direct drivers.

The **DOUBLE ARROW** indicates traffic may pass on either side of the obstacle.
The **HAZARD MARKERS** channel traffic to the lower end of the stripes: to the right or to the left.

2

HILL SIGNS

The **HILL** sign is posted in advance of a downgrade that requires some special precautions. Supplemental plaques with respect to the grade and the length may also be installed.

Drivers should check their brakes by applying the brake pedal and also prepare to downshift to an appropriate gear to take advantage of engine compression on the slope.

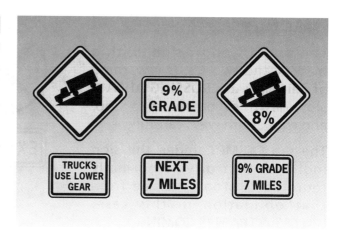

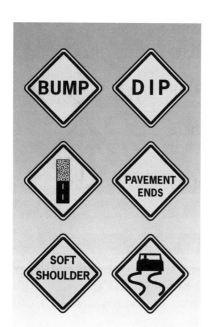

HAZARDOUS ROAD SIGNS

BUMP or **DIP** signs warn of a sharp rise or depression that creates discomfort for passengers or may deflect a vehicle from its true course. Drivers should reduce speed to minimize any possible effect on their vehicle.

PAVEMENT ENDS warns of a change in the road surface ahead. Drivers should slow down prior to the change as road traction will decrease and the danger exists of potholes at the end of the pavement.

The **SOFT SHOULDER** advises that the shoulder cannot safely support the weight of a vehicle. Drivers should avoid using the shoulder and proceed to a paved area if they must leave the roadway.

The **SLIPPERY WHEN WET** sign warns of a section of roadway where traction is severely reduced when wet. Drivers should reduce speed when wet.

SAFETY TIPS

WARNING SIGNS ALERT YOU TO SITUATIONS ON OR NEAR THE ROADWAY AHEAD.

- *You should reduce your speed and proceed cautiously.*
- *You should increase your visual search pattern to locate the hazards.*
- *You should manage your speed, time, and space to reduce the level of danger.*

3 - GUIDE SIGNS

GUIDE SIGNS are essential to direct drivers along roadways; to inform them of interesting routes; to guide them to cities, towns or villages; to identify nearby rivers, streams, parks, or historical sites; and to inform them of available roadside services. These signs are usually square or rectangular and color-coded as to their purpose.

ROUTE MARKERS

ROUTE MARKERS are used to identify and mark all numbered highways. The markers for each system, which are distinctive in shape and color, are used only on that respective system and the approaches thereto. Even numbers denote east-west; odd for north-south highways.

Auxiliary tabs such as TO, arrows, cardinal directions, or distances are often added to form trailblazer assemblies. The use of the tab with the word TO indicates that where the marker is posted is not a part of the indicated route, merely a progressive direction to the route in question.

These trailblazers inform road users and guide them to the nearest access point of the designated facility.

INTERSTATE ROUTE MARKER — INTERSTATE ROUTE MARKER — OFF-INTERSTATE ROUTE MARKER — US ROUTE MARKER — GENERIC STATE ROUTE MARKER — TRAILBLAZER — COUNTY ROUTE MARKER — FOREST ROUTE MARKER

DESTINATION SIGNS

DESTINATION SIGNS are green horizontal rectangles of varying sizes with white lettering, symbols, and numbers. They are posted to assist travelers to their destination. Arrows to indicate the direction as well as the distance to travel to the destination. The number of the roadway to be used may also be included. The word EXIT at top indicates which side to exit. On major highways, there are at least 3 signs posted prior to the exit that is identified.

Drivers should have plenty of time to prepare to exit.

2

RECREATION SIGNS

A brown background (square, rectangle or trapezoid in shape) with white lettering or symbols is reserved for **RECREATIONAL** and **CULTURAL INTEREST** signs.

They may be posted on any **conventional roadway** or **expressway** to direct motorists to facilities; to identify recreational areas and services; and to inform of cultural interest structures and places.

The concept is to guide motorists to a general area and then to specific amenities within the area without confusing these signs with other traffic control signs.

ROADSIDE SERVICES

On conventional highways, services are generally within sight and available to the traveler at reasonably frequent intervals along the route. The blue square or rectangular **SERVICE** signs are not posted on these roadways.

When such services are infrequent and are found on intersecting highways and at crossroads, these signs will be posted to advise travelers as to the location, distance, and direction.

The service legends may be either symbols or word messages - they should not be mixed.

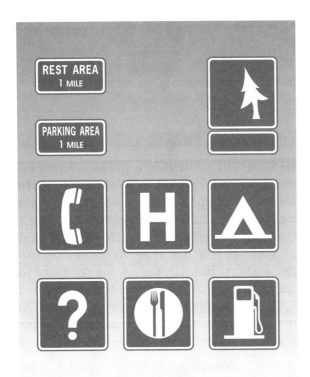

4 - CONSTRUCTION / WORK ZONE SIGNS

Signs with an orange background and black symbols or lettering are used when traffic must be moved through or around road construction work, maintenance operations, utility work, and special sporting events on or adjacent to the roadway. These signs (both construction and temporary signs) have to control a wide variety of situations and conditions and as such they present a wide assortment of messages.

SPEED

A **FLAGGER** (flag person) **AHEAD** may slow or stop the traffic (see 2-E Traffic Control Persons) as the situation requires.

The driver is well advised to reduce speed to the **POSTED SPEED LIMIT**, **SUGGESTED SPEED**, or to a speed in keeping with the abnormal driving conditions.

WORK ZONE LIMITS

These signs indicate the **DISTANCE TO THE WORK AREA**, the **LENGTH OF THE WORK SITE** and the **END OF THE ZONE**.

A **DETOUR** sign indicates that traffic must deviate around the work in progress up ahead. Square detour signs are posted to delineate the route to be followed.

CONDITIONS IN THE WORK ZONE

These signs inform of the type of activity in the area, the conditions, changes in the number or position of lanes, etc.

A reduced speed and increased visual scanning will permit the driver to adapt. This will produce extra time to judge, decide and react to these conditions.

2

International Signs

As more people travel internationally, the need to recognize international signs increases every year. Local auto clubs should be consulted prior to road excursions in foreign lands; they can supply pertinent information with respect to signs and laws for the country where you intend to travel. INTERNATIONAL signs convey their message with symbols, colors, numbers, and shapes rather than words.

MINIMUM SPEED   SPEED LIMIT   SPEED LIMIT

SPEED LIMIT SIGNS

White numbers on a blue circle indicate the minimum speed. Black on a white circle with a red border indicate maximum speed.

In some cases, the words maximum replace the words speed limit. Remember the speed limit is posted in kilometers per hour.

REGULATORY SIGNS

PROHIBITION SIGNS- a white circular sign with a red border and slash means NO. The black symbol indicates what is prohibited.

OBLIGATION SIGNS, white squares with green circles and black symbols oblige all of the traffic to proceed in the indicated direction.

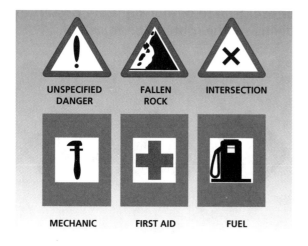

UNSPECIFIED DANGER   FALLEN ROCK   INTERSECTION

MECHANIC   FIRST AID   FUEL

WARNING AND GUIDE SIGNS

WARNING SIGNS- white triangles with red borders warn of hazards. The black symbol illustrates the upcoming danger.

GUIDE SIGNS- white squares on blue rectangular backgrounds provide information about services that are adjacent to the roadway. The symbols indicate the services.

Pavement Markings

L ines, lettering, symbols and occasionally shading painted directly on the road surface make up **PAVEMENT MARKINGS**. Sometimes special markings may also be painted on curbs and other surfaces. They are normally white or yellow in color and are used to assist in regulating the flow of traffic. These markings define lanes, delineate roadways, reinforce information given by signs or signals, and sometimes warn of possible dangers.

The most common pavement markings are lines. They are painted in two colors: **yellow lines** that separate traffic traveling in opposite directions and **white lines** that separate lanes of traffic traveling in the same direction (the thicker the line, the more hazardous the situation).

YELLOW LINES

A **CENTER LINE**, yellow in color, need not be at the geometric center of the roadway. It may be a single **BROKEN LINE** which permits passing if the way is clear; or a **SOLID YELLOW LINE** which prohibits passing (except in special cases: slow-moving vehicles, bicycles, etc.).

Center lines composed of double lines with one broken line and one solid line permit passing for drivers traveling beside the broken line and prohibit passing for drivers beside the solid line.

While driving on a two-lane roadway, you are required to use the right lane. You may use the left lane to pass another vehicle or in the event that your lane is obstructed or closed to traffic.

Before entering the left lane, you must yield the right-of-way to any oncoming traffic. The complete procedures for all passing maneuvers will be discussed later in the text in Chapter 15.

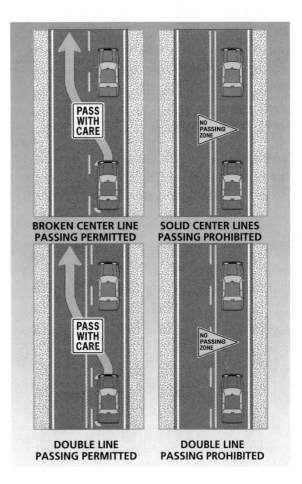

BROKEN CENTER LINE PASSING PERMITTED

SOLID CENTER LINES PASSING PROHIBITED

DOUBLE LINE PASSING PERMITTED

DOUBLE LINE PASSING PROHIBITED

2

 SAFETY TIPS

When driving, if you ever notice that a yellow line is on your right, you are traveling the wrong way. Immediately move onto the shoulder and when it can be done safely, turnabout, and drive in the opposite direction.

Many highways use raised lane markers (reflectors attached to the pavement or Pott's Dots) to guide motorists in their lane. They should appear white or yellow depending on the color of the line which they represent. Should they appear red in color, you are traveling in the wrong direction.

REVERSIBLE LANES

A **DOUBLE BROKEN YELLOW LINE** on either side of a lane indicates this lane is designed to carry traffic in one direction at certain times, and in the opposite direction at other times.

Before entering such a lane, check for signs posted at the side of the road and/or special lights installed above the lanes (see Page 2.23) to see if you may drive in them at this particular moment.

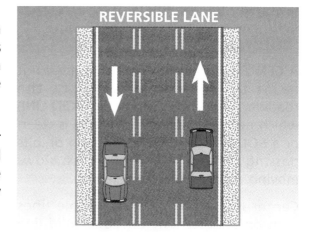

FOUR LANE ROADWAYS

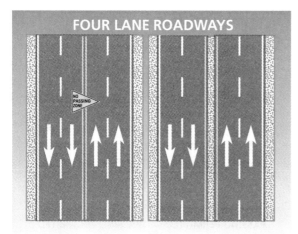

FOUR LANE ROADWAYS

On 4-lane roadways, a double yellow median line or divider (median strip) should not be crossed in either direction.

Drive in the right lane and follow the traffic flow. The left lane should be used when passing or to avoid hazards on the shoulder, as well as when you approach hidden entrance ramps or entrance ramps where vehicles are entering the roadway.

SIX LANE HIGHWAYS

The center line may be a double-yellow, though usually a median strip or concrete divider.

Drive in the right lane in order to exit or to drive at less than the posted speed limit. The second lane should be used when driving at the speed limit as well as to pass or avoid dangers from the right. The left lane should be reserved for passing. Check for reserved lanes, left exits and vehicles at high speed approaching from the rear before entering the left lane.

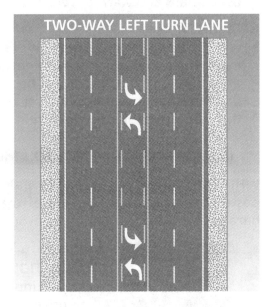

SHARED LEFT TURN LANE

Often called TWO-WAY LEFT TURN LANES, the lane is delineated by double yellow lines (one solid and one broken) on either side. This lane is reserved for vehicles turning left driving in both directions, as well as turning left into the roadway from alleys, driveways, and parking lots (*not at intersections*) (or U-turns when they are legal). At major intersections, the lane markings may change to highlight left turning bays.

Before entering this lane, check carefully for vehicles already in the lane, as well as vehicles about to enter from either side of the road and from both directions. **DO NOT DRIVE IN THIS LANE FOR MORE THAN 300 FEET!**

RESERVED LANES

One or more lanes may be reserved for special vehicles. They are delineated by double yellow lines and a white diamond on the pavement. Signs posted at the side of the road designate their use for "**Bus**," "**Bicycle**," or "**HOV**" (high occupancy vehicle and the number of occupants required), etc. Do not drive in these lanes unless your vehicle qualifies.

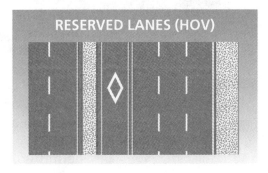

2

WHITE LINES ON THE PAVEMENT

WHITE LINES separate traffic moving in the same direction. They channel traffic into orderly lanes and assist drivers to control their path of travel. Lines are also used as:

EDGE LINES:
- mark the right edge of the roadway
- on one-way streets, the left edge line should be painted yellow but is often white in color

CROSSWALKS:
- horizontal or perpendicular wide lines delineate walkways to guide pedestrians and warn drivers

STOP LINES:
- wide lines that mark where vehicles must stop at red traffic signal lights and stop signs. These lines will be painted from one curb to the other (all the way across) on one-way streets.

OBSTRUCTION MARKINGS:
- guide traffic around fixed obstructions
- slanted stripes indicate where vehicles should not pass.

PARKING SPACES:
- controlled by white lines on the pavement. They encourage an orderly and efficient use of space while preventing encroachment on bus stop zones, fire hydrant zones, etc.

CURB MARKINGS:
- white, yellow, blue, green and red may be used to control parking.

WHITE LETTERING AND SYMBOLS ON THE PAVEMENT

WHITE LETTERING or **SYMBOLS** painted on the pavement may supplement signs posted overhead or at the side of the roadway. They may designate lanes, warn of hazards, provide information, etc. Some examples are:

LANE DESIGNATION:
- arrows indicate to drivers in a given lane, the direction that they must travel.
- the word **ONLY** indicates one direction of travel is permitted.

RAILROAD CROSSINGS:
- are delineated by a white crossbuck and double R.

SCHOOL ZONES:
- indicated by the word SCHOOL.
- SCHOOL X ing indicates where students cross.

WARNINGS:
- stops and signal lights may be lettered on the pavement.

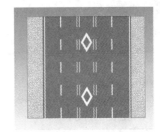

RESERVED LANES:
- white diamonds painted on the lane identify lanes reserved for special vehicles.

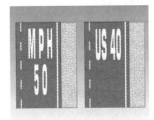

INFORMATION:
- speed limits, route numbers, and other information may be painted on the roadway.

RESERVED PARKING:
- handicapped symbol in a space reserves that space.

Traffic Signals

Traffic control signals are valuable devices for the regulation and orderly movement of vehicular and pedestrian traffic. They control traffic at one location and are clearly visible, mounted on posts at the corners of intersections or hung over the roadway. The position and colors of the signals are standardized. **When lights are inoperative, drivers should stop (proceed as if it were a four-way stop intersection).**

RED SIGNAL LIGHT

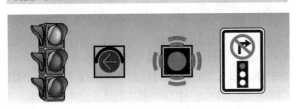

The **RED** signal light is located at the top when mounted vertically or on the left when horizontal. If the **RED LENS IS LIT,** drivers must stop their vehicles at the indicated stop line; if none is marked, before reaching the crosswalk on the near side of the intersection.

Unless a sign indicates otherwise, the driver may then cautiously enter the intersection in order to turn right. (Also to turn left from a one-way street to another one-way street.)

WARNING: turns on red lights are not universal; check with local authorities when driving in other countries.

2

If the driver intends to proceed straight ahead, he must wait for the signal to change before continuing.

RED ARROW:
- stop. Turns prohibited in the direction of the arrow.

FLASHING RED LIGHT:
- stop, then proceed only when it is safe to do so. (Similar to a stop sign)

YELLOW (AMBER) SIGNAL LIGHT

The **AMBER** signal light is located in the middle whether mounted vertically or horizontally. If the **YELLOW LENS IS LIT**, the green signal has ended and the signal is about to change to red. Drivers are required to stop. However, if the light changes to yellow and you cannot stop safely, you may continue.

Crossing an intersection on a yellow amber signal is a hazardous maneuver, it is highly recommended to stop. In order to do this, good drivers are continually aware of the traffic situation, the signals ahead as well as the traffic ahead and behind. Approaching intersections, you should "cover the brake" ready to stop.

How long has the signal been green? Will the traffic behind be able to stop?

How much space will you need to stop? These questions should be considered while nearing any green signal.

The basic concept is, when a signal light changes to yellow, **you should stop!**

YELLOW ARROW:
- if you were intending to turn, you should stop.

FLASHING YELLOW:
- slow down, proceed with caution, check before crossing the intersection.

GREEN SIGNAL LIGHT

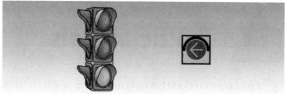

The **GREEN** signal light is at the bottom when mounted vertically and on the right when horizontal. When the **GREEN LENS IS LIT**, the driver is authorized to proceed into the intersection. This does not guarantee that the way is clear.

When a red light changes to green (fresh green), you should yield to any other vehicles or pedestrians that have not cleared the intersection. There is also a possibility of late arrivals who tried to "run the yellow." **Check the traffic to the left, center, right and left again before entering** (count of three technique). Do not enter if other road users do not appear to be stopping or are still engaged.

When approaching a green signal light, is it a "stale green?" (It has been green for some time, since you first noticed it. It might be ready to change to yellow any second.) "Cover the brake" and check traffic to the rear, be prepared to stop safely prior to entering the intersection.

If the light is still green when you pass the "point of no return" (the last chance to stop safely prior to the intersection), check the cross traffic and then proceed to cross the intersection while returning to your normal cruising speed.

GREEN ARROW:
- you may turn in the direction of the arrow after checking and yielding to pedestrians.
- this light may accompany a red signal. You may move in the direction of the arrow.
- a protected left turn.

SAFETY TIPS

In many major cities, a device called an "OPTICON" may be installed at intersections with traffic signal lights.

The device resembles a camera with a white lens. In reality, it receives a signal from approaching emergency vehicles and is intended to assign right-of-way to them (preemptive control of traffic signal operation).

At the same time, it flashes to indicate an emergency vehicle traveling along this road (either direction), or it is a steady white when an emergency vehicle is crossing the intersection.

PEDESTRIAN SIGNALS

PEDESTRIAN SIGNALS are used at intersections or crossings for the exclusive purpose of controlling pedestrian traffic.

The concept is to regulate the flow of traffic in order to allow pedestrians time to cross while minimizing the possibility of conflicts. Pedestrians are still required to check traffic with due care before crossing and to avoid causing untoward delays for traffic.

Drivers must yield to pedestrians and pay special attention to those who are visually (white cane) or hearing impaired.

- The illuminated **WALK** or a walking person symbol indicates pedestrians may enter the crosswalk.

- The illuminated **DON'T WALK** or orange hand symbol prohibits entering the crosswalk.
- When flashing hurry to safety.

In some areas, an audio signal assists the visually impaired - continuous sound to cross; intermittent sound when the lights flash; and no sound at all when they should not cross.

2

LANE-USE SIGNALS

Special overhead signals control the use of lanes on bridges, in tunnels, reversible lanes, etc. They inform road users of the availability of the lanes ahead.

 A STEADY RED X identifies the lane below the signal as a lane that you may not use.

 A STEADY DOWNWARD GREEN ARROW, indicates you are permitted to drive in the lane under this signal.

 A STEADY YELLOW X means you should prepare to vacate, in a safe manner, the lane under the signal.

 A FLASHING YELLOW X identifies a lane reserved for left turns in both directions.

 A FLASHING HORIZONTAL YELLOW OR GREEN ARROW indicates the direction in which you should direct your vehicle to change lanes in complete safety.

2-E Traffic Control Persons

Traffic control persons are authorized to direct and control the traffic flow for a specific purpose. Failure to obey them is hazardous, as well as entailing penalties similar in most states to passing a traffic signal. Some examples:

FLAGGERS (FLAG PERSONS):
- using a flag or a standard, they control traffic at construction or work sites, etc.

CROSSING GUARDS:
- using a stop sign symbol, they control traffic to protect students while crossing.

POLICE OFFICERS:
- using hand signals and/or a whistle, they direct traffic.

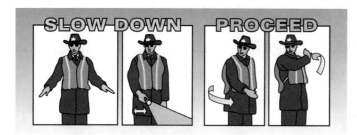

In any situation where there is a traffic signal or sign, as well as a peace officer or other traffic control person, you must obey the directions given by the person directing the traffic.

Hand Signals

Hand signals must be used to communicate road users intentions on vehicles that are not equipped with electronical signals or when the signals may be inoperative for any reason.

Road users may supplement the mechanical signals with a manual signal. This adds a personal aspect to the communication and can be more effective. Positive results from other drivers and other road users are much more likely.

You must signal your intentions (by law) with respect to any maneuvers - turns or lane changes - by signalling steadily for a sufficient distance (100 feet at 30 mph; 500 feet at higher speeds), in order to permit other drivers to react and be able to take appropriate action should it be necessary.

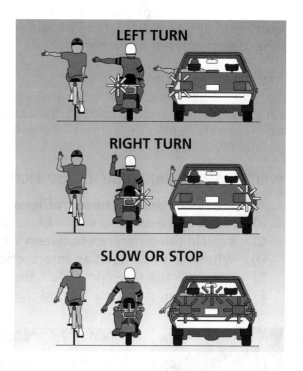

SAFETY TIPS

COMMUNICATION IS ONE OF THE ESSENTIALS TO SHARING THE HTS SAFELY. Hand signals can be used in conjunction with the electric turn signals. They often result in a more positive response from other road users. Other hand signals can be used as well - a gesture to proceed at a an intersection, for example.

2-G Review

VOCABULARY - WRITE A SHORT DEFINITION FOR THE FOLLOWING :

- Yield
- Basic speed limit
- Absolute speed limit
- Hazardous cargo

- Trailblazer
- Reversible lane
- Reserved lane
- Flagperson

- Regulatory sign
- Warning sign
- Construction sign
- Guide sign

SUMMARY

TRAFFIC SIGNS:
inform of rules, warn of hazards and provide information to assist drivers. Colors, shapes, and symbols provide a language that is easier to interpret.

PAVEMENT MARKINGS:
define lanes, delineate roadways, reinforce information provided by signs and signals, and sometimes warn of possible hazards.

TRAFFIC SIGNALS:
regulate movement of traffic at a specific location to facilitate the use of the HTS. When lights are not operating, all drivers must stop (proceed as if it were a four-way stop intersection).

TRAFFIC CONTROL PERSONS:
direct and control traffic movement for a specific reason. They override other traffic control devices.

WRITE A SHORT PARAGRAPH ANSWERING / EXPLAINING THE FOLLOWING.

1. A) Why does the HTS have traffic control devices?
   B) Name and explain the four basic categories of traffic signs.
   C) Explain the difference between white and yellow lines on the pavement.
   D) What must you do at an intersection if the traffic signals are inoperative?
   E) What are the three possible hand signals?
   F) When should you use a hand signal?

TODAY'S HANDBOOK PLUS WORKBOOK

Check your comprehension and mastery of the contents of this chapter by completing the corresponding exercise that is found in the complement to the TODAY'S HANDBOOK PLUS:

TODAY'S HANDBOOK PLUS WORKBOOK

Complete the exercise on Pages 4 through 17. If necessary, review the chapter when uncertain of an answer and refer to your instructor for further guidance.

Administrative Laws

The adoption, promulgation, and enforcement of new laws is an important step towards road safety. These laws, whether federal, state, or municipal, are compiled under a variety of names. For simplicity, the title, "THE HIGHWAY CODE" refers to all the laws that govern the operation of the HTS.

This highway code establishes norms for all motorized vehicles and their manufacturers. Rules for road sharing and safety, from professional truckers to pedestrians, are specified in these laws.

Law enforcement is the responsibility of the police agencies who patrol the HTS. Judges and the court systems will apply the penalties. Failure to obey the norms will result in fines, demerit points, possible jail terms, and/or the loss of the driving privilege.

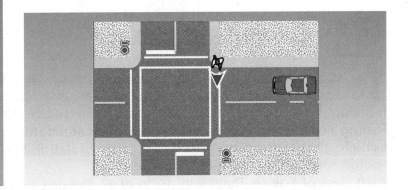

AFTER COMPLETING THIS CHAPTER, THE STUDENT MUST DEMONSTRATE KNOWLEDGE OF AND WILLINGNESS TO ACCEPT PERSONAL RESPONSIBILITY FOR:

- the licensing procedures and vehicle registration requirements.
- the rules of the road and license control measures.
- required duties in case of a collision.

3

General Information

Federal, state, and local governments cooperate to enact legislation that governs the use of the HTS.

THE FEDERAL GOVERNMENT passes laws that set general standards for the operation of the HTS. Some examples are:

- THE NATIONAL TRAFFIC AND MOTOR VEHICLE SAFETY ACT- legislating regulations for vehicle manufacturers; such as safety features, vehicle emissions and recall of defects.
- THE NATIONAL HIGHWAY SAFETY ACT- establishing general guidelines for state regulations concerning vehicle registration and inspection, driver licensing and traffic laws.
- THE UNIFORM TRAFFIC CONTROL DEVICES ACT- regulating the shape, color, and location of road signs.

STATE GOVERNMENTS, following the guidelines set by federal laws, enact statutes that regulate all aspects of the HTS: the ownership, registration and inspection of vehicles; the licensing of drivers; traffic laws and courts; and highway construction/maintenance.

LOCAL GOVERNMENTS, cities and towns, pass by-laws that regulate the use of the HTS within their regions. They govern the speed limit, one-ways, particular rules at intersections, parking rules, etc.

It is your responsibility to know the rules. Your state Department of Motor Vehicles issues a handbook on the specific rules and regulations that apply in your state. **IGNORANCE IS NO EXCUSE!**

Driver's Licenses

The state authority, the Department of Motor Vehicles (DMV), authorizes individuals to operate motor vehicles by issuing licenses according to the class of vehicle that will be operated. Certain requirements must be met to apply for each class of license. Rules vary from one state to another. Most are considering or preparing legislation, that will be called **graduated licensing**, for new drivers.
The new driver may be prohibited from driving on freeways or at night, must

have a zero BAC and be accompanied by an adult/parent. **The main concept is to increase driving privileges as the candidate demonstrates responsible and violation-free driving behavior.**

YOUR FIRST DRIVER'S LICENSE

All states have minimum age requirements (parental consent for minors) to apply for a driver's license. You must fill out an application, pass a vision screening test, a general health questionnaire, and a knowledge test (traffic signs, signals, laws, and safe driving practices) evaluated either in a written or computerized format. If you satisfy requirements and pay the necessary fees, an instruction permit will be issued.

You may then practice driving, with this permit in your possession, while accompanied by a qualified instructor or other licensed adult (in some states you may not drive at night). Once you have mastered the necessary vehicle control skills, you may go to (or book an appointment at) the registry office (DMV office) for the road test (provided you meet the legal age requirements in your state).

If you pass the in-vehicle exam, you must pay the required fees and you will receive your driver's license.

When you drive, this license must be in your possession and you must present it when requested by any police officer.

Certificate of Title/Registration

States issue a certificate of title when you purchase an automobile. It lists the owner, make, model, vehicle identification number (VIN), and engine number of your vehicle. The state retains a copy. Whenever you sell your vehicle, you must supply the new owner with this certificate.

When you purchase a vehicle, you must apply for a registration certificate from the DMV. The state will issue a registration card along with the license plates for your vehicle. This is renewable according to the procedures required by your state government.

In most states, you will be required to show proof of financial responsibility in order to receive the registration card. Proof is usually a certificate from your insurance company (Chapter 21). When you drive, you must have the registration card, insurance certificate and your license in your possession and be prepared to present it if requested or if you are involved in a collision.

License Control Measures

A driver's license is a privilege, not a right, that is granted by the state. This also means that the DMV may refuse to issue or renew a license to individuals who don't meet the necessary standards.

Those persons who will be refused are :
- not of legal age
- unable to show, by examination, reasonable knowledge of the vehicle code, signs and signals (and simple English used in traffic control signs)
- unable to show minimum competence in operating a motor vehicle
- who are chronic and excessive alcohol and/or drug abusers (alcoholics/addicts unless participating in treatment)
- who are subject to a physical/mental disability that may cause lapses of consciousness, confusion, disorientation, etc. unless under medical control
- whose license from another state or legal jurisdiction is under suspension or revocation
- who refuse to surrender a valid license issued by a foreign jurisdiction.

The state also has the power to take away licenses from any drivers who have demonstrated a disregard for the rules and regulations. Because of this and the devastating toll of carnage on American highways, most state legislatures have enacted laws empowering the DMV to regulate drivers with a track record of improper use of the HTS.

The two most common methods are a system based on demerit points with prescribed penalties and a system based on automatic penalties for certain infractions over and above court imposed sanctions, usually entitled Admin Per Se.

DEMERIT POINT SYSTEM

The DMV is required to maintain a record of every individual who operates a motorized vehicle in the HTS. The system inscribes points on the driver's record for moving-vehicle violation as well as, in some states, for collisions in which the driver is held responsible by the DMV.

Upon conviction by the court or payment of the fine, a report is forwarded to the DMV and the demerit points are added to the driver's record. These points remain on record for a specified period of time or, in some states, a specified number of points can be removed for each year of point-free driving and/or a court approved Violator's Program.

The intention of this system is to identify negligent drivers by the accumulation of points. Once identified by records that have a specified number of points, they are warned by a form letter of their status and of the possible penalties that may be imposed on them. The purpose is to encourage modification of the drivers' attitudes and behavior and thereby allow them to retain the driving privilege.

Any addition of points after the warning letter will cause the DMV to send another letter announcing the intention to suspend the driving privilege if any further infractions are committed.

If a driver does not change and more points are accumulated to reach the specified level, the license will be suspended for a period of time (usually 30 to 90 days) and an administrative fee will be charged to reinstate the license once the suspension has ended. If the driver continues to commit infractions after the license is reinstated, the driving privilege can be suspended a second time for a longer period or it may be revoked for a year or more. The person will then have to apply for another license.

The revocation can be made permanent for offenders whose record demonstrates repeated serious traffic violations.

ADMIN PER SE

Many states have passed legislation that has created an administrative license suspension law (commonly called Admin Per Se) over and above any sanctions that the court may impose.

This law applies to any driver who:

a) refuses to submit to or complete the required impairment test
b) takes a breath test that shows a BAC exceeding the legal limit
c) takes a urine or blood test and the officer believes the results will show impairment

d) is driving while under suspension
e) fails to show proof of financial responsibility when requested.

The Admin Per Se law specifies that:

- the officer arrest the driver
- the driver's license is confiscated and/or the vehicle is impounded
- a suspension form is completed and served on the driver (suspension to begin 30 days later)
- the officer forwards a sworn statement of the facts as well as all required documentation to the DMV.

The DMV will review the documentation and may set aside the action against the driver if all conditions have not been met. If not set aside, the driver may request a hearing or a court review. Needless to say, if all conditions are met by the police officer, it is highly unlikely that these reviews will alter the situation.

IMPLIED CONSENT

Most states, have also enacted legislation which stipulates that any person who drives a motor vehicle is deemed to have given his/her consent to be tested for the purpose of determining the alcohol/drug content of his/her blood.

Usually, the person may choose the type of test if available; the officer may also request a blood test if evidence suggests drug usage. The person does not have the right to consult an attorney prior to deciding nor to have counsel present during the testing procedure.

3

FINES AND PENALTIES - DUI / DWI

Due to statistical data and the actions of many interest groups, society has become much less tolerant toward driving while impaired and legislation has been enacted that reflects this attitude. As a result, stiffer fines, jail terms and other penalties are imposed on any driver convicted of this infraction besides the Admin Per Se procedures.

FIRST OFFENSE
- a fine from $300 to $1,000
- possible jail term - 48 hrs. to 6 mos.
- suspension of license - up to 6 mos.

The vehicle may be impounded and the driver will be billed for storage. An alcohol rehabilitation program may be imposed. An ignition interlock device, that prevents operation of the vehicle when alcohol is detected in the driver's breath, may be required. A fee when the suspension is completed is required.

SECOND OFFENSE (within 7 years)
- a fine from $500 to $1,000
- mandatory jail term - up to one year
- suspension of license - up to 18 months
- probation - up to 5 years

The vehicle may be impounded for up to 90 days. An ignition interlock device will be required. The driver must file proof of financial responsibility with the DMV and pay the re-instatement fee before the license will be re-issued.

ADDITIONAL PENALTIES ARE ADDED IF CONVICTED OF FAILURE TO SUBMIT TO OR COMPLETE A TEST.

MISDEMEANOR VS. FELONY DUI/DWI

DUI / DWI is usually a misdemeanor; however, if anyone were injured as a result of a collision while a driver is impaired, the charge becomes a felony. A felony is punishable by a heavy fine, an automatic jail term, an extended probationary period and a permanent criminal record (just like bank robbers, murderers, etc.).

Rules of the Road

Traffic laws are important because they promote the orderly operation of the HTS. They govern the behavior of all road users and assist in predicting what others will do. They include basic driving rules, rules of right-of-way, and speed laws.

BASIC DRIVING RULES:
- Always drive to the right of the center on a two-way roadway.
- Obey all posted signs and signals

- When traffic signal lights are defective, all drivers must stop (four-way stop).
- Pass other vehicles on the left only when the way is clear (on multilane or one-way roadways, passing or overtaking on the right is permitted).
- Always communicate your intention to turn or change lanes by using your turn signals over a sufficient distance (usually 100 feet).
- Make sure maneuvers can be performed

3

safely before executing them.

- Drive at a careful and prudent speed not greater than, nor less than is reasonable and proper, having due regard to the traffic, surface, and width of the highway and any other condition then existing. Do not drive at a speed greater than that which will permit a stop within the assured, clear distance ahead.
- When following another vehicle, you must maintain a reasonable and prudent distance, taking into account vehicle speed, the road, the weather, and traffic conditions.
- Drivers must yield to pedestrians on a marked or unmarked crossing.
- When turning, drivers should turn from the closest lane to the closest lane (right to right, left to left).

RIGHT-OF-WAY

Right-of-way is the privilege of the immediate use of the roadway. **The prime directive requires all road users to yield the right-of-way to avoid a collision.**

The right-of-way rules are designed to determine who should go first when two road users want to occupy the same space. **The rules specify who shall yield to whom. They never specify who has the right-of-way.** This distinction is important. You never have the right-of-way; SOMEONE ELSE MUST GIVE IT TO YOU.

INTERSECTIONS:

- Drivers must obey all traffic control devices/signals unless otherwise directed by police/traffic officer.
- Drivers must yield to avoid a collision or to any other vehicles approaching on a road without traffic controls.
- Vehicles approaching at the same time must yield to the vehicle on the right; this rule also applies at a 4-way stop. (Exception: vehicles at a terminating road such as at a T-intersection, should yield.)
- Drivers turning left (U-turn, private property, intersection turn) must yield to oncoming vehicles.

- **GREEN LIGHT**- Drivers may proceed if the way is clear; however, they must yield to other road users (lawfully within the intersection) and allow them to complete their movements, as well as stop for pedestrians.

- **YELLOW LIGHT** - Drivers must stop before entering the nearest crosswalk

3

at the intersection or at a limit line when marked. If the stop cannot be made safely, proceed cautiously through the intersection.

- At a **flashing yellow light**, drivers may proceed with caution.

- **RED LIGHT** - Drivers must stop at a clearly marked stop line and wait for the signal to change to green before proceeding. When turning right (and there is no sign or signal prohibiting the maneuver), they must stop completely and then yield to pedestrians and vehicles already in the intersection as well as **any road users close enough to present a hazard**. (Left turns onto a one-way street may also be permitted - same rules apply.) Pay special attention to cross traffic that may change lanes into a lane that may conflict with a right turn as well as oncoming vehicles turning left.
- Treat a **flashing red light** as a stop sign.

In some cases, the lights may be **controlled by a switch in the pavement** - movement over the switch in a left turn lane, for example, will activate the left turn arrow.

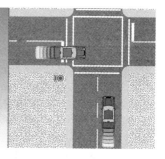

Drivers approaching an intersection MUST YIELD to road users already in the intersection.

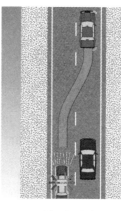

Drivers must yield to emergency vehicles when these vehicles have their sirens activated and/or lights flashing.

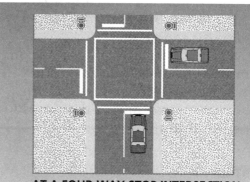

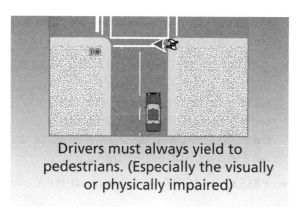

Drivers must always yield to pedestrians. (Especially the visually or physically impaired)

AT A FOUR-WAY STOP INTERSECTION

1. The vehicle that stops first, should go first.
2. The vehicle that enters first, should go first.
3. If two or more vehicles stop simultaneously, the vehicle on the left should yield to the vehicle on the right.

AFTER STOPPING, ROLL SLOWLY FORWARD TO ANNOUNCE YOUR INTENT TO PROCEED WHEN IT IS YOUR TURN.
OTHER DRIVERS CANNOT READ YOUR MIND.

3

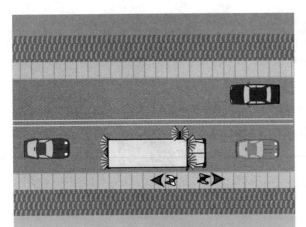

**Drivers must stop in both directions when a school bus is stopped with its red signal lights flashing.
(Some exceptions:**
oncoming vehicles **are not required to stop** when the roadway:
a) is separated by a median or physical divider [most states];
b) has four or more lanes [some states].
They should still proceed with caution.)

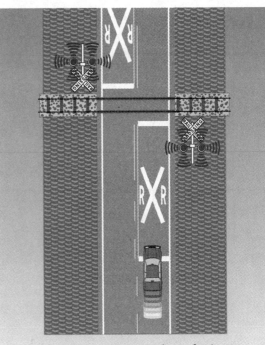

Drivers must stop when facing a railroad crossing with the lights flashing, gates down, or a train is approaching.

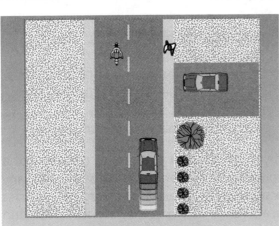

Drivers exiting private property (gravel roads meeting paved roads, lanes, etc.) must stop before the side walk, and yield to road users on the roadway.

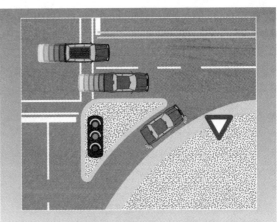

Drivers facing a yield sign must reduce speed and yield to any traffic close enough to present a hazard.

3

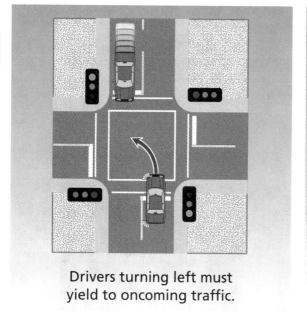

Drivers turning left must yield to oncoming traffic.

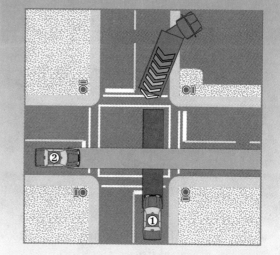

Drivers must not enter until they can cross and exit the intersection in safety.

 3-F # In Case of a Collision

Despite your best intentions, you may be involved in a collision. Loss of time, human suffering, damage to your vehicle, and legal problems resulting in great expense can be the result. Remain calm.

- Stop immediately.
- Warn others if possible.
- Enlist the assistance of others to warn and/or direct traffic.
- Give aid to the injured within your abilities.
- Call for the police and medical aid.
- Exchange information.
- Write down the names and addresses of witnesses.

- Remain at the scene.
- Make an accident report.
- Do not admit fault or sign any documents other than those requested by the police.
- Have a medical check-up.
- Report the collision to your insurance.

If you are the first to arrive at the scene of a collision, be prepared to stop and render any assistance possible. When emergency vehicles are already at the scene, reduce speed and be prepared to stop if necessary.

State law may require further reporting of the collision: DMV report showing proof of financial responsibility (insurance).

Review

TERMS TO REMEMBER - WRITE A SHORT DEFINITION FOR THE FOLLOWING :

- Vision screening test
- Knowledge test
- Instruction permit
- Road test

- Certificate of title
- Registration card
- Insurance certificate
- Point system

- Suspension
- Revocation
- Yield
- Right-of-way

SUMMARY

The highway code is a body of rules that govern the operation of the HTS. A valid driver's license, proper registration and proof of insurance are necessary to operate a vehicle. The rules of the road assist all road users to anticipate and share the roadway. Traffic violators will be prosecuted and may find their driving privilege suspended. In case of a collision, proper procedures must be followed.

TEST A - WRITE "T" BESIDE STATEMENTS THAT ARE TRUE AND "F" BESIDE THOSE THAT ARE FALSE.

_____ **1.** With a learner's permit, you must be accompanied by an instructor.

_____ **2.** Loaning your driver's license to someone else is permitted.

_____ **3.** You must inform the DMV of any change of address.

_____ **4.** It is illegal to drive while impaired by drugs or alcohol.

_____ **5.** Criminal code traffic infractions entail a minimum one year revocation.

_____ **6.** When a license is suspended for demerit points, all points are erased.

_____ **7.** Right-of-way is always given to the vehicle on the right.

_____ **8.** Using turn signals before a maneuver is always required by law.

_____ **9.** At a railway crossing, all vehicles are always required to stop.

_____ **10.** After a collision, you are always required to call for a peace officer.

TEST B - MATCH THE ITEMS IN COLUMN B TO THE ITEMS IN COLUMN A BY WRITING THE CORRECT NUMBER IN THE SPACE PROVIDED.

COLUMN A

_____ A) Graduated license

_____ B) Learners permit

_____ C) Registration

_____ D) Demerit system

_____ E) Admin Per Se

_____ F) Implied consent

_____ G) Right-of-way

_____ H) Four-way stop

_____ I) Yield

_____ J) Witness

COLUMN B

1) An administrative license suspension law over and above court imposed sanctions.

2) Card identifying ownership of a vehicle.

3) New driver license with some limitations, such as zero BAC.

4) The immediate use of a portion of the HTS.

5) An individual who is willing to provide details or information as to what he/she has seen.

6) To give another road user the immediate use of the roadway.

7) A license control measure used to identify and correct negligent drivers.

8) An intersection with stop signs controlling the flow of traffic in all directions.

9) Legislation requiring every driver to submit to an alcohol/drug test upon request.

10) A learning license permitting a beginner to drive accompanied by a licensed adult.

TODAY'S HANDBOOK PLUS WORKBOOK

Check your comprehension and mastery of the contents of this chapter by completing the corresponding exercises that are found in the complement to the TODAY'S HANDBOOK PLUS:

TODAY'S HANDBOOK PLUS WORKBOOK

Complete the exercise on Pages 18 through 29. If necessary, review the chapter when uncertain of an answer and refer to your instructor for further guidance.

Physical & Mental Health

Road conditions, the driver, and the vehicle are all elements in the safe and proper operation of the Highway Transportation System. Despite the many administrative rules and controls, the corner-stone of traffic safety is the driver. The physical and mental fitness of the human being who will sit behind the steering wheel will be the final determination of the efficient and safe use of the HTS.

Medication, physical impairments, alcohol, drugs, fatigue, vision, and visual skills are some of the factors that can affect the driver's degree of attention, alertness, and ability to drive. In this chapter, we will examine some of these factors in detail. The following chapters will deal exclusively with the problem of road rage and then alcohol and the driving task.

AFTER COMPLETING THIS CHAPTER, THE STUDENT MUST BE ABLE TO DEMONSTRATE COMPETENCE IN HIS/HER KNOWLEDGE OF:

- **physical health factors affecting driving skills.**
- **mental health factors affecting driving skills.**
- **the attributes of human vision and the other senses.**
- **controlling distractions and limiting their effect on the driving task.**

Physical Health

The driving task is not simply a robotic execution of maneuvers. Though not seemingly physically demanding, driving requires attention, decision making, coordination, and proper action. Many factors may have a profound influence on a driver's ability to perform.

Your nervous and muscular systems combine to provide the coordination necessary to drive. Different people have different levels of ability. The key is to adapt your driving to the level of your personal skills. As well, it is important to drive when your condition is at its best and to refrain from driving whenever it is not. Know your own limits.

AGE affects coordination and vision. Young drivers have the advantage; and yet, statistics demonstrate that younger drivers have more collisions. Older drivers, having slower reflexes and reduced hearing and vision, have fewer collisions because they adapt by driving more slowly. They depend on their experience to avoid critical situations.

YOUNG NOVICE DRIVERS with quick reflexes and excellent vision have to learn to control their impulsiveness, develop their judgment, and build up their experience, thus avoiding the pitfalls that produce collisions.

Some physical disabilities are temporary in nature, yet the driver must be able to compensate for them.

SOMETIMES THE DECISION NOT TO DRIVE IS THE ONLY INTELLIGENT CHOICE.

FATIGUE

Driving is very much a mental activity, mainly involving seeing and thinking. Anything that affects your ability to see and think will make driving more challenging. Young drivers have a harder time maintaining accurate situation awareness, which will influence how attention is directed, how information is perceived, and how it is interpreted.

All of these elements can be impaired, either individually or in combination, by fatigue. It makes it harder for you to perceive, interpret, judge, and choose. If you suddenly face a hazard, and do manage to overcome the fatigue and choose a course of action, your reduced coordination may let you down anyway.

4

The result is that thousands are injured or killed each year by drivers who fall asleep at the wheel. About half of the victims of these crashes are under the age of 25. And because it is difficult to determine whether drowsiness was a cause, fatigue may play a role in many other crashes that are attributed to other factors. Even during day-to-day driving, such as to work or school, fatigue can fairly quickly lead to a driver dozing off. A tired driver may not actually cause a crash, but may have less than adequate reaction times when an incident does occur. These events may not make the news headlines, but they are occurring with alarming frequency.

You may not be able to avoid one or more of the above factors, but by being aware that each factor may contribute to or intensify fatigue, you can take steps to counteract the enhanced risk.

Causes of fatigue

Fatigue (mental and physical) indicates a need for rest or sleep. If you must drive, plan ahead to avoid or minimize as many of the following factors as you can:

- Lack of sleep.
- Boredom or monotony.
- Stress.
- Alcohol or drugs.
- Illness.
- Overeating (heavy or fatty foods).
- Sun glare.
- Prolonged, uninterrupted driving.
- Fixating on a single thing such as the hum of the tires or engine.
- Driving during normal sleeping hours.
- A long day at school or work.
- Time of day, especially between 1:00 and 5:00 p.m. and early morning hours.
- A day of hard exercise, such as swimming or snowboarding.
- An overheated vehicle interior.

WHAT HAPPENS WHEN FATIGUED?

Fatigue affects everyone differently, and it may affect you differently on different occasions. But by understanding the various effects below, you can see how your driving risks increase:

- Blurred vision.
- Lower vision capability.
- Misjudge speed.
- Seeing double.
- Easily irritable.
- Poor timing of actions.
- Loss of depth perception.
- Taking unusual risks.
- Drowsiness.
- Loss of control or falling asleep.

Note that drowsiness is just one of the 10 factors listed. *When you first notice any of the warning signs of drowsiness, take them seriously, find a safe place to pull off the road, and rest.*

4

WARNING SIGNS OF DROWSINESS

- Trouble keeping your eyes open.
- Difficulty maintaining a constant speed.
- Trouble keeping your head up.
- Your vehicle keeps drifting lanes.
- You cannot remember the last few minutes of your drive.

If you find that your brain refuses to scan ahead or check the mirrors frequently, then it is time to pull over and rest. The only safe way to counteract fatigue is to sleep.

IF YOU MUST STOP TO REST:

- Find a safe roadside rest area.
- At night, locate a well-lit, highly visible area.
- Turn off the engine.
- Open the window a crack to get fresh air.
- Lock the doors of your vehicle.
- Leave parking lights on and turn off all other accessories.
- Relax and just try to rest. Don't worry if you fall asleep.
- After resting, before you leave, walk around the vehicle to wake up.

MEDICATION

Many temporary illnesses may require medication. Whether "prescription" drugs (prescribed by a doctor) or "over-the- counter" drugs (purchased at a pharmacy), **ALL DRUGS MAY HAVE SIDE-EFFECTS THAT MAY AFFECT YOUR ABILITY TO DRIVE**. Care should be taken to check the labels on over-the-counter medicines. Ask your pharmacist or your doctor to ensure that you will be capable of driving while taking any particular medication.

In your everyday lifestyle, there are other drugs such as nicotine or caffeine that can adversely affect your ability to drive.

Illegal drugs are just that: illegal. Driving under the influence of drugs can result in severe penalties for anyone convicted of this infraction. Penalties usually include the suspension of the driver's license, as well as heavy fines or imprisonment, or both.

People who suffer from chronic illnesses (diabetes, heart disease, etc.) may be issued licenses, providing their condition is under medical control. Proof of their status may be required by the Department of Motor Vehicles in your state.

The physically disabled can also drive, provided they have special controls to compensate for their particular disability. These drivers must learn to adapt their driving habits and procedures.

SAFETY TIPS

Approximately 1.46 million drivers were arrested in 2006 for driving under the influence of alcohol or narcotics. This is an arrest rate of 1 for every 139 licensed drivers in the United States. NHTSA - DOT HS 810 809

Mental Health

Strong emotions can interfere with your ability to think and reason. Anger, fear, joy, and depression are some examples of these. They can affect your alertness, concentration, and decision-making - all aspects central to your safety. When strong emotions take hold, postpone driving. "TAKING A DRIVE" to solve your problems may involve you in a more serious situation.

Some techniques for coping with emotions:

- Postpone driving - or let someone else drive.
- Drive in a rational manner - apply your concentration and skills.
- Identify situations well in advance.
- Adjust your expectations.
- Avoid heavy traffic areas.
- Stop driving and rest if emotions get out of hand.

4

ALCOHOL

The effects of alcohol on driving have become a matter of great social concern. Collision statistics demonstrate a drastic toll in deaths and injuries where alcohol was a major factor (in almost one-half of all collision fatalities).

This is especially the case when teenage drivers are involved, even though they may not be of drinking age. The leading cause of death for teens aged 16 to 19 is motor vehicle crashes. In recent years, there has been a decline in fatalities due to collisions. This is due in part to developments in vehicle safety features (air bags, ABS, etc.) and also in part because of societal factors. There is, however, still a long way to go. As a responsible driver, you should **NEVER DRINK AND DRIVE**, and work to keep others from doing so.

Vision

Most of the information you need to drive is collected by your vision. The eye receives images by utilizing reflected light through the iris - like a camera - and transmits these images to the brain by the optic nerves. Each eye captures "30 to 40 images" per second.

To become a skilled driver, you must develop this eye quickness, by practice, so

that you can effectively search the roadway.

VISUAL ACUITY

Visual acuity refers to the clarity of your vision, or your ability to distinguish details up close and from afar.

Most states require a vision test to acquire a license (minimum 20/40). Most

4

problems can be corrected with glasses. Some defects result in license restrictions, and in extreme cases, a license cannot be issued.

The responsible driver should have an eye examination at least every two years or at any time that vision becomes blurred or there is trouble focusing.

FIELD OF VISION

Your field of vision includes all the area that you can see. It includes two basic types of vision:

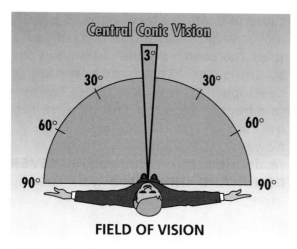

FIELD OF VISION

CENTRAL VISION: a 3 degree conic range that identifies details, color, etc.

PERIPHERAL VISION: vision to the left and right up to a total of 180 degrees for most people. It detects movement, masses, and shapes.

Your peripheral vision acts as radar to attract your attention; the central conic vision searches and identifies. The images transmitted to the brain by your two eyes

are transformed into a three-dimensional image. This produces "stereoscopic vision," enabling you to judge distance, depth perception, and measure relative speeds. All of these abilities are affected when driving at night. In Chapter 17, vision under many adverse conditions will be discussed in detail.

SELECTIVE VISION

The beginning driver, having developed the ability to search the roadway, is now faced with a situation that is called **INFORMATION OVERLOAD**. The eyes are delivering images to the brain at the rate of a couple of thousand per minute. The human brain is incapable of dealing with all of these.

You must develop a technique called selective seeing, the capability of the brain to retain and concentrate on only those images it considers important to the situation at hand. These signs, hazards, and signals relate to your driving.

A pedestrian on the sidewalk is seen; a pedestrian walking towards the roadway is seen and verified again as a potential hazard. This ability is essential to becoming a proactive driver.

VISUAL DISABILITIES

MONOCULAR VISION
People who have suffered the loss of an eye or have an inherent eye problem have to learn to assess distance, speed and safety margins

without 3-D vision. They should center their good eye on the road ahead and search more frequently. In cases of fatigue, monocular vision can develop. This is extremely dangerous because the affliction is temporary and the driver has not adapted to this problem.

COLOR PERCEPTION

Many people suffer from some form of color blindness. They must learn how to identify signs and signals by shape and position.

TUNNEL VISION

Normal peripheral vision is reduced to 140 degrees or less. People with this vision problem must search the roadway more frequently.

As you increase your speed on freeways, your normal field of vision decreases. The higher the speed, the narrower the field of vision becomes. All drivers must learn to search further ahead and more often to compensate.

4

Other Senses

On many occasions when you are driving, you will have to rely on senses other than your vision to detect problems or to enhance vehicle control.

HEARING

The ability to hear sounds can often warn you of situations both from outside your vehicle and from the vehicle itself.
A honking horn, a siren, a train whistle, the sound of squealing tires, etc. will all warn you of possible danger even before you may have spotted the hazard with your eyes. Noises from your vehicle may alert you to mechanical problems.

With this in mind, you should make sure the sound system (radio/CD or tape player) does not interfere with your ability to hear the sounds around you. People who are deaf are permitted to drive, but they must compensate by

searching the roadway and the mirrors more frequently. Often, a hearing aid may help to correct hearing deficiencies.

SMELL

Your sense of smell can also alert you to some problems while driving. The smell of smoke can warn you of a fire or an overheated engine. Carbon monoxide is odorless; however, other exhaust gases do have an odor and can warn you of the presence of exhaust fumes in the vehicle.

KINESTHETIC SENSE

The ability to sense a change in vehicle balance or motion is correctly referred to as your kinesthetic sense. This permits you to feel acceleration, deceleration, and vehicle weight transfer. At the same time, this sense will alert you to tire, steering, or braking problems which could then be corrected.

Distractions

4

While driving, you must be totally aware of the driving environment around your vehicle. The SIPDE System is based on a continuous searching of the road ahead, to the rear, and to the sides.

This information will then be used to identify hazards, predict, and then decide what vehicle control inputs are needed to reduce risk. This requires your complete attention. With this in mind, you must consciously try to avoid any distractions that will divide your attention span and thinking processes.

INSIDE VEHICLE DISTRACTIONS

A wide variety of items can distract you while driving:

MUSIC / CD PLAYER
If you are playing a favorite song on an excellent sound system, you may immediately raise the volume. The result may be that you can't hear traffic as well or that your mind is recalling some past event, thus you are not concentrating on your driving. The time it takes to insert and select music is a major distraction - plan the music prior to starting out or ask a passenger to look after it.

PASSENGERS
Whether a conversation that attracts your attention, a child that starts to act up, or a few friends that start to rough house in the vehicle, all of these situations can also distract you.

You are responsible for your safety and the safety of your passengers. Tell them to behave. Bring along distractions to amuse children. Let them know you are merely trying to concentrate on your role as driver.

PETS
Transporting pets can be a problem. This can be solved by bringing someone along to control the animal with a leash or using a pet carrying case. Plan ahead and this distraction can be solved.

CELL PHONES
More and more common today, cell phones can be a lifesaver in an emergency (car jacking, breakdown, etc.). They can also be a major distraction if the driver tries to call, take or answer text messages, etc. while driving. It is highly recommended to purchase a hands-free system with pre-programmed speed dialing. *The best suggestion is to pull over and park in a safe place before using a cell phone or text messaging.*

4

OUTSIDE VEHICLE DISTRACTIONS

The most common distractions outside the vehicle involve unusual sights that capture your attention. They cause you to stare (rubberneck) and forget the driving task for a short time. Examples of these are very numerous: collision scenes, construction zones, crowds of people, unusual vehicles, etc.

The trick is to glance at the scene and return your eyes to searching the traffic situation immediately. You can always return for another quick glance later, after you have checked your driving environment and ascertained that the glance can be performed safely.

Carbon Monoxide

Carbon monoxide is a colorless, odorless, tasteless gas that is a by-product of the internal combustion engine. It is a deadly poison. The bloodstream absorbs it faster than oxygen and it sedates the person without warning. It can cause headaches, drowsiness, dizziness, unconsciousness and, if in a large enough quantity, death.

To protect yourself and your passengers, check your exhaust system periodically and repair any leaks. Always drive with fresh air circulating in the passenger compartment. The fumes can enter through an open rear window.

Never run an engine in an enclosed space such as a garage or underground parking lot for extended period of time. In heavy traffic or tunnels, be aware of the danger and limit outside air by turning off the heater or ventilation system.

Should anyone succumb to carbon monoxide gas by falling asleep, move them out into fresh air immediately, lay them down, apply artificial respiration, if necessary. Call for emergency medical services even if they seem to revive.

SAFETY TIPS

Carbon monoxide is a silent killer! Check the exhaust system regularly and, as well, whenever increased engine noise signals a possible problem. Always drive with fresh air circulating in the passenger compartment (never the recirculation setting). Don't idle the engine for long periods in an enclosed space!

Review

4-G

- Fatigue
- Prescription drugs
- Chronic illness
- Emotions
- Visual acuity

- Field of vision
- Central vision
- Peripheral vision
- Selective seeing
- Information overload

- Monocular vision
- Tunnel vision
- Kinesthetic sense
- Cell Phones
- Carbon monoxide

SUMMARY

Your mental and physical well-being is essential to your ability to drive properly. To ensure this, avoid drugs, alcohol, stress, fatigue and anything else that may diminish your faculties.

When either your physical or mental condition are not 100%, DO NOT DRIVE.

Practice your visual skills to develop good scanning and selective seeing habits. Since most of the data you need to drive is collected through the eyes, learn to use your eyes to their utmost.

Carbon monoxide is a toxic gas that is odorless, tasteless and colorless.

TEST A - COMPLETE THE SENTENCES BY FILLING IN THE BLANKS.

1. The most important factor in all driving situations is the _____ of the driver.

2. When a doctor prescribes medication and you know you will be driving, you should _____ the _____ or pharmacist if the medication will affect your driving ability.

3. After driving for several hours, you are feeling tired, the best solution is to stop and _____ or to _____ drivers.

4. On the freeway, your normal field of vision _____ as you increase speed.

TODAY'S HANDBOOK PLUS WORKBOOK

*Check your comprehension and mastery of the contents of this chapter by completing the corresponding exercise that is found in the complement to the **TODAY'S HANDBOOK PLUS:***

TODAY'S HANDBOOK PLUS WORKBOOK

Complete the exercise on Pages 30 to 35. If necessary, review the chapter when uncertain of an answer and refer to your instructor for further guidance.

Road Rage

Aggressive driving, commonly referred to as "Road Rage," is a new arrival on the public agenda, but its roots parallel the advent of the proliferation of the automobile.

Pressures derived from employment or school, meeting the needs of our loved ones, a crowded driving environment, and declining time for personal interests and relaxation all contribute to rising stress in our modern world. More and more often, these pressures are turning to anger on our nation's roadways.

Any driver can become possessed because of the accumulation of stress and frustration. You must learn to control your emotions to avoid becoming an aggressive driver.

At the same time, you must develop strategies for coping with others who do not control their anger, or who do not drive correctly.

AFTER COMPLETING THIS CHAPTER, THE STUDENT MUST BE ABLE TO LIST AND TO IDENTIFY :

- the dangers of aggressive driving.
- the characteristics of an aggressive driver.
- the common errors made by aggressive drivers.
- the strategies for responding to aggressive drivers.

A Major Concern

The National Highway Traffic Safety Administration (NHTSA) suggests that one third of the three million injury crashes and two thirds of the resulting fatalities can be attributed directly to aggressive driving or road rage.

Realize that you are at risk from these aggressive drivers. Recent studies (the NHTSA study quoted above is only one example of many) show that thousands are reported injured or killed in North America every year due to confrontations based on road rage or with aggressive drivers.

Do not underestimate the potential for violence. Millions of drivers are armed with weapons (firearms, knives, clubs, etc.), and every driver is armed with a much more lethal weapon, their vehicle. Anyone, old or young, male or female, rich or poor, from any racial background, can become an aggressive driver and attack you. A highly stressed, angry driver is capable of incredible acts of violence, including assault and murder.

CAUSES
The Highway Transportation System is more congested than it has ever been. Despite massive construction of new roads to alleviate rush hour traffic jams, the volume of new vehicles that are manufactured and then licensed every year, exceeds the new space that has been created for existing road users.

Chronic traffic congestion is the everday commuter's biggest headache. The scenario of sitting in rush hour traffic jams for extended periods of time creates stress.

In general, people today have more stress in their lives than was common a decade ago. Whether from pressure to succeed (on the job or in the classroom) or from personal obligations (to friends and family), psychologists identify rising stress as a major factor in the many problems facing society. They have also identified an increasing disrespect for others and attitudes that condone hostility as major factors in aggressive driver behavior.

People are always rushing to get somewhere (meetings, appointments, sports or cultural activities, etc.). They tend to depart with barely enough time to reach their destination, hoping to make up time while driving; their driving becomes more aggressive in a futile attempt not to be late. This type of behavior creates more stress.

Most drivers consider their vehicle a prized and symbolic possession. It is part of their self-image. Any perceived slight to their vehicle is taken as a personal affront. With the increased driver interactions required in the congested HTS, they feel that they are being insulted on a regular basis. This creates more stress.

5

In recent years, the incidence of, or at least the reporting of, aggressive driving behavior has become more common. When we see other motorists acting in this manner, most drivers respond by picking up on the behavior and responding with similar actions. Anger and aggressive driving can be energizing, even exhilarating. The action of venting anger normally escalates the response to a higher level. Aggressive thoughts occurring in sequence provoke greater intensity of anger. Continued escalation can lead to unreasonable violence, oblivious to any consequences.

When all of these factors interact, as they do in the HTS every day, the impact on motorists is self-evident. Road rage and the conflicts between road users has become a cause of major concern. Many states have enacted laws applying more severe penalties for drivers convicted of road rage behaviors. You must develop a strategy to deal with this problem.

SAFETY TIPS

An aggressive driver will intentionally aggravate other drivers, and in some cases will cause bodily injury, property damage, and death. You must not respond to these provocations; it will only make matters worse. IT TAKES TWO TO TANGLE!

Types of Aggressive Drivers

When traffic safety experts and psychologists examined the road rage phenomenon, they have identified aggressive driving behaviors that lead to these conflicts.

Many of the early symptoms, which are suggested to contribute to the problem, are common to many drivers who have never been involved in a road rage incident in their lives. If they do not change their driving behavior, they are considered prime candidates for future incidents.

QUIET ROAD RAGE
The first level of road rage behavior, which is common to many road users, involves continually complaining about the conduct of other motorists, always rushing to get to a destination, treating driving as a competitive activity (trying to beat the other drivers), and actively

resisting the attempts of other road users to maneuver. These types of behavior do not create conflicts of themselves; however, they are the building blocks for confrontations between road users. Though other road users may not notice them immediately, ergo the name quiet road rage, they produce the environment in which aggression can easily escalate.

VERBAL ROAD RAGE

In the second level of aggressive driving behavior, drivers verbalize or exhibit their frustrations and anger. They yell, curse, and honk (a long blast of the horn) at other road users. Often, they will deliberately pull alongside another motorist and glare at him/her. Angry gestures and hand signals (not the turning or stopping variety) are used to let others know they are upset.

The aggression or anger is communicated to other road users. It has escalated to a personal confrontation. At the extreme, drivers have been known to pull over,

exit their vehicles, and proceed to have a verbal argument at the side of the roadway. How easily could this situation escalate further? Can physical assault be far away? Is violence inevitable?

EPIC ROAD RAGE

A wide variety of behavior is included in this level of road rage. Most of them involve drivers using their vehicle to frighten or to attack other road users (as a weapon), or using an actual weapon.

They cut off another motorist. They drive in front of others, deliberately slam on the brakes to get even or to scare, and then block their path of travel. Two motorists chase each other for several miles, waving and cursing at each other. A motorist rams his/her vehicle into another vehicle, or into a building where the victim is located. An enraged driver exits his/her vehicle and smashes the other's windshield.

Two drivers arguing at the side of the road end up in fisticuffs, or worse, use

5

weapons, which they keep concealed under the driver's seat, to attack one another. A motorist pulls out a firearm and shoots another road user.

All of the above-mentioned scenarios are examples of epic road rage. They have all actually occurred in the United States in recent years. This is why road rage has become a matter of major social concern.

SAFETY TIPS

As with all aspects of driving, you cannot control the environment or other road users. You do, however, have control of yourself and your actions. This is where you must start to protect yourself from possible road rage involvement. You must control your emotions and avoid offending other motorists. Correct any bad habits that may infuriate others who are already over-aggressive or angry!

Driving Errors

Traffic safety experts and psychologists suggest that you should follow the rules of the road and be polite and courteous to others. Furthermore, you should correct any unsafe driving habits that are likely to antagonize or to infuriate other road users and may lead to a road rage confrontation.

Among the identified behaviors that have resulted in violence in the past are:

LANE BLOCKING
Remember, the passing lane is for faster moving traffic. Stay out of the passing lane as much as possible. If you are in the left lane and the driver behind wants to pass, move over and let him/her pass. If he/she is speeding, it is better that they are unhappy with a citation rather than angry at you.

DON'T DOUBLE PARK

Never block the roadway or a lane in order to ask for directions or to talk to a pedestrian or other road user for any reason whatsoever. Pull over and park out of the traffic flow before conversing. Don't double park (stop beside the vehicles parked near the curb) while you, or your passenger, runs into a store to pick something up. Find a parking space and move your vehicle out of the traffic flow before running that important, quick errand. Be considerate, don't block the flow of traffic.

If you are towing a trailer (or driving slowly) and traffic builds up behind you, pull over (onto the shoulder, if necessary), and allow the vehicles behind you to pass before proceeding on your way.

If you find yourself in a turning lane, don't block the path of other drivers waiting to turn. When the traffic signal indicates protected turns may proceed, turn even though you had not intended to do so. Never block the lane by waiting for another signal.

INVADING SPACE

Other road users feel threatened when a driver cuts in too close or occupies their space cushion (putting them at risk). You react in the same way when someone else invades your space.

Don't tailgate. You must always maintain a safe and reasonable following distance. At freeway speeds, a minimum of 4 or more seconds in ideal driving conditions, more in bad weather or heavy traffic.

When preparing to pass another vehicle, don't get too close to the vehicle ahead. If you do, you will lose your speed superiority, block your field of vision, and moreover, you risk aggravating the driver ahead.

When completing the passing maneuver, don't cut back into the right lane too soon. Make sure the whole front of the vehicle is visible in your rear-view mirror before returning to the right lane. Also, do not slow down after entering the lane; it is infuriating to have to slow down because someone passed you. Maintain speed until you have a comfortable space behind you.

In merging situations, leave plenty of space between your vehicle and other motorists. When another driver is merging into traffic, cooperate and change lanes, if possible, or adjust speed to create a gap.

When changing lanes, don't cut in too close. Do not weave back and forth, from lane to lane, performing several lane changes one after another. Both of these actions cause an angry reaction from other road users. Switch lanes only when

DON'T TAILGATE

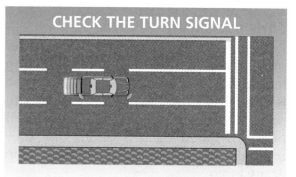
CHECK THE TURN SIGNAL

5

necessary and always follow the correct procedures.

COMMUNICATION ERRORS

Communication is one of the keys for the safe and cooperative use of the HTS. Failure to communicate, improper communication, or communicating aggressive attitudes have all created confrontational situations.

The most common aggravation is failure to signal your intentions. Always signal your intentions early, without confusing other road users; it is required by law (for the last 100 feet or 2 seconds prior to a maneuver) and is essential to reduce risk.

On some turns and all lane changes, you don't turn the steering wheel sufficiently for the turn signal automatic cancel device to function. Driving along with a turn signal flashing is both confusing and aggravating to other motorists. Remember to check the turn signal after completing a maneuver and/or use the lane changer device for lane changes.

HIGH INTENSITY HEADLIGHTS

When meeting an oncoming vehicle or when approaching close to a vehicle

HIGH BEAMS - FLASH DON'T ABUSE

ahead, driving with the high beams creates a blinding glare for the other motorist. Remember to dim to the low beams, as it is required by law and will reduce the risk of a collision, as well as a potential confrontation.

When faced with high beams, resist the impulse to get even, or to teach a lesson. Flash your high beams once, and then look far ahead towards the right edge of the roadway (oncoming), or change the rear-view mirror to the night setting (vehicle behind). Then ignore the discourtesy and continue driving.

Flashing the high beams repeatedly, whether to signal the driver to move over or to advise of high beams, is very irritating. Use this very effective communication tool sparingly; one or two quick flashes will suffice. If the other road user does not get the message, forget it, and don't get aggravated.

HORN USAGE

Honking the horn is another excellent communication device that must also be used in moderation. Use two short taps (a continuous blast is very offensive), and only when necessary. Never use the horn to attract people's attention for reasons other than road safety.

Honking the horn as soon as a light changes to green has been the cause of scores of violent road rage incidents. Avoid this aggressive habit; instead, be patient for several seconds. When you are waiting at a red light, pay attention, check cross traffic, and you'll be ready to move when the light changes.

HAND GESTURES

Using gestures to communicate the right-of-way to another road user is an excellent form of communication. However, demonstrating your emotions by shaking a fist, or even shaking your head is a definite No No! Motorists have been beaten, stabbed, and shot for this type of communication.

PARKING

When parking, make sure you park using ONE space; do not encroach on the other spaces. Never use the spaces reserved for the disabled (unless you are entitled). Avoid making any contact with other vehicles when you open the door of your vehicle. Never fight over a parking space. Let the other motorist have it if the situation arises. A parking space is not worth risking your life.

CELL PHONES

If you own a cellular phone, don't let the phone distract you while driving. Cell phone users are perceived as careless drivers and a hazard by the general public. Any error on your part while using a cellular phone may elicit a

violently unprecedented reaction from some road users.

Have your cell phone equipped with hands-free, speed dialing, and voice recognition options to reduce the possible distraction. Ideally, stop your vehicle in a safe place before using your cell phone or text messaging.

VEHICLE ALARMS

If your vehicle is equipped with a car alarm (this is an excellent idea to reduce the risk of car theft), know how to turn off the alarm. Preferably, purchase one that shuts off automatically after a short period of time. If the alarm goes off at the slightest provocation, have the sensitivity adjusted so that it does not sound unnecessarily.

SAFETY TIPS

Correct unsafe driving habits that may antagonize or infuriate other road users. Follow the rules of the road. Be polite and courteous to other road users. Give the other motorist the benefit of the doubt. Nobody is perfect.

CHALLENGING SLOGANS

Bumper stickers, flags, and slogans are common on many vehicles. Refrain from attaching any to your vehicle that other road users may find offensive and cause a confrontation.

Anger Management

Strong emotions can interfere with your ability to think and reason. Anger is a prime example. It can also affect your alertness, concentration, and decision-making; all of which are aspects that are vital to your safety behind the wheel. (It can also cause heart problems.)

You need to devise a plan of action that will maintain your self-control when you are driving. You cannot control the environment or other road users; but you can learn to control your reactions to it.

STEP ONE

You must acknowledge the fact that you can feel anger and frustration. A bad or stressful day can create a scenario where your anger can be easily escalated to the point of affecting your ability to drive.

When strong emotions take hold, for whatever reason, postpone driving. *Wind down before you crank up.* You should find a way to return to a more normal emotional level before climbing behind the wheel. If this is not possible, don't drive. It is very irresponsible to drive when you are not in complete control of yourself.

STEP TWO

Pay attention to your thoughts and feelings (anger and frustration) while driving. While driving, realize you cannot control traffic; you can control your reactions to it! When anger increases to the point that rational behavior is no longer possible, hostile behavior will be the result. Learn to spot the warning signs of stress, fatigue, and anger before the chain reaction occurs. Develop positive coping strategies.

Keep your cool in traffic! Recognize the absurdity of traffic disputes. It is important to challenge anger provoking thoughts before the successive waves of anger can compound the problem. Encased in protective metal (your

5

vehicle), don't become aggressive; realize that your vehicle is not bullet-proof, and you will have to get out of the vehicle eventually.

STEP THREE
Change the way you feel gradually, one step at a time. If you have a history of stress or anger while driving (or otherwise), *take a course in anger management.*

Plan your time wisely, instead of trying to beat the clock all of the time. Plan your trip in advance and allow extra time in case your vehicle breaks down, or in case of traffic congestion due to a crash, road construction, or rush hour traffic. Alter your schedule to avoid rush hour traffic. These adjustments will avoid stress that creates an atmosphere of competition with other motorists.

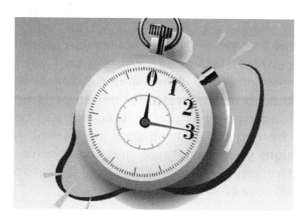

Create a soothing environment in your vehicle. Play softer, more soothing music (that you like) or some type of audio cassette (ideally dealing with stress). Use the climate and seat controls to improve your comfort zone. Concentrate on relaxing; stretch your arms and legs occasionally. If you get caught in traffic, don't get angry. Realize the delay is temporary and you'll soon be on your way.

Be courteous. Do unto others as you would have them do unto you. Courtesy is contagious and may help to diffuse a bad situation. Whether it be leaving a sports event parking lot, or a major tie-up on the freeway, calm and level heads combined with a little courtesy can work wonders. One driver's little courtesy becomes infectious. Other drivers begin to yield even when not required to by law.

A little hand signal to proceed first, combined with a friendly smile, replaces the "dog eat dog" mentality. Drivers smile and become more cooperative than usual. The situation suddenly becomes more livable for everyone concerned. Courtesy makes order out of chaos.

Give other drivers the benefit of the doubt. Don't think that other drivers do things deliberately to antagonize you. You have made mistakes while driving; so can other road users. Try putting yourself in their shoes.

Researchers tell us that young drivers are more egocentric. You see things from your point of view and you have trouble understanding how the world looks from the point of view of other people. You have to put extra effort into overcoming this problem. You are not perfect by any means. How many times have you inadvertently made the same mistake?

So, why should you expect others to be perfect? You should expect that other road users are going to make mistakes from time to time. You must try to avoid a conflict or crash, regardless of whose "error" or "fault" it was. Don't take it personally. Forget whatever happened, and proceed on your way.

SAFETY TIPS

Learn to control your emotions. While driving, look for the preliminary symptoms that warn of your anger and frustration beginning to rise. Apply the strategies that are most effective for controlling this emotion.

What To Do When Confronted

The best way to prevent road rage incidents is not to respond in kind. Don't react to provocation. Don't acknowledge the other driver and escalate the situation. Do not up the ante into a personal insult which will provoke righteous indignation and retaliation. One driver cannot start a fight alone. It takes two to tangle.

Disassociate yourself from problems that occur while driving. Keep your distance from erratic drivers. Avoid all conflicts. Don't make eye to eye contact with aggressive or confrontational road users. If challenged, swallow your pride, relax, and get out of the way. Take a deep breath. Try being tolerant and forgiving.

As a general rule, lock all doors while driving. Keep the window and/or sunroof only partially open. When stopped behind a vehicle, leave space so you can pull out and escape if someone approaches your vehicle. As a rule, follow the posted speed limits, and avoid accelerating to "run yellow traffic lights."

If another motorist pursues you, don't go home, and don't get out of your vehicle. If you have a cell phone, call for help. Drive to a police station, shopping center, or other popular location where there will be witnesses or you can get help. Once there, honk the horn or sound the car alarm to attract attention.

When you see an aggressive driver, get the license number and report the incident to the authorities. If the individual is involved in a crash, stop a safe distance from the collision, wait for the police to arrive, and then report the driver's behavior to the officer.

Review

5-F

TERMS TO REMEMBER - WRITE A SHORT DEFINITION FOR THE FOLLOWING :

- Aggressive drivers
- Quiet road rage
- Verbal road rage
- Epic road rage
- Lane blocking
- Invading space
- Communication errors
- Cell phones
- Bumper stickers

SUMMARY

With the increased stress that is prevalent in modern society, road rage has become a major concern. You must do whatever you can to control your own emotions, to correct unsafe driving habits that may provoke others, and to develop strategies to diffuse confrontations when they may occur.

TEST A- ANSWER THE FOLLOWING QUESTIONS.

1. A) Why has road rage become a major concern in recent years?
   B) What types of driving behavior characterize aggressive drivers?
   C) What are the causes of increased stress in today's society?
   D) How has increasing disrespect for others affected the problem of road rage?

2. A) What is meant by the name, "Quiet Road Rage?"
   B) Describe three behaviors that would be classified as verbal road rage.
   C) What differentiates epic road rage incidents from the other types?
   D) Identify three epic road rage incidents.

3. A) Name three examples of lane blocking behavior.
   B) When passing, what can be done to prevent invading space errors?
   C) Identify three communication errors that can cause road rage incidents.
   D) Explain how to correct the three communication errors identified.
   E) When parking, what can be done to avoid offending other motorists?
   F) What can be done about the problem of cell phones and road rage?

4. A) When confronted by a road rage incident, what should you do?
   B) If you see an aggressive driver, what should you do?

TODAY'S HANDBOOK PLUS WORKBOOK

Check your comprehension and mastery of the contents of this chapter by completing the corresponding exercise that is found in the complement to the TODAY'S HANDBOOK PLUS:

TODAY'S HANDBOOK PLUS WORKBOOK

Complete the exercise on Pages 36 to 39. If necessary, review the chapter when uncertain of an answer and refer to your instructor for further guidance.

Alcohol & Other Drugs

The use and abuse of drugs, whether alcohol or any other type, has a profound effect on the human neuro-muscular system. The driving task needs the full concentration of a person who is in ideal physical and mental condition. Any reduction in one's abilities is not acceptable.

Society has become much less tolerant. Much stiffer fines and penalties have been enacted in an attempt to deter individuals from drinking and driving and zero tolerance laws have been enacted for minors.

The media (movies, T.V., magazines, etc.) bombard society with alcohol-related campaigns paid for by the alcohol industry. By the time you become a young adult, you have been brainwashed by their message. As a future driver, you must re-evaluate your thinking regarding alcohol.

AFTER COMPLETING THIS CHAPTER, THE STUDENT MUST BE ABLE TO SYNTHESIZE INFORMATION AND APPLY PROBLEM-SOLVING SKILLS :

- **for making health-promoting decisions regarding impaired driving.**
- **to evaluate the nature of the impaired driving crash problem.**
- **to the physiological and psychological effects of alcohol (and other drugs) and demonstrate comprehension of the affect on the driving task.**

6-A Introduction to Alcohol

Where do laws originate? Are all laws in written form? Glance at the chart below which briefly summarizes the most common regulations (laws or rules) that govern your everyday life.

As the chart points out, there are many rules that are not written. This does not make them any less important, nor mean that they can be ignored. The natural laws, for example, are not; failure to heed them can lead to dire consequences, especially with respect to the driving task.

Many of the rules governing your lifestyle are absorbed by osmosis; the daily observation of others (parents, peers, siblings) obeying them. Conversely, bad habits are also acquired in this way.

A person is considered responsible when actions are in accord with the norms, whether explicit or implicit. This suggests that a person who is responsible, is accountable for his/her actions and the consequences thereof. Proper actions are rewarded; the authority in question places trust in the individual and allows more freedom of action. Improper actions, on the other hand, are penalized by removal of privileges or some other form of punishment relative to the severity of the offense.

In our daily existence, we are surrounded by rules and regulations of all kinds. Civil liabilities (tort) resulting in lawsuits, as well as government penalties, may result from irresponsible behavior.

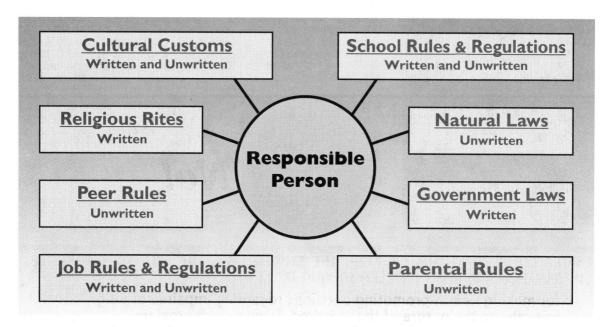

Alcohol & Other Drugs

The use and abuse of drugs, whether alcohol or any other type, has a profound effect on the human neuro-muscular system. The driving task needs the full concentration of a person who is in ideal physical and mental condition. Any reduction in one's abilities is not acceptable.

Society has become much less tolerant. Much stiffer fines and penalties have been enacted in an attempt to deter individuals from drinking and driving and zero tolerance laws have been enacted for minors.

The media (movies, T.V., magazines, etc.) bombard society with alcohol-related campaigns paid for by the alcohol industry. By the time you become a young adult, you have been brainwashed by their message. As a future driver, you must re-evaluate your thinking regarding alcohol.

AFTER COMPLETING THIS CHAPTER, THE STUDENT MUST BE ABLE TO SYNTHESIZE INFORMATION AND APPLY PROBLEM-SOLVING SKILLS :

- for making health-promoting decisions regarding impaired driving.
- to evaluate the nature of the impaired driving crash problem.
- to the physiological and psychological effects of alcohol (and other drugs) and demonstrate comprehension of the affect on the driving task.

Introduction to Alcohol

Where do laws originate? Are all laws in written form? Glance at the chart below which briefly summarizes the most common regulations (laws or rules) that govern your everyday life.

As the chart points out, there are many rules that are not written. This does not make them any less important, nor mean that they can be ignored. The natural laws, for example, are not; failure to heed them can lead to dire consequences, especially with respect to the driving task.

Many of the rules governing your lifestyle are absorbed by osmosis; the daily observation of others (parents, peers, siblings) obeying them. Conversely, bad habits are also acquired in this way.

A person is considered responsible when actions are in accord with the norms, whether explicit or implicit. This suggests that a person who is responsible, is accountable for his/her actions and the consequences thereof. Proper actions are rewarded; the authority in question places trust in the individual and allows more freedom of action. Improper actions, on the other hand, are penalized by removal of privileges or some other form of punishment relative to the severity of the offense.

In our daily existence, we are surrounded by rules and regulations of all kinds. Civil liabilities (tort) resulting in lawsuits, as well as government penalties, may result from irresponsible behavior.

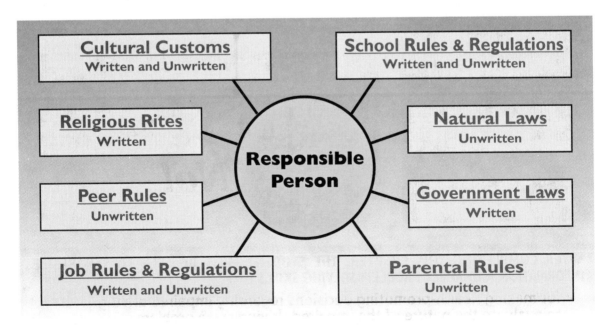

Cultural Customs Written and Unwritten	**School Rules & Regulations** Written and Unwritten
Religious Rites Written	**Natural Laws** Unwritten
Peer Rules Unwritten	**Responsible Person**
Job Rules & Regulations Written and Unwritten	**Government Laws** Written
	Parental Rules Unwritten

DRIVER RESPONSIBILITY

As a driver, you have a responsibility to obey the law, cooperate with other road users, etc. Your liability for improper action is a fine, loss of user privileges and, most seriously, the possibility of personal injury, as well as the injury or even death of other road users. In addition, you are faced with many added responsibilities which have been discussed throughout the text. In point form, they are:

PERSONAL RESPONSIBILITY
Imposed by customs, parents, peers and personal values:

- Self-preservation,
- Vehicle preservation,
- Parents' trust, and
- Passengers' trust.

LICENSING AND PREPARATION
Imposed by government.

- Vehicle operational skill,
- State rules and regulations,
- Willingness to operate within guidelines, and
- Vehicle preparedness.

FINANCIAL RESPONSIBILITY
Imposed by government and insurance.

- Ability to make restitution for errors in judgment that cause property damage, injury, or death; and
- Ability to provide a monetary pool to share costs.

TORT LIABILITY
Tort is defined as a wrong or wrongful act. Courts determine who is at fault in an action committed by an individual or driver, with government and/or civil liability as a consequence.

- Roadway property,
- Other user personal injury/death,
- Personal property of other users, and
- Personal well-being and security of other users.

You must understand that operating a vehicle allows for greater freedom and may open doors of opportunity; however, the opposite side of the coin is much more serious responsibility for a great number of decisions that affect many other road users. Poor choices lead to uninvited, serious, and sometimes long-term consequences.

Alcohol and other drugs create very serious problems related to decision-making and operating a motor vehicle. Statistical evidence demonstrates that combining alcohol with the driving task is the leading problem among youthful drivers. What is the potential for injury or death if you decide to mix drinking and driving? *Drunk driving is the number one killer of teenagers.* As a responsible driver, what choices will you make?

Although alcohol use is a choice made by individuals, use of alcohol and other drugs is controlled by laws and enforcement agencies. What will be the consequences if you choose to drink and drive? Review Chapter 3 for the short and long term penalties provided under the law for drinking and driving.

OTHER CONSEQUENCES

A conviction for drinking and driving will have many other repercussions on the life of a normal citizen. They are:

• PERSONAL CONSEQUENCES

The inconvenience of being unable to drive (alternate transportation) and the embarrassment of the conviction. If it is a felony, you may lose your voting rights, the right to own a firearm, the ability to travel to certain countries, and any future employer will regard you as a felon. This may not only be embarrassing, but downright painful.

• FINANCIAL CONSEQUENCES

Besides the lawyer's fees, fines, vehicle seizure/forfeiture, alcohol/drug assessment and information course, license reinstatement, and all the other fees related to the trial, conviction, and rehabilitation, your insurance premium will skyrocket for several years after you reapply for your license.

If someone had been injured or died, you may also face a civil lawsuit placed by the injured party or a relative of the deceased. The court judgment can exceed your earning ability for the rest of your life and/or require forfeiture of property or any other assets you may possess.

Is the short term "pleasure" of drinking

worth all of the short and long term consequences that are most likely to result? Any discussion of risk assessment and decision-making stresses three major concepts. They are:

- *Never risk more than you can afford to lose!*
- *Do not risk a lot for a little!*
- *Consider the odds and your situation!*

How would these concepts apply to decisions regarding drinking and driving?

The criminal justice system is designed to protect society from those people who are unable to make responsible decisions, or who make irresponsible decisions and choices. The consequences of high risk decisions are sometimes not known by young drivers until after the crash occurs. Ignorance is no excuse; it will not affect the consequences. Consider the facts that have been presented, you should now be in a position to make a responsible, risk-reducing decision. *Just say NO!*

Alcohol-related Crashes

The effects of alcohol on driving have become a matter of great social concern. Accident statistics demonstrate a drastic toll in deaths and injuries where alcohol was a major factor (in almost one-half of all fatal collisions). This includes both drivers and pedestrians.

This is especially the case when teenage drivers are involved, even though they may not be of drinking age. The leading cause of death for teens aged 16 to 21 is motor vehicle crashes.

In recent years, there has been a decline in fatalities due to collisions. This is due in part to developments in vehicle safety features, and also in part because of increased police surveillance, the severity of court penalties, and the actions of public groups to prevent impaired driving (MADD, SADD, etc.), as well as improved traffic safety education.

In 2006, in the United States, there were an estimated 5,973,000 police-reported crashes, in which *42,642 people were killed* and **2,575,000 people were injured**, 4,189,000 crashes involved property damage only. This works out to an average of **117 motor vehicle fatalities each day in 2006** – *one person died every 12 minutes*.

Impaired driving fatalities fell to 13,470 - 32 percent of all traffic fatalities for the year. It represents an average of *one*

impaired driving fatality every 39 minutes (a decrease compared to 2005), and approximately *one alcohol-related crash every 2 minutes*. (Source: DOT HS 810 801, US Department of Transportation, National Highway Traffic Safety Administration).

Alcohol-related crashes accounted for 17,602 fatalities in 2006 - 41 percent of traffic fatalities. No data is available, for drug-related crashes (lack of uniform and comprehensive testing). **Does this mean there were none?** What do you think?

These statistics do not talk about the emotional scars which often outlast the physical, legal, and moral consequences of crashes. The impact on the friends and families of the people affected are not mentioned either.

Since all states have enacted 21 year-old minimum drinking age laws, NHTSA estimates that these laws have reduced traffic fatalities involving drivers 18 to 20 years old by 15 percent, and have **saved an estimated 25,509 lives since 1975**.

In 2006, an estimated 990 lives were saved by minimum drinking age laws. (Visit the NHTSA - the fact sheets and annual Traffic Safety Facts report can be accessed online at www-nrd.nhtsa. dot.gov/CMSWeb/index.aspx.)

Despite the fact that the legal drinking

6

age is 21 years of age, there were 3,723 under legal drinking age drivers involved in alcohol-related incidents in 1995 (in Texas, for example). This represented almost 40 percent of all drivers involved in alcohol-related crashes.

Teen drivers are at a much greater risk of being involved in a fatal motor vehicle crash when alcohol is involved. The risk for drivers age 16 through 19 is higher than all other age groupings at any BAC level studied (age-specific analysis of data). In addition, as BAC levels increase, risk of death rises faster for this age group (see chart below).

The fact that young drivers are at such a high risk when they drink and drive was one of the prime reasons for legislators enacting the Zero Tolerance For Minors Law and raising the legal drinking age to 21 years of age. NHTSA estimates these laws have **saved an estimated 20,970 lives since 1975. You must decide never to drink and drive.**

OVER-INVOLVEMENT OF TEENS

In Texas in 1998, there were 1,054,120 under legal-drinking-age licensed drivers; **this equalled 7.8% of all licensed drivers.**

3,350 under legal-drinking-age drivers were involved in alcohol-related crashes in 1998; **this represented 12.7% of all alcohol-related crashes.**

This is a 63% over involvement by teen drivers in alcohol-related crashes in 1998.

Statistics in recent years indicate improvement. There is, however, still a long way to go. **One fatal collision** in which alcohol is a contributing factor is one too many! There is no possible justification for a responsible teenager taking the wheel, unless in complete control of his/her faculties. **The risk of injury, disfigurement and death is too real.**

As a responsible driver, you should NEVER DRINK AND DRIVE.

PERCENT OF BAC	AGE - SPECIFIC		INCREASED RISK OF DEATH	
.015 to .049	20 +		NONE	
		Teens 15 to 19		2.5 TIMES
.05 to .079	20 +		2 TIMES	
		Teens 15 to 19		9 TIMES
.08 to .099	20 +		7 TIMES	
		Teens 15 to 19		40 TIMES
.10 to .149	20 +		13 TIMES	
		Teens 15 to 19		90 TIMES
.15 and over	20 +		110 TIMES	
		Teens 15 to 19		420 TIMES

Physiological Factors

It is essential that every teen realize that consuming, purchasing, and possessing alcoholic beverages is illegal for them in every state in the United States.

AS A DRUG

Alcohol is a drug. It's a chemical (ethanol or ethyl alcohol) which is the result of fermentation. Fermentation is a process similar to digestion, but it occurs outside the body. When the pulp of grapes or grains has been literally digested by yeast, the result is ethyl alcohol or ethanol.

Because alcohol is the result of fermentation, unlike food which must be digested, it is absorbed directly into the bloodstream. It is then absorbed by all of the fluids in the body tissues. The human brain has a larger concentration of body fluids and thus absorbs a greater percentage of the alcohol.

The liver must eliminate 90% of this absorbed alcohol, at its own steady rate. **You cannot speed up the process.** The liver oxidizes the alcohol present in the bloodstream - converting it into water and carbon dioxide; approximately one alcoholic serving per hour.
(1.5 OZ. HIGHBALL, 12 OZ. OF BEER, 5 OZ. OF WINE)

There is no miracle cure. Once alcohol is imbibed, **TIME IS THE ONLY REMEDY.**

STAGES OF ALCOHOL INFLUENCE

All of the negative consequences of alcohol **start with the first drink!** They increase as each extra alcoholic beverage is consumed. They are also aggravated by your mood and fatigue. At what point are you unable to drive? At what point will the risk become unacceptable?

YOU SHOULD NEVER DRINK AND DRIVE!

What is the legal limit for an adult? What is the legal limit for a minor?

BLOOD ALCOHOL LEVEL
The amount of alcohol in a person's bloodstream can be measured by a chemical analysis of the blood, urine, or breath. In most states, a test of either breath or blood is permitted under the law and accepted by the courts as proof of impairment. The amount of alcohol present (grams of alcohol per two hundred and ten liters of breath) is expressed as a decimal and is referred to as blood alcohol concentration (BAC).

Many factors affect your BAC :
Your ideal weight, your sex, what you drink, if you eat before and while drinking, how many drinks you consume, and the elapsed time while consuming the alcoholic beverages.

Consult the charts on the next page. Base the calculations on an ideal weight

ESTIMATED BAC BY NUMBER OF DRINKS IN RELA

FEMALES

BODY WEIGHT	NUMBER OF DRINKS									
LBS	1	2	3	4	5	6	7	8	9	10
100	.050	.101	.152	.203	.253	.304	.355	.406	.456	.507
125	.040	.080	.120	.162	.202	.244	.282	.324	.364	.404
150	.034	.068	.101	.135	.169	.203	.237	.271	.304	.338
175	.029	.058	.087	.117	.146	.175	.204	.233	.262	.292
200	.026	.050	.076	.101	.126	.152	.177	.203	.227	.253
225	.022	.045	.068	.091	.113	.136	.159	.182	.204	.227
250	.020	.041	.061	.082	.101	.122	.142	.162	.182	.202

MALES

BODY WEIGHT	NUMBER OF DRINKS									
LBS	1	2	3	4	5	6	7	8	9	10
100	.043	.087	.130	.174	.217	.261	.304	.348	.391	.435
125	.034	.069	.103	.139	.173	.209	.242	.278	.312	.346
150	.029	.058	.087	.116	.145	.174	.203	.232	.261	.290
175	.025	.050	.075	.100	.125	.150	.175	.200	.225	.250
200	.022	.043	.065	.087	.108	.130	.152	.174	.195	.217
225	.019	.039	.058	.078	.097	.117	.136	.156	.175	.195
250	.017	.035	.052	.070	.087	.105	.122	.139	.156	.173

1 DRINK = 12 oz Beer / 5 oz Wine / 1,5 oz Spirits

HOURS SINCE FIRST DRINK	1	2	3	4	5
SUBTRACT FROM BAC	.015	.030	.045	.060	.075

of 150 lbs. Presume you have consumed four alcoholic beverages over a two hour period. Deduct for how much time has elapsed since you started drinking.

WHAT WOULD YOUR BAC BE ?
For a male, the answer is .086
For a female, the answer is .105

It is commonly accepted that by a BAC of .03 to .05, a driver's abilities are impaired.

By .08 in most states (any discernable amount under 21), the driver is driving under the influence, and can be charged under the Criminal Code with all of the possible penalties.

EFFECTS OF ALCOHOL ON REACTION TIME

Your ability to react to any unusual situation is reduced starting from the first drink. It deteriorates further with any continued consumption of alcohol and subsequent increase in your BAC. Needless to say, you may be slow to understand (attention), or you may understand the wrong thing. You will be slow to decide (aggression, risk-reduction decision-making) and react (or react improperly), and then the muscles will not respond normally. What a recipe for a disaster. What could the consequences be? What is the crash potential?

COLLISION POTENTIAL / STATISTICS
If your BAC exceeds .08 (red zone), you would be seven and a half times more likely to be involved in a collision; at .15, the chances increase to twenty five times. At what point does the risk of injury or death become unacceptable to you as a driver? The answer should be that you should learn to say **"NO - I'm driving."**

Any increased risk of a collision should be unacceptable! Any reduced ability to apply the SIPDE system to manage the driving environment, to make proper decisions, and to input proper driver control should not be considered at any time!

SYNERGISTIC EFFECT

NEVER MIX DRUGS AND ALCOHOL.

Alcohol, when combined with other drugs, produces a result referred to as a synergistic effect; which will be far greater than one would normally have expected. It is greater than the sum of each of the parts.

Alcohol is a primary drug. When present in your body, your system concentrates on the alcohol and ignores any other substances. Any other substance then produces a much greater effect than usual because a normal dose takes into account that some of the drug will be eliminated by your system.

Moreover, the alcohol may react with the other chemical and produce a new combination. In either case, it will have very dangerous effects and should be avoided at all costs.

EFFECTS OF ALCOHOL ON THE BODY

Alcohol has both immediate effects on the body and long term effects when the body and the internal organs are consistently assailed by the ravages of alcohol present in the bloodstream.

The immediate effects are of the most interest to you because they affect driving ability and substantially increase the risk of a collision.

ORGANS

Long term, heavy use of alcohol can lead to addiction (alcoholism). The liver, brain, and other organs can become damaged. Cirrhosis of the liver usually leads to internal bleeding, liver failure, and death.

The brain can be damaged to the point where the individual cannot function normally in society. Problem drinkers continue to abuse alcohol and create problems for themselves, their families, and their communities.

VISION

Alcohol is a depressant. It has a relaxing effect on all muscles of the body. This applies especially to the fine, delicate muscles of the eye that focus and move the eyes. When these are relaxed, the resulting image loses its sharp focus. The more relaxed the muscles, the fuzzier the picture becomes (double vision).

Rather than search the roadway ahead, to the sides, and the rear-view mirror (as a driver should), a driver under the influence of alcohol tends to stare at a point straight ahead or at any object that attracts his/her attention.

Glare from oncoming headlights or the environment produces a greater effect on the impaired driver, and the time required to recover from the glare is much longer than normal.

Possible results are:
- a tendency to stare straight ahead;
- a narrowing of the field of vision;

6

- a reduction in depth perception;
- a reduction of adaptability to darkness;
- increased sensitivity to glare; and
- a longer time to readjust after glare.

BRAIN
The activity of the brain is also slowed, thus affecting judgment, reflexes, and muscular coordination. The image from the eyes is unclear and the brain is not functioning normally due to the presence

of alcohol in combination with the body fluids in the brain tissue. What a great recipe for disaster!

Other effects of alcohol are:
- reduced awareness of danger;
- over-confidence (more reckless);
- difficulty recognizing potential hazards;
- difficulty making decisions; and
- a reduction in balance (equilibrium).

SAFETY TIPS

Summarize the adverse effects consuming alcohol produces, and you should decide never to drink and drive! JUST SAY NO!

Psychological Factors

The statistics on alcohol-related crashes indicate a need for more action to deter drinking and driving. With all this evidence, why do teenagers drink?

FACTORS INFLUENCING DRINKING

PEER PRESSURE: Many times teenagers (and even adults) do not like to admit that they are influenced by others. In reality, one of the most common reasons for drinking is because "everyone else is" or someone you wish to impress asks you to "just have one drink."

INFLUENCE OF PARENTS: Parental influence can be for good or bad. If a

teen comes from a home where alcohol is abused, this could lead the teen to also abuse alcohol.

SOCIAL ACCEPTANCE: Our culture is one which, for the most part, readily accepts drinking. Even the word "drink" has often come to mean "drink alcohol." The onslaught of media advertising, paid for by the alcohol industry, glorifies the party atmosphere and success of people who drink.

ANXIETY/FRUSTRATION: Worries about school, athletics, boy/girl friends, jobs, family, etc. are all part of growing up and normal life. Alcohol is often portrayed as a means of coping with these problems. In reality, alcohol usually makes things worse.

HAVING A GOOD TIME: Drinking is associated with "partying" for a large percentage of teenagers. This is partly due to the myth perpetuated by the alcohol industry that you will always have a good time when you consume their brand of beer, alcohol, etc. Nothing could be farther from the truth. Abuse of alcohol creates situations that are far from a "good time" (drunkenness, throwing up, being arrested, hangover, etc.).

PSYCHOLOGICAL EFFECTS

Alcohol is a drug. When consumed, it enters the blood stream and circulates to all the parts of the body. A given amount of alcohol affects each person differently and may not affect the same person in the same way every time.

ATTENTION
Alcohol affects the brain first and foremost because of the concentration of fluids in that area of the body. It usually affects a person's ability to concentrate, and especially when several sources of incoming information are present at the same time; the divided attention problem which occurs frequently while driving.

MEMORY
Under the influence of alcohol, the brain is less capable of storing and retaining information. The ultimate example of this is the "blackout"; where a person who was under the influence of alcohol cannot recall what transpired after he/she was drinking.

EMOTIONS
From simple observation of people who drink, it is obvious that emotional control tends to be lost as more alcohol is consumed. There is conflicting research in this area as to what exact effects and how serious the effects can be.

AGGRESSION
There is a direct correlation between alcohol and aggression; the more alcohol consumed, the more a person becomes aggressive. In a social situation this may lead to uncomfortable situations. In the driving environment, this can have deadly consequences.

TOLERANCE
Tolerance is defined as the need to consume more of a drug to reach a given effect, or the body's ability to eliminate the drug faster. In the case of alcohol, the body cannot eliminate it any faster, as we already explained. **What it does refer to is the person's ability to mask the effects of alcohol.** In other words, someone who drinks regularly does not seem to get as drunk; he/she does not exhibit the normal signs (slurred speech, poor coordination, etc.). This does not mean they are not affected. If they were to take an intoxilyzer (breath) test, the test would show the actual blood alcohol concentration (BAC).

6

Other Drugs

Other than alcohol, there are a wide variety of drugs, some legal and others illegal, that have a profound effect on the human body. Almost any one of these can have a harmful effect on your ability to drive.

Although limited research has been conducted on the specific effects of these drugs on the driving task, specific drug effects on humans are known. These have the potential to negatively affect driving. It is important to remember that any change a drug produces may also cause a lessening of driving ability.

KINDS OF DRUGS

Most drugs are classified according to how they affect the central nervous system and other bodily functions.

Some slow down the central nervous system and are called **depressants**. Others speed up the nervous system and are called **stimulants**. (Alcohol, for instance, is a depressant.)

OVER-THE-COUNTER DRUGS

Drugs, such as aspirin and other pain relievers, cold and allergy remedies, as well as medicines for back pain and arthritis, can be purchased at a local pharmacy, and are referred to as **over-the-counter (OTC)** medications. These drugs do not require any special permission to acquire them. Any individual may purchase them at a variety of stores.

Although these OTC drugs are not "controlled," they can cause drowsiness, dizziness, slower reaction times, reduced coordination, and other side effects that impair your ability to drive safely.

By law, OTC drugs must be labelled to warn the purchaser of any side-effects. It is important to read the package label (or ask the pharmacist) for any possible side-effect that could affect your driving ability. The dosage recommended should also be checked on the label; exceeding the dosage may cause adverse results.

DRUGS	HOW OBTAINED	POSSIBLE SIDE EFFECTS
Central-nervous system stimulants (such as diet pills, pep pills) Examples: amphetamines (Benzedrine, Dexedrine)	• Prescription only for chronic fatigue, mild depression, overweight, narcolepsy (sleep compulsion)	• Depression, headache, dizziness, decreased ability to concentrate, irritability, hallucinations, hyperactivity
Analgesics(painkillers) Examples non-narcotic - Aspirin, Exedrin, Anacin	• Over-the-counter for pain	• Bleeding in the stomach and intestines
Anti-infective agents Examples: sulfa drugs, antibiotics (Aureomycine, Penicillin, Steptromycin)	• Prescription only for infections	• Nausea
Antihistamines (in many cold pills, hay fever pills) Examples: Atarax, Benadryl, Chlortrimeton, Dramamine, Pyrilamine	• Prescription and over-the-counter for colds, motion sickness, control of allergies, nasal congestion insomnia	• Drowsiness, inattention, confusion, dizziness
Sedatives-hypnotics (sleeping pills) Examples: barbiturates Amital, Luminal, Nembutal, Noctec, Seconal, Sominex	• Prescription only for insomnia, high blood pressure, epilepsy, emotional conditions	• Mental confusion, poor muscle coordination, irritability, drowsiness
Local anesthetics	• Minor surgery, oral surgery	• Poor reflexes/judgement, fatigue
Anti-anxiety agents Examples: benzodiazepines (Valium, Tanxene, Serax)	• Prescription only for mild and moderate anxiety	• Drowsiness, blurred vision, fatigue
Tranquilizers Examples: Equanil, Halcyon, Librium, Mellaril, Miltown, Navane, Phenothiazine, Thorazine, Valium	• Prescription only for severe anxiety, emotional problems, alcoholism	• Drowsiness, faintness, vomiting, tremors, dizziness
Narcotics Examples: morphine, codeine (cough syrup). Darvon, Demerol, Dilaudid, Percodan, Vicodin (painkillers)	• Prescription and over-the counter for deadening pain, inducing sleep	• Inability to concentrate, apathy, euphoria, stupor, dimness of vision, drowsiness, nausea
Cannabinoids Examples: marijuana, hashish	• Illegal, only for medical research uses	• Less coordination, distorts distance, hallucinations, depression, panic, fear
Hallucinogens Examples:LSD, peyote, mescaline, DMT, STP	• Illegal, only for emotional illness, alcoholism (experimentally)	• Hallucinations, striking distortions in senses, hands / feet shake, floating sensation, panic, depression

6

PRESCRIPTION DRUGS

Any drug that requires a doctor to order it (on a special form with a signature) in order to purchase it legally is called a **prescription** medication.

Whether because they contain higher dosages of the same active ingredients as OTC drugs, or because they contain other, more potent elements, they are controlled by law. Records are kept of their use because these drugs can have a very strong effect on the human system.

It is vital that you ask your doctor about any possible side-effects especially relating to your ability to drive.

DEPRESSANT DRUGS

Barbiturates, tranquilizers, and sleeping pills are all depressant drugs (as is alcohol). They are prescribed to relieve tension, to calm nerves, as well as to treat high blood pressure.

Driving while taking these depressants can cause the driver to become very relaxed, lose their inhibitions (take more risks), and have difficulty applying the SIPDE System.

The "major" tranquilizers (neuroleptics) impair information processing, especially at the onset of treatment. The "minor" tranquilizers (benzodiazepines) can slow

6

reaction time, decrease eye-hand coordination, and interfere with one's judgment.

Because of the risks associated with barbiturate abuse, and the availability of safer drugs (such as the benzodiazepines), barbiturates are less frequently prescribed today than in the past. Nonetheless, they are still available, both on prescription and illegally. Even in moderate doses, they affect motor skills, coordination, vision, and vehicle handling ability.

Depressants are particularly dangerous if alcohol is also consumed (**Synergistic Effect**) because the mixture increases the collision risk enormously (particularly strong is the interaction between alcohol and diazepam - Valium). When an antihistamine (in cold, cough, and allergy remedies) is taken with a depressant drug, the resulting synergistic effect can also be hazardous due to the disruption of certain physical, intellectual, and perceptual functions.

ANTIDEPRESSANTS

The sedative effect of antidepressants (e.g. Elavik, Tofranik, Sinequan) can impair vigilance, significantly increase reaction time, and seriously affect a person's ability to handle a vehicle properly. These side-effects are especially dangerous when the driver must perform multi-tasks (divided attention), which occurs frequently when operating a vehicle in the HTS.

STIMULANTS

Any drug that can speed up, or stimulate, the central nervous system belongs in this category. Some people misuse these drugs to attempt to "stay awake" when driving at night, or over long distances. Initially, the user gets a feeling of alertness and high energy. However, the stimulant effect soon wears off (usually very suddenly), and the driver becomes very tired, very quickly (often fast asleep at the wheel).

Caffeine, in coffee, tea, and cola drinks, and **nicotine**, in cigarettes, are examples of stimulants. It is an enduring myth that caffeine in coffee can sober one up (after consuming alcohol). This is totally false, only time can lower alcohol concentration in the blood. Drinking coffee will produce a wide-awake drunk, instead of a sleepy drunk.

Amphetamines are another example. Although laboratory data indicate that most of the basic driving skills involved in in driving are not negatively affected by medical doses of these drugs, there is some evidence that they can result in over-confidence leading to risk-taking behavior. High doses make many people hostile and aggressive.

Cocaine affects the users perception, mood, and thinking. The most dramatic effect is on vision. It may cause a higher sensitivity to light, halos around bright objects, and difficulty focusing. Users have reported blurred vision, glare problems, and hallucinations (visual - weak flashes or movement of light in the peripheral field causing swerving toward or away from the light; auditory - the ringing of bells; olfactory - the smell of smoke or of gasoline).

Users claim cocaine actually improves driving ability, which is not surprising since it induces euphoria and feelings of increased mental and physical abilities. These "false" effects are short-lived, and are often followed by fatigue and listlessness. The drug also heightens irritability, excitability, and startle response (resulting in severe anxiety coupled with sudden braking or steering reactions to noise, even when far away).

Suspiciousness, distrust, and paranoia - other reactions to cocaine - have prompted users to flee in their vehicles or drive evasively. All users surveyed reported attention lapses while driving and ignoring relevant stimuli (traffic lights).

HALLUCINOGENS

Often called mind-altering drugs, hallucinogens are very dangerous. They can have unpredictable results - alter personality, cause panic or terror, distort the way a person thinks, sees, and acts.

For these reasons, selling, possessing, or using them is against the law.

Marijuana is the drug most often found in drivers involved in crashes (after alcohol). It takes only a small quantity of the active chemical in marijuana or hashish to impair the user's ability to see, steer, brake, and make correct driving decisions. The chemical can remain in the body for weeks; drug tests with positive results can result in citations and criminal charges.

Users can become drowsy and have problems judging speed, time, and space. They have been known to sit and stare while completely unaware of their surroundings. They may think that the effects have worn off when they are still impaired. When mixed with alcohol, it may mask the feelings of nausea that accompany intoxication, resulting in continued drinking (to the point of alcohol poisoning, coma, or death).

LSD and **PCP** (angel dust) are among the strongest of the hallucinogens. Users can become confused, forget who they are, where they are, and what they are doing. They have an altered sense of speed, space, time, and direction.

6

? SAFETY TIPS

Statistical evidence demonstrates that 36% of fatalities, that were tested, were under the influence of drugs (other than alcohol). Ask your physician or pharmacist before taking any prescription or over-the-counter drug. Never consume any "street" drugs!

Intervention Strategies

Every year the alcohol manufacturing community spends billions of dollars to promote and sell their products. They advertise on television, in magazines, in newspapers, etc.

They promote, sponsor or advertise at almost every major sports event, most of which are televised. If you think about it, it is almost impossible not to be influenced by this all pervasive campaign in a normal, everyday lifestyle.

ADVERTISING TARGET

The target market for this media blitz is the new drinker. Advertising agencies and the advertisers themselves design advertising campaigns, not so much to influence the existing market to change brands, but rather to enlarge the market by attracting new consumers (drinkers). These new consumers (the young) will become life-long buyers.

CAMPAIGN MESSAGE

The message is, in order to be financially successful, glamorous, have a good time, be attractive to the opposite sex, and be successful with the opposite sex (or at least appear to be), you must drink their brand of alcoholic beverage.

Very few of these ads ever mention the responsible use of alcohol, or the dangers involved in drinking and driving. The devastating toll of deaths and injuries, and the social cost of collisions that are a direct result of drinking drivers are never shown. These statistics would be a sobering message.

As a new driver and as a member of the target group for this advertising campaign, you must not be hoodwinked by the message. You must develop the proper attitude with respect to this serious problem.

You should never drink and drive. Never let a friend drink and drive. Friends don't let friends drive drunk!

INTERVENTION STRATEGIES

The question is: "What can I do?" The answer is that every individual, if he/she is so inclined, can have a profound effect on the people around them and, by a concerted campaign, on society, in general. Writing letters to legislators, the media, etc. is just one such example.

ALCOHOL ADVERTISING

The airwaves are regulated and licensed by your government, whose legislators are very responsive to public pressure. A concerted letter campaign to the legislators by concerned organizations and a large number of citizens could have the desired effect. The proposal should be for a gradual reduction in advertising that glorifies drinking, replaced by advertising which targets the responsible use of alcohol.

6

DRUNK DRIVERS

Drunk drivers identify themselves by riding the lines, weaving, driving at inconsistent speeds, intermittent braking, misjudging stops (too soon or too late), driving without headlights, etc.

When you see a driver that seems to be impaired, turn off the road into a parking lot or side street. Keep away from that vehicle; the driver could involve you in a serious crash.

Try to get the license number of the vehicle. Call the police immediately and report it along with the color, make, model, and direction of travel. In so doing, you will be instrumental in removing an impaired driver from the HTS and possibly preventing a collision involving injuries or fatalities. We are all responsible for the safety of other road users who share the HTS.

ALTERNATIVES TO DRINKING AND DRIVING

As a responsible driver, you should **NEVER DRINK AND DRIVE**.

Many other options are open to you if you are in a situation where drinking of alcoholic beverages is occurring:

THE DESIGNATED DRIVER - The person who will drive abstains from drinking alcoholic beverages and receives complimentary non-alcoholic beverages and/or food.

Encourage your friends and favorite establishments to participate in the program. (Contact your local police department for materials/info.)

S.A.D.D. or M.A.D.D. - Organized groups that support people who have been drinking and do not wish to drive. A contract is signed by the two parties stating they will come to get you - no matter what, no questions asked.

ABSTINENCE - Refuse to drink alcoholic beverages when you will be driving. Try to assist others who are drinking.

ALTERNATE TRANSPORTATION - Take a cab! Get a ride! Call home and ask a family member to come and get you! Let someone else drive who has not been drinking. Don't ride with someone who has been drinking. Try to get the car keys. Friends don't let their friends drive drunk. Do your best to convince friends not to drive; offer alternate transportation. If you can't convince them, don't ride with them.

SLEEP OVER - Stay the night at a friend's place. If you are the host, encourage impaired people to sleep over if any other alternate transportation cannot be found.

In situations where alcohol is being consumed, follow the recommendations above and encourage others to do likewise. Choose one of the options; any one you like; however, **if you consume alcoholic beverages, don't drive**.

Moreover, don't accept a ride from someone else who has been drinking.

PARTY SITUATIONS

If you host a party and the guests are not of drinking age, make sure that they are aware that alcohol will not be served and will not be acceptable. Plan a wide selection of non-alcoholic beverages, appropriate entertainment and food. You can refuse entrance to individuals who appear to have been drinking prior to their arrival.

Encourage individuals that appear to be impaired to sleep over or arrange alternate transportation. Get their keys! If guests are of drinking age, don't force drinks on them or mix drinks that are stronger than normal. Space any alcoholic beverages out (one per hour). Have a large selection of non-alcoholic beverages available.

Serve various food items throughout the evening. Discourage any pressure on guests to drink. Stop serving alcoholic beverages at least one hour before the end of the evening. Pay special attention to known drinkers.

Encourage drinking guests to sleep over or take alternate transportation home. Don't allow any impaired person to drive. If necessary, pay for the taxi.

PUBLIC HEALTH

The cost to the American public in health care, lost productivity, injuries, permanent disfigurement, etc. due to alcohol-related collisions is estimated to exceed $100 billion annually. This does not include the loss of lives, each of which would have provided some productive contribution to society.

This massive drain on American citizens, and on the American economy, cannot be allowed to continue.

ASSESSMENT OF RISK

The first step in correcting this untenable situation is for each driver to realize that he/she increases the risk of a collision and all the possible ramifications (injury, death) every time alcoholic beverages or drugs are consumed prior to driving.

The odds of it happening to you must be accepted and understood. No victim of a collision knew that it was going to happen; if this were the case, they would have done something differently to avoid the situation; **and yet, thousands die**.

This indicates that every driver is always at risk; however, alcohol/drugs increase the risk. It is like playing "Russian Roulette." At what point is the loaded chamber lined up with the firing pin and barrel? Would you play this fatal game?

WILL YOU DRINK AND DRIVE?

SAFETY TIPS

Approximately 1.46 million drivers were arrested in 2006 for DUI -alcohol or narcotics. This is an arrest rate of 1 for every 139 licensed drivers in the United States. Don't become part of the problem! BE PART OF THE SOLUTION! NHTSA - DOT HS 810 809

6

ACTIONS TO REDUCE RISK

The **SIPDE** system is applied to reduce risk. Alcohol/drugs affect the human body and diminish your ability to implement the system (the **APE** system - **ASSESS**, **PREPARE,** and **EXECUTE**) in reaction to the driving environment.

The second step is to realize that you can take positive action to reduce risk. In this case, **never drink and drive**, thereby keeping your physical and mental condition in top form to permit you to implement the SIPDE system and avoid collisions.

Over and above looking after yourself, you can also do whatever you can to reduce the incidence of others driving drunk. Assist your peers who might otherwise succumb to social pressure to drink, or who might need a lift when they have been drinking.

On a societal level, report impaired drivers to the authorities to get them off the streets (that you or your loved ones may be using). Join letter-writing campaigns and organizations that are implementing programs to reduce the incidence of driving while impaired.

SEVERE CONSEQUENCES

The third step is the realization of the severity of the unnecessary results that driving after consuming alcohol/drugs are very likely to produce.

You have a choice. You can take a stand. You never have to drink and drive.

Death, injury, and/or impairment are consequences that occur very frequently to impaired drivers; the odds of these happening are enormous. The penalties for being caught driving while impaired and the other consequences which result are also likely to happen. These potentially severe results need not occur.

You can decide, immediately, that you will never drink and drive. This decision will eliminate any severe consequences.

6-G Review

VOCABULARY - WRITE A SHORT DEFINITION FOR THE FOLLOWING :

- BAC
- Under 21 BAC limit
- Intervention strategies
- Zero Tolerance Law

- SADD
- Tort liability
- Vehicle seizure
- Synergistic effect

- Depressant
- Coordination
- Designated driver
- MADD

SUMMARY

The use of drugs (alcohol or others) by drivers will no longer be tolerated by society. The costs are enormous. The intelligent driver, realizing the effects of alcohol on the abilities that are required for vehicle operational control input and implementation of the SIPDE system, will decide to say NO.

The alcohol advertising campaigns have brainwashed the public. A re-evaluation of their message by individuals, as well as concerted action by society to curtail the message, are needed. Further strategies to reduce the incidence of drinking and driving, especially among the young, must be supported by all interested parties.

TEST A- ANSWER THE FOLLOWING QUESTIONS.

1. A) What is the legal blood alcohol concentration (BAC) limit for novice drivers?
   B) What are the penaties if novice drivers disobey the law?

2. A) What is the Criminal Code blood alcohol concentration (BAC) limit for drivers?
   B) What are the criminal penaties if they disobey the law?
   C) What other consequences may be involved in a DUI conviction?

3. A) What are the effects of alcohol on driving ability?
   B) What is meant by the "over-involvement of teens" in alcohol-related crashes?

4. A) What intervention strategies can be used to reduce drinking and driving?
   B) What can you do to help prevent drinking and driving?

TODAY'S HANDBOOK PLUS WORKBOOK

*Check your comprehension and mastery of the contents of this module by completing the corresponding exercises that are found in the complement to the **TODAY'S HANDBOOK PLUS**:*

TODAY'S HANDBOOK PLUS WORKBOOK

Complete the exercise on Pages 40 through 45. If necessary, review the chapter when uncertain of an answer and refer to your instructor for further guidance.

7

7 - A
Approach to the vehicle

7 - B
Pre-driving Protocol

7 - C
Blind Spots

7 - D
Pre-Drive Inspection and Maintenance

7 - E
Review

Preliminaries

Before approaching your vehicle to drive, it is important to get in the habit of planning your route. Weather conditions, temporary road work areas, traffic congested areas should be taken into consideration in order to choose the safest route to your destination. Collisions, vehicle break downs etc. can create unexpected difficulties but even these tend to occur more frequently on certain roadways. Keep your radio tuned to radio stations that transmit traffic reports. Plan your route logically if several steps are required. When driving to unfamiliar areas plan the route using familiar landmarks.

Then you can approach the vehicle with a clear mind and concentrate on the task at hand. This chapter will deal with the preliminary steps involved in setting out to drive your vehicle.

AFTER COMPLETING THIS CHAPTER, THE STUDENT MUST BE ABLE TO LOCATE, DESCRIBE AND PERFORM:

- **the proper approach to the vehicle, the pre-drive inspection, as well as the adjustments necessary when preparing to drive.**
- **the blind spots and the necessary checks thereof.**

Approach to the Vehicle

As you walk towards your vehicle, begin to think like a driver, make sure that nothing is in the blind zone around the vehicle.

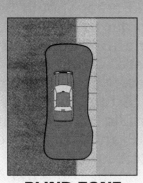   

BLIND ZONE

- Make sure that the path of travel is clear of debris, children, animals, etc.

- Check under the vehicle for any possible fluid leaks.

- Visually check the inflation of the tires and the position of the front wheels.

- Check the body of the vehicle for any damage - vandalism, hit and run, or theft.

- Check that the windows are clear and clean and the wipers are not stuck to the windshield (heat or ice).

- Verify that lights, turning signals, license plate are clean and clear.

If your vehicle is parked at the curbside, approach the driver's door from the front of the car thereby facing the traffic and

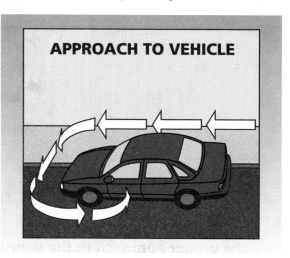

APPROACH TO VEHICLE

allowing you to check for other vehicles, bicycles, etc. before unlocking and opening your door.

Once inside, close and lock the door. Insert the key in the ignition switch while you make the remaining pre-driving checks. (Avoid mislaying it, free your hands) make sure there are no loose objects lying about on the front or rear window ledges; the seats, the floor, hanging from the rear-view mirror, sun visors, etc. These loose objects may become "flying objects" in the event of sudden braking or a collision. Objects on the floor can roll under the pedals and prevent their proper operation. Other loose or hanging objects can create reflections and/or obscure the driver's vision. (On some vehicles, the large A pillar - beside the window - can block your view of a pedestrian crossing the street.)

When transporting cargo, extra care must be taken to secure the parcels in vehicles,

BLOCK VISION   **"FLYING OBJECT"**

particularly station wagons, hatchbacks, and other vehicles, where the trunk area is open to the passenger compartment. If carrying clothing on hangers, use the hook on the left rear side of the car. Never use the right one; as the clothing will obstruct your view of the right blind spot. Make sure the windows are clean inside and out.

Paying attention to these items in detail may seem like a chore at first, but if performed regularly, they will quickly become a safety habit. They will then be done automatically without thinking.

Pre-Driving Protocol

With respect to pre-driving habits, it is "improper" to get behind the wheel and drive without being physically and emotionally ready to drive and without having made the proper adjustments. You should develop a pattern for your vehicle that you follow every time. It may differ slightly from that suggested here. Check your owner's manual.

A) Close and lock the doors:
   To protect you against intruders.
   To prevent the door from opening in a collision.

B) Insert key in the ignition switch:
   To free your hands.
   To avoid mislaying the keys.

C) Secure loose objects:
To prevent obstruction of field of vision.
To prevent reflections.
To ensure free use of the controls.
To prevent any "free flying objects."

D) Adjust your seat position:
Your seating position determines your ability to see properly, use the controls for the vehicle, and thereby effectively control the vehicle while driving. Seat yourself comfortably, making sure that your back and hips are firmly against the seat backrest.

Can you see over the steering wheel comfortably? Some cars have "tilt-steering columns" or electric seats; both of these are helpful. If your car is not so equipped, you may need a firm cushion to raise your eye position.

Hold the steering wheel with one hand while using the other to release the seat locking lever. (Depending on the location of the "adjustment lever," you may need to use either hand.) Slide the seat forward or backwards until your right foot can comfortably reach the floor under the brake pedal (as if the brake pedal were depressed to the floor), with your right leg still slightly bent, not stretching. This will allow your right foot to control the brake and gas pedals comfortably, but with good pressure when needed. On a vehicle with a standard transmission, the left foot should fully depress the clutch pedal for this adjustment.

Your left foot should be positioned on the far left against the foot-rest or **"dead pedal."** If your car does not have an actual pedal, the floorboard will have a flat plasticized area on the far left. It should be used to brace yourself to maintain your balance (arms free to control steering). With a standard transmission, as soon as the clutch pedal is released, the left foot should rest on the dead pedal.

The backrest is also adjustable on most vehicles. Think of the steering wheel as a clock, and place your wrists on the steering wheel at 12 o'clock. Adjust the backrest so that your elbows are slightly bent. Now lower your right hand to the 3 o'clock position and your left to 9 o'clock to ajust for air bag inflation.

E) Adjust the head restraint:
If adjustable, adjust the head restraint so that the top reaches just above the top of your ears. While driving, your head should not lean on the restraint.

SAFETY TIPS

Special care should be taken with the seating position, as this will determine your comfort and, more importantly, your ability to properly control your vehicle while driving. As a result of reported air bag injuries, a space of approximately 10 inches from your chest to the steering wheel is highly recommended. Visit www.nhtsa.dot.gov/ for more info.

F) Adjustment of the mirrors:

Use your mirrors to search behind your vehicle regularly (every 6-8 seconds), in reaction to traffic, prior to braking, and prior to performing all maneuvers. It is vital that they be adjusted so they can be used comfortably and easily, as well as reflecting the largest view to the rear of your vehicle.

INTERIOR REAR-VIEW MIRROR: Without moving your head from the driving position, grasp the mirror by the frame and adjust it so that you can see out the rear window with the right edge of the mirror aligned with the right edge of the rear window. This adjustment reflects a clear view to the rear and to the right rear of your vehicle.

EXTERIOR LEFT REAR-VIEW MIRROR: Turn your head slightly from the driving position and align it so that the right edge of the mirror shows a little of the side of your car. This mirror can be adjusted by a remote control lever or by manually moving the mirror frame

EXTERIOR RIGHT REAR-VIEW MIRROR: Turn your head and align the mirror with a little of the side of your car showing in the mirror. Remember this mirror (optional on some models) is convex and distorts distance.
RECHECK ALL MIRRORS BEFORE PROCEEDING.

G) Ensure good ventilation (HVAC):

Adjust the climate controls to the preferred setting for the weather conditions. Lower the side window slightly (3/4 inch). Even with air conditioning, the danger of carbon monoxide (exhaust) accumulating in the passenger compartment requires that proper ventilation be maintained.

H) Fasten your seat belt:

Fasten your safety belt properly and **make sure that all passengers do likewise** (for their as well as your safety).

I) Driver's Compartment Drill

Review the location and operation of gauges and controls. Check that the parking brake is applied.

Blind Spots

Before proceeding to the basic maneuvers (Chapter 9), you must understand a vital fact. Despite proper mirror adjustment and a normal field of vision, there are two areas around your vehicle that you cannot see. They are called "blind spots."

Blind spots are located to the left and right of your vehicle, just behind your normal field of forward vision. They extend behind the car on either side until the rear-view mirrors reflect the lanes beside your car. Trucks and large vehicles have an extra blind spot behind the vehicle.

7

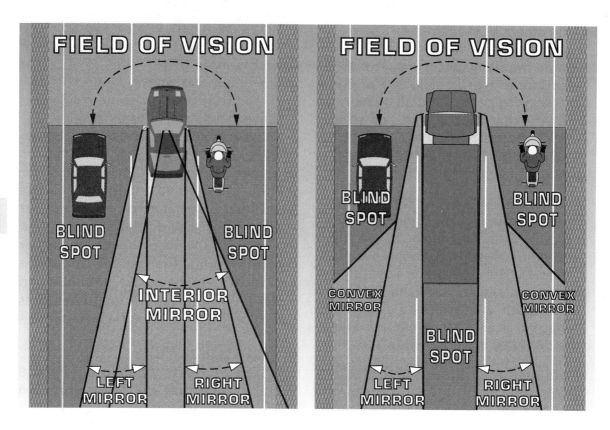

Once you realize the size and location of the blind spots (see illustrations above), **there are two things you should learn:**

A) Anytime you wish to maneuver (change lanes, turn, etc.) it is essential, after checking in the mirrors, to glance at your blind spot on the side where you wish to move. To do this, you must practice turning your head till your chin reaches your shoulder and glance to the side towards the rear. Practice left and right so that it can be done quickly yet correctly. To the right, glance out the right side rear window; on the left, glance out the driver's side window. **Practice until it feels natural.**

B) Also note: if you have these two blind spots, all other drivers have them as well and large vehicles have a third just behind them. **How many drivers don't bother to check their blind spots?**
Avoid driving in other people's blind spots. Reduce speed and drop back or accelerate to pass out of their blind spots. With respect to the rear blind spot on large vehicles, slow down and back off until you can see the driver in the left-side rear-view mirror.
Never place your safety in other driver's hands. They make mistakes and may involve you in a collision. **Keep your safety and the safety of your vehicle in your control.**

Pre-Drive Inspection and Maintenance

The inspection and maintenance of your vehicle is vital to the proper operation, avoidance of breakdowns and keeping your vehicle roadworthy. In the long term, this will not only reduce operating expenses and extend the span of time that the vehicle may be utilized safely; but will also help retain the value (reduce depreciation) of your vehicle when you decide to trade or sell it.

PRE-DRIVE INSPECTION

On the approach to the vehicle, as already mentioned, check for fluid leaks, tire inflation or damage and physical damage to the body or glass. If there are any abnormalities, identify (and rectify) the cause of the problem.

Should you spot a leak under the vehicle, identify whether it is coolant, brake fluid, air conditioner condensation, motor oil, transmission fluid, etc. Is it a problem that you can repair yourself? Will it cause a breakdown if not corrected immediately?

If you are not sure, do not take a chance; proceed to your service center and have a professional service technician check and repair the problem should immediate attention be recommended. Breakdowns on the roadway are much more costly than repairing a problem when your vehicle is driven to the service center: the towing charges, damaged parts, etc.

WEEKLY INSPECTION / MAINTENANCE

At least once a week, you should take the time to inspect your vehicle more completely; this could be done at the same time as you wash the vehicle. The items are:

TIRE PRESSURE: use a tire gauge to check the pressure in each tire. Note the pressure recommended on the tire sidewall (maximum) as well as in your owner's manual (smooth ride).

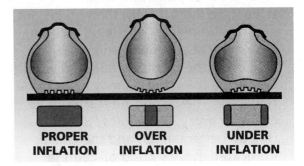

PROPER INFLATION   OVER INFLATION   UNDER INFLATION

TIRE WEAR PATTERN:
- tread wear indicator showing
- balding spots
- cuffing (uneven wear on outside or inside tread areas)
- worn tread (in middle or at side)
- stone or metal fragments.

TREAD WEAR INDICATOR

SAFETY / COMMUNICATION ACCESSORIES:
- lights and signals
- emergency lights and markers
- emergency kit
- wipers
- HVAC

MONTHLY INSPECTION / MAINTENANCE

At least once a month, you should take the time to check:

MOTOR OIL: the engine must be off for several minutes with the vehicle on level ground; pull out the dipstick, wipe it, reinsert it fully, then pull it out and check the level of the oil slick on the gauge at the lower end. Reinsert. Add oil of the correct grade if needed. Check the color, the oil may need to be replaced. The oil and filter should be changed every 3,000 miles / 3 months (see owner's manual) and the chassis lubricated every second oil change.

WIPER FLUID: check the fluid level in the reservoir. Add fluid appropriate to the season as needed. Keep a container in the trunk so that you may add while on the road when driving conditions may require frequent use.

COOLING SYSTEM: check the level of the coolant in the expansion tank and then (only if the engine is cold) open the radiator cap and check the level in the radiator. Add anti-freeze as needed. Check the hoses (softness and swelling, brittleness and cracking) and the drive belt (condition and tension). The system requires major service - flushing and coolant replacement - every 30,000 miles or 24 months.

BRAKE SYSTEM: check the brake fluid level in the master cylinder; add when necessary. The second time you add fluid, have the brakes checked for wear and possible replacement. Lubricate and adjust the parking brake cables every second oil change. Check the operation (parking brake) every time you park by applying it and then EASING UP on the service brake while still in drive - vehicle should not move.

POWER STEERING: check the fluid in the reservoir; add if low. Check the condition and tension of the power steering drive belt.

SIX MONTH INSPECTION / MAINTENANCE

FLUID LEVELS: check the level and condition of the transmission fluid and differential fluid if so equipped (automatic- dip stick, engine running in Park; standard- access bolt on side of transmission, ask service technician)

SERVICE MANUAL PERIODIC SCHEDULE

A regular maintenance schedule is required to validate the manufacturer's warranty and to ensure that your vehicle is roadworthy. Check the owner's guide for specific requirements for your vehicle. Some items are:

TIRE and WHEEL INSPECTION / ROTATION: at 6,000 miles and then every 15,000 miles or as necessary.

IGNITION SYSTEM: spark plug replacement, EGR and plug wire inspection every 30,000 miles.

FUEL SYSTEM: inspection every 30,000 miles.

Review

TERMS TO REMEMBER - WRITE A SHORT DEFINITION FOR THE FOLLOWING :

- Blind zone
- Vandalism
- Pre-driving protocol
- Backrest
- Seat squab

- "Dead" pedal
- Head restraint
- Rear-view mirror
- Left exterior mirror
- Right exterior mirror

- Convex mirror
- Ventilation
- Seat belt
- Blind spots
- Clothing hooks

SUMMARY

Proper preparation is conducive to effective driving control. Planning your route, performing the necessary checks as you approach your vehicle and once in the vehicle, following your pre-driving protocol are all essential components of this preparation. Practice doing all of these every time you drive so they will become automatic, a habit that you will eventually perform without thinking.

TEST A - STUDY THE DIAGRAM AND THEN ANSWER THE FOLLOWING QUESTIONS.

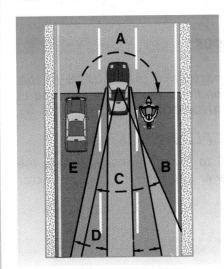

1. **Match the letters in Column A (from the diagram) with the number corresponding to the correct description in Column B**

COLUMN A
A _____
B _____
C _____
D _____
E _____

COLUMN B
1. Your forward field of vision.
2. The view in the interior rear-view mirror.
3. The view in the exterior rear-view mirrors.
4. The left blind spot.
5. The right blind spot.

2. **Name three situations when should you check these blind spots.**

a) _____

b) _____

c) _____

Student notes

_____
_____
_____
_____
_____
_____
_____
_____
_____
_____
_____
_____
_____
_____

TODAY'S HANDBOOK PLUS WORKBOOK

Check your comprehension and mastery of the contents of this chapter by completing the corresponding exercise that is found in the complement to the **TODAY'S HANDBOOK PLUS:**

TODAY'S HANDBOOK PLUS WORKBOOK

Complete the exercise on Pages 46 to 51. If necessary, review the chapter when uncertain of an answer and refer to your instructor for further guidance.

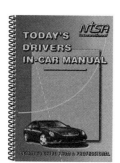

TODAY'S DRIVERS IN-CAR MANUAL

Before any in-car session, prepare yourself and facilitate the development of proper driving skills and habits by reading the corresponding lesson in the complement to the **TODAY'S HANDBOOK PLUS:**

TODAY'S DRIVERS IN-CAR MANUAL

Your instructor will evaluate your progress in the manual. Licensed parents or guardians should supplement your practice by following the manual procedures and coordinating with your in-car instructor.

Knowing Your Vehicle

Finally, the keys and the car... Your dream has come true! You climb in behind the wheel, the engine starts and purrs. Wow! Shift into gear and you're off. The sky darkens, rain starts to fall... Where is that wiper switch? Oops, not that one. Oh, There it is! And now, the headlights. What does that bright blue light mean? Why is that oncoming car flashing high beams? My gosh... the car in front is braking... You're sliding!! Your heart is pounding!

Now what?!

Good or bad habits are acquired through repetition. Familiarity with controls must be acquired before driving. Any other course of action could be fatal. Don't wait for experience to teach you, start with the right technique. Know your controls and practice.

AFTER COMPLETING THIS CHAPTER, THE STUDENT MUST BE ABLE TO LOCATE, OPERATE AND DESCRIBE:

- the information devices and symbols on the instrument panel.
- the control devices for operating the vehicle.
- the procedures when a warning device indicates abnormal operation.

The Driving Compartment Drill

Whether you are a novice driver or merely driving a different car for the first time, you need to be familiar with the instruments, gauges, and controls of the vehicle **before you drive**.

The first step: identify the location and function of all indicators/gauges in the instrument panel. Practice glancing at them (1/2 sec.), returning your eyes to the road ahead.

The second step: identify, locate and, further, use the hand controls. Practice using them until you can do so without taking your eyes from the road ahead.

The final step: perform the same practice with the vehicle controls.

Practice this driving compartment drill on the vehicle you will drive once you are licensed. This drill will assist you to feel more comfortable and be more competent in your vehicle. Also, when you take your behind-the-wheel lessons, it can be performed more quickly.

Remember, whenever you drive a new vehicle, perform this short drill. You'll never regret those few moments. When you need to use a control device urgently, you won't have to search for it.

The Instrument Panel

The instrument panel cluster, part of the dash in front of the driver, has various indicators and gauges mounted on it to let you know at a glance how your vehicle is operating.

The diagram and the chart (opposite page) describe some of the basic items that are normally present in most dashes. You should consult the owner's manual for your vehicle (preferably while seated in the driver's seat and parked in a safe area) in order to acquaint yourself with the gauges, alert lights, and indicators that are mounted on the vehicle you will be driving. Make sure that you understand what each means and what should be done if it should become lit.

In general, alert lights or warning lights that are yellow in color denote a warning; whereas those that are red denote immediate danger, you should stop your vehicle as soon as possible.

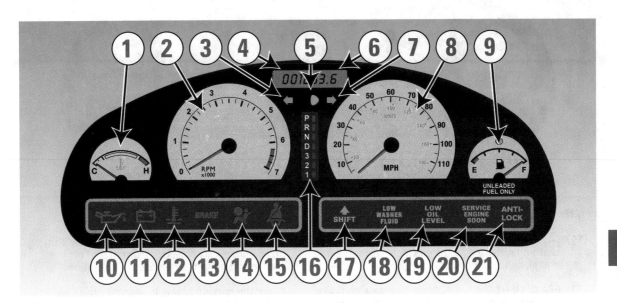

INDICATOR	FUNCTION	INFORMATION
(1) TEMPERATURE (gauge **(1)**, alert light **(12)**, & chime)	Indicates the operating temperature of the engine coolant.	The light comes on when the engine overheats SHIFT TO NEUTRAL, DEPRESS THE GAS PEDAL SLIGHTLY TO REV MOTOR (DON'T OVER-REV). Set the heater at maximum heat. If no improvement, turn off engine (see Chapter 18).
(2) TACHOMETER (Up-shift light **(17)**)	Indicates the engine revolutions per minute (RPM x 1000).	Check to shift at appropriate moment (standard). Avoid entering red zone, as it may cause engine damage. Upshift light signals when to shift gears.
(3) TURN SIGNALS (Left **(3)**, right **(7)**)	Flashes if the turn signal or hazard lights are activated.	If the light or arrow does not flash normally, this indicates a burnt bulb or faulty wiring.
(4) ODOMETER	Displays total mileage since vehicle was manufactured.	Check for vehicle maintenance schedule. Check when purchasing a used vehicle.
(5) HIGH BEAM	When lit, it indicates the high beams are activated.	Check when activating the headlight switch.
(6) TRIP ODOMETER	Displays the mileage since it was reset to zero.	Useful in calculating fuel consumption and trip mileage. (Button to activate and to reset.)
(8) SPEEDOMETER	Indicates the vehicle speed in miles per hour (kilometers).	Check frequently while driving to remain within the posted speed limits.
(9) FUEL GAUGE (light and chime when near empty)	Indicates the fuel level in the gas tank when the . ignition is on.	CHECK BEFORE STARTING OUT! Always keep more than 1/4 full. Keep almost full in winter (TO PREVENT IMPURITIES AND GAS LINE FREEZING)!
(10) OIL PRESSURE (gauge, light, chime)	Indicates the oil pressure in the engine	The light comes on when the oil pressure is too low. STOP SAFELY AND TURN OFF THE ENGINE!

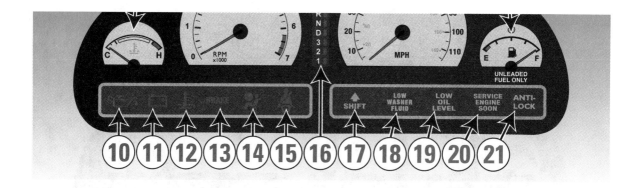

INDICATOR	FUNCTION	INFORMATION
(11) BATTERY/ALTERNATOR (charging system) (gauge, light, chime)	Indicates the intensity of the electrical current.	The light comes on if the current is abnormal. Turn off all unnecessary accessories, do not shut off the engine and go to the nearest service station.
(13) BRAKE LIGHT (may have more than one light)	Indicates the parking brake is activated or the brake system is faulty.	Check the parking brake. If released, stop your vehicle safely and check the brake fluid level. If this is also normal, have your vehicle towed.
(14) AIR BAG LIGHT	Indicates the air bag system readiness.	The light flashes when you start your vehicle and will then go out. If it stays on or comes on when driving, the system is defective. Have it serviced.
(15) SAFETY BELT (light and chime)	Reminder to fasten the safety belts.	The light comes on (then flashes) and a chime sounds for several seconds (unless belts buckled).
(16) SELECTOR LEVER (automatic transmission)	Indicates which gear has been selected by shifting the selector lever.	The shift or selector lever is usually located on the console between the front seats. Complete operation explained later in this chapter.
(18) LOW WASHER FLUID (light and chime)	Indicates washer fluid level is below one-third full.	Illuminates during starting, then goes out. If it comes on (and chimes), you need to refill fluid.
(19) LOW OIL LEVEL (light and chime)	Indicates the engine oil level is too low.	Illuminates during starting, then goes out. If it comes on (and chimes), check the oil level.
(20) SERVICE ENGINE SOON (light and chime)	Indicates the operation of the fuel, ignition, and emission control systems.	Computer monitors fuel, ignition, and emission control systems. The light alerts you to problems even before they may be apparent. Service is required. (Flashing indicates misfire condition, steady indicates emission control problems.)
(21) ANTI-LOCK BRAKE (ABS system)	Indicates the condition of the Anti-Lock Brake System	Illuminates during starting, then goes out. If it comes on while driving, it indicates the ABS is inoperative (pump, sensor, computer). (Regular brakes still operative.) Service in the near future.

Many new vehicles have a control center which illustrates the outline of the vehicle. Lights will illuminate for low washer fluid, door ajar, burnt out lights, change oil, etc.

SAFETY TIPS

When an alert light illuminates while driving, do not search for the owner's manual and fumble through it for emergency answers, nor think you know what it means (all manufacturers do not use the same symbols and meanings).
Read and understand the operating manual in advance (plan a mental course of action for each emergency), and then you can be calm and cool if and when the unexpected should happen.

8-C The Vehicle Controls

8

In addition to the instrument panel, vehicles are equipped with a number of other controls such as lights, comfort controls, steering, braking, and controls for safety.

RHEOSTAT (A) :

- Regulates the intensity of backlighting in the instrument panel.
- Lower the intensity in unlit areas; raise the intensity in well lit areas.

MULTI-FUNCTION LEVER
Turn signal / Headlights / Flash

MULTI-FUNCTION LEVER (B)

This lever **(B)** on the left side of the steering column includes the following:
- Turn and Lane-Change Signals.
- Headlights and High/Low Beam Changer.
- Flash-to-pass Feature.

TURN SIGNAL LEVER (B):
- Use to communicate your intentions for **turning maneuvers** - move using fingers (hand on wheel) in the same direction as you will move the steering wheel.
- Activates the turn signal lights and an indicator light in the instrument panel.
- When the turn is completed, the lever will normally return automatically. (May have warning chime if remains on.)

LANE-CHANGE SIGNAL (B):
- Use fingertips to move the lever until the arrow starts to flash. Hold it there until you complete the lane change. (Move in same direction as above.)

HEADLIGHT CONTROL (B):
Turn the outside part of the lever with the symbol on it, to operate the lights.

FIRST POSITION:
- Turns on the parking lights - amber lights in front, red in rear, use when parking if you must ensure the vehicle is visible to other road users.
- NEVER use alone when in motion.
- The instrument panel, license plate, and side marker lights will also come on.

SECOND POSITION:
- Turns on headlights as well as those mentioned in the first position.
- Always check the high beam indicator.
- High or low beams may be on.
- **Daytime Running Lights (DRL)** are becoming more common (state law).

HIGH BEAM DIMMER SWITCH (B)
- Push or pull the lever to change intensity of the headlights.
- The blue high beam indicator light informs the driver when the high beams are lit.

FLASH-TO-PASS FEATURE (B):
- Pull the multi-function lever toward you until the high-beam headlights are illuminated; release lever to turn them off. (Signal driver ahead of your intention to pass.)

HORN (C and F)

You can sound the horn by pressing the symbol on the steering wheel **(C & F)** :
- A warning device used to alert other road-users of your presence.
- May be located on the end of the signal lever.
- Do not overuse or abuse.

STEERING WHEEL (D)

The steering wheel:
- Controls the position of the front wheels.

- Turning the wheel to the right will direct your vehicle to the right; to go left, turn the wheel to the left.
- Avoid turning the steering when the vehicle is stationary (dry steering).
- TILT steering (optional) allows you to adjust the position of the wheel before driving.

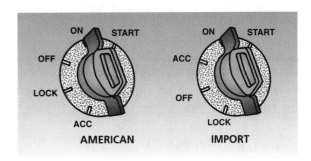

AIR BAG (E)

A frontal driver air bag, located in the hub of the steering wheel (E), is designed to protect the driver in a frontal collision. Some precautions with seating position (Chapter 7) and checking Air Bag Readiness light are advised (see Chapter 13).

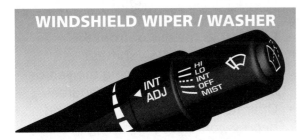

WINDSHIELD WIPER / WASHER

WINDSHIELD WIPER/ WASHER (G)

Use the windshield wiper and washer located on the right of the steering column (may also be located on the dash) to operate wipers.

- Use to clear the windshield.
- Turn outside of lever to positions - OFF, INTERMITTENT (optional), SLOW, FAST. (Never use when the windshield is dry.)
- Push end of stalk for washer fluid to clean the windshield (check reservoir).
- Install winter blades when necessary.
- Rear-window wipers and washer are available on some models.

IGNITION SWITCH (H)

The more square-looking of the two keys, the ignition key, may be inserted or removed in the lock position only. (On many vehicles may be located on the right side of the steering column.)

"LOCK" POSITION:
- The steering is locked. Most electrical systems are inoperative.
- Transmission must be in Park (auto.).

"OFF" POSITION:
- Most electrical systems are inoperative. The steering is not locked.

"ACC" POSITION:
- Electrical accessories are operative .

"ON" POSITION:
- All electrical systems are operative.
- Indicator lights and gauges can be checked for any malfunctions.

"START" POSITION:
- Spring-loaded, a slight extra pressure must be exerted to turn the key to this position.
- Activates the starter motor.
- Release the key and switch when the engine is operating (sound of motor).
- Never hold engaged for more than 10 seconds.
- **IF THE ENGINE IS NOT OPERATING, WAIT SEVERAL SECONDS BEFORE RE-STARTING.**

(Some vehicles require returning to "OFF" before re-starting.)

Some vehicles are equipped with a safety button that must be depressed to return to the "LOCK" position.

COMFORT CONTROL (I)

- To control the temperature in the passenger compartment.
- To direct air at the windshield and windows to help keep them clear.
- Air conditioner to cool air is optional.
- CONTROLS PERMIT DIRECTING THE AIR - VENT, HEATER, DEFROST.
- Temperature - from cold to hot.
- Air recirculation or from the exterior.
- Fan control - to increase air flow.

HAZARD SWITCH (J)

Pressing the button activates warning flashers but disables turn signals. The turn signals in both directions will flash simultaneously. Use to alert other road users of danger. (Button also flashes.)

REAR-WINDOW DEFOGGER (K)

Activates electric (heat) wires to clear the rear window (automatic shut-off).

THE ACCELERATOR PEDAL (or Gas Pedal)

- Controls the speed of the engine.
- Operate using right foot, heel on the floor, exert pressure using the "ball" of foot.
- Pressure supplies more fuel to engine causing increased speed when in gear.
- Releasing pressure will cause the vehicle to decelerate gradually.

THE BRAKE PEDAL (or Service Brake Pedal)

- Controls the service brake system to slow or stop the vehicle.
- Operate using right foot, heel on the floor (if possible).
- Exert pressure using the "ball" of the foot.
- Pressure activates the service brake system slowing the wheels thus, in turn, slowing the vehicle.
- Different brake systems (power brakes) may require less pressure to activate.
- Test the pressure required several times at slow speeds.

THE CLUTCH PEDAL:

- Found on cars with standard transmissions only.
- Disengages the motor from the transmission to allow shifting (changing) gears, stopping the vehicle and during the "start" procedure.
- Operate using left foot ("ball") and depress completely to disengage.
- Pedal must be fully depressed to start the engine (most cars are equipped with a "clutch safety switch" that prevents starting unless the pedal is fully depressed).

THE PARKING BRAKE (or Emergency Brake)

- Controls the "mechanical" brakes.
- Usually applies on the rear wheels.
- Use when parking, after stopping, to restrain the vehicle (prevent movment).
- An instrument panel indicator light (brake) will come on when the parking brake is in applied position.

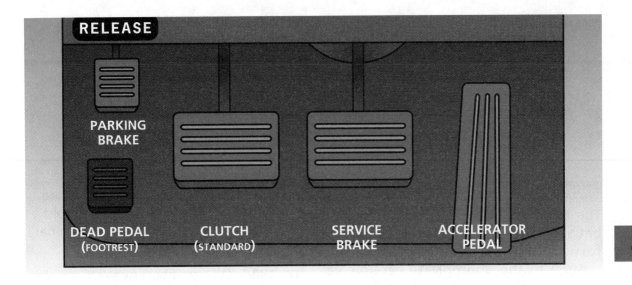

RELEASE

PARKING BRAKE

DEAD PEDAL (FOOTREST)   CLUTCH (STANDARD)   SERVICE BRAKE   ACCELERATOR PEDAL

TO ENGAGE

TYPE A (above)
- Operate using left foot, depress foot pedal firmly (pump to increase pressure on some models / press to release - no release handle - on other models). Check your owner's manual for the operation of the parking brake in your family vehicle.

TYPE B (right)
- Operate using your right hand, pull firmly (hand lever) locks in the applied position.

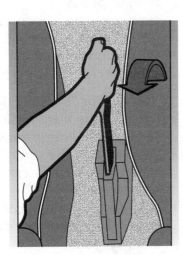

TO RELEASE, TO SET THE VEHICLE IN MOTION, ONCE IN GEAR.

TYPE A
- Pull the release lever (located above the pedal) with the left hand (or press the parking brake pedal on some models). The indicator light should go off.

TYPE B
- Raise the lever slightly with the right hand, depress the lock mechanism (button), then lower the lever completely. The indicator light should go off.

In emergency situations, if the service brakes fail, the parking brake may be used to stop the vehicle. While keeping the lock mechanism released, pump the parking brake to bring the vehicle to a stop.

The stopping distance will be longer as only the back brakes are functioning; however, *the vehicle will STOP*. This emergency maneuver should be practiced in a quiet, traffic-free area.

THE AUTOMATIC TRANSMISSION:

The transmission controls the connection between the engine and the wheels. In forward motion, it will automatically change to the appropriate economical gear - hence the name. The driver may override the system by selecting a specific gear position.

SELECTOR LEVER POSITIONS:
"P"-PARK:
- After stopping and applying the parking brake, the selector is placed in park.
- Locks transmission to prevent rolling.
- Must be in this position for ignition switch to move to **"lock"** position and remove the key (most vehicles).
- Allows starting the engine.
- To move out of park, must depress the lock button (red arrow). Some vehicles require depressing the service brake (called a **"Shifter Lock"**).

"R"-REVERSE:
- Used to back the vehicle.
- Must be at a standstill before engaging.
- Activates "**REVERSE**" lights (**white lights**) on rear of vehicle.

"N"-NEUTRAL:
- No connection to the drive wheels.
- The vehicle will roll.
- Allows starting the engine (if engine stalls when in motion, shift to neutral and restart while rolling).

" ☐D☐ " or OVERDRIVE (up to 8 gears):
- Optional position (may be electric) (on many newer model vehicles).
- Extra forward gear for cruising more economically (speeds above 45 mph).
- In stop and go situations "D" (normal drive) should be selected.

"D"-DRIVE (CVT - continuously variable transmission):
- Fully automatic forward gear position.
- The transmission will select the appropriate gear (3 to 8 gears or CVT).
- May be engaged while stopped or rolling forward.

"2" or "D2" or "L2"-SECOND GEAR:
- Prevents the transmission from selecting high forward gear.
- Used to slow a vehicle from high speed or when descending a steep hill at higher speeds.
- Used to obtain more power than high gear to climb a steep hill at higher speed.
- Used in poor traction conditions - mud, snow, etc.

"1" or "D1" or "L"-FIRST GEAR:
- Prevents the transmission from selecting any other forward gear.
- Used to slow the vehicle at lower speeds or when descending a steep hill at slow speed.
- Used to maintain maximum power at slow speed to climb a steep hill or pull a heavy load.

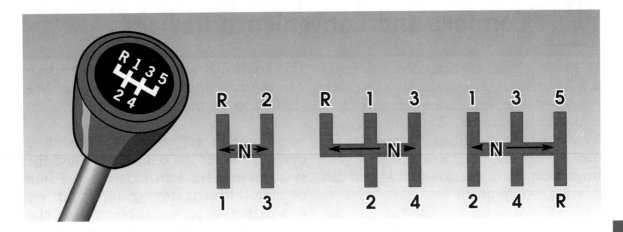

THE STANDARD TRANSMISSION:

Standard transmissions are available in three, four, five, or six speed models. With experience, the standard affords the driver superior control of the vehicle but requires more work by the driver.

"N"-NEUTRAL:
- The shifter lever moves easily from side to side.
- Use this position to start the engine - make sure the clutch pedal is fully depressed (clutch safety switch).
- The engine is not connected to the drive wheels.

"R"-REVERSE:
- Used to back the vehicle (reverse lights).
- Make sure the vehicle is at a standstill.

"1"-FIRST GEAR:
- Lowest forward gear - most power.
- Use to start from a stopped position until speeds of 10 to 15 mph.
- Use to climb steep hills or pull heavy loads at slow speed.

"2"-SECOND GEAR:
- Less power - more speed.
- Use when shifting out of 1st until speeds of 10 to 20 mph.
- Use when rolling slowly to pick up speed rather than return to 1st gear.
- Use to turn corners when in motion.
- Use to climb long, steep hills or pull heavy loads at slow speeds.

"3"-THIRD GEAR:
- On a 3-speed transmission, use to cruise at speeds over 25 mph.
- On a 4 or 5 speed transmission, use to accelerate to 35 to 40 mph.

"4"-FOURTH GEAR:
- Use for steady driving in the 40 mph and over range.

"5"-FIFTH GEAR:
- Use for steady expressway cruising to save fuel and engine wear.

8

Comfort and Convenience Devices

Most vehicles are equipped with other controls that increase the comfort, convenience as well as the safety for you and your passengers. These devices are located where the driver can reach them easily. Make sure you include them in your driver's compartment drill so that you can operate them properly.

TILT STEERING

Many vehicles have an adjustable (tilt) steering wheel which allows you to alter the position to one that provides maximum comfort and control. Be careful not to block your view of the dash gauges and warning lights. (Aim air bag at chest to prevent facial injury.)

AIR CONDITIONING

An option on most vehicles, you can use the air conditioner climate control to cool or heat the interior and reduce the humidity to make driving more comfortable. You can also regulate the fan speed to increase air circulation. The air can be directed through the floor outlets, the defroster nozzles, the dash vents, or a combination of these.

This control is also useful on a trip, or when your emotions (road rage) are starting to get the better of you.

Some models are computer controlled (HVAC); you set the temperature and the system adjusts automatically. Some provide different settings for the driver and passenger (in an automobile) or the front and back passengers (in a minivan or SUV).

CRUISE CONTROL

An optional feature on most vehicles, cruise control allows you to maintain a desired speed while removing your foot from the accelerator pedal after you set the control (at speeds above 30 m.p.h.).

The controls are located on the steering wheel or a stem on the left side of the steering column (check your owner's manual). The available control options include on/off, set/accelerate, coast, and resume. To activate the system, you must push the "on" button, then accelerate to the desired speed (using the foot pedal or "accelerate" button), and then push the "set" button.

SAFETY TIPS

Before releasing one hand from the steering wheel to adjust any control, communication, convenience, or comfort device, you should place your other hand in a position on the steering wheel for balanced steering control and consciously hold it steady to avoid the "Hand-Eye-Coordination" phenomenon.

CRUISE CONTROL MOUNTED ON STEERING WHEEL

RESUME
ACCELERATE

CANCEL

COAST
SET

You must tap the brake pedal (the clutch pedal as well on a standard, or in some vehicles, shifting to neutral) or push the "off" button to return the vehicle speed to normal foot control.

After braking (using the clutch or shifting to neutral, in some vehicles), pressing the "resume" button activates a memory circuit that will automatically return your vehicle to the previously set speed (unlike the "off" button). (On vehicles equipped with ETS - Enhanced Traction System - or traction control, when the computer limits wheel spin, the cruise disengages.)

Some vehicles will allow you to return to your set speed even after using the "off" button, provided the button is reset to "on" and you press the "resume" button.

You should never drive with the cruise "on" unless you are using it (it could cause you to accelerate unexpectedly), nor activate the system unless you can cruise at the pre-set steady speed without unnecessary risk (volume of traffic, road conditions, curves, etc.).

ENGINE IMMOBILIZER SYSTEM

The engine immobilizer system is a theft prevention system (one of many now available on modern vehicles). The engine will start only when the electronic code in the transponder chip (located in the key) corresponds to the registered ID code for the particular vehicle.

The system is set automatically when the key is removed from the ignition switch. An indicator light will flash to show that the system is set (check your owner's manual).

PASSENGER AIR BAG SWITCH

The passenger air bag cut off switch permits the driver to disengage the mechanism which activates the air bag. With the switch in the "off" position, the air bag will not inflate in a frontal collision.

8

SAFETY TIPS

Most owner's manuals issue a warning or caution concerning activating the cruise control mechanism on slippery roads (winding roads as well) because of possible wheel spin which could initiate a skid or destabilize the vehicle. You should never activate the cruise when driving on these road conditions.

The switch is usually located on the center console (check your owner's manual). Many models are now available from dealers with passenger air bag cut off switches already installed. Dealerships and repair garages with authorization from NHTSA can install such a switch on existing models.

ELECTRICAL OR LEVER REMOTE CONTROLS

Power windows, optional on many vehicles, provide switches to open and close the windows electrically. The driver can control all of them; each passenger can control their window. Often the driver can lock the controls to prevent children from playing with the switches.

Power door locks will secure all doors by means of switches. Once again, the driver can lock the controls for safety purposes. Some models automatically lock all of the doors when the transmission is shifted out of Park into any gear selector position. **Child-proof door locks** are available (switches located on the rear door frames) on some models preventing the rear doors from being opened except from the outside handle.

Power seats offer the driver, and often the front passenger, several switches that can control the position of their seats.

The height of the seat from the floor, the position of the seat relative to the pedals, as well as the angle of the back rest are all adjustable. The controls may be located on the console, the side of the seat, or the door (check your owner's manual). These adjustments allow for the best possible driving position.

Some vehicles provide adjustments for lumbar and side support as well. In some advanced systems, two programmable settings can be stored in a memory chip which, at the touch of a button (or insertion of the key), will then move the seat to the predetermined position.

The driver should never adjust the seat position while in motion. Stop your vehicle in a safe location, then adjust the seat position. Can you imagine what would happen, if at the moment you were moving the seat, you needed to make an emergency stop?

A trunk release button or lever, which can be locked on some vehicles, allows the driver to open the trunk from the passenger compartment.

The interior hood release lever, an additional protection against theft, opens the first latch on the hood (security against the hood flying up).

SAFETY TIPS

Comfort and convenience items are just that; they are there to assist you and improve your enjoyment of your vehicle. Make sure they do not distract you, nor lull you into a false sense of security. You are the driver; you are responsible for your safety.

Review

TERMS TO REMEMBER - WRITE A SHORT DEFINITION FOR THE FOLLOWING :

- Driving compartment drill
- Instrument panel
- Headlight switch
- Windshield wiper

- Ignition switch
- Accelerator pedal
- Brake pedal
- Clutch pedal

- Parking brake
- Automatic transmission
- Manual transmission
- Cruise control

SUMMARY

THE DRIVING COMPARTMENT DRILL:
Practice using and checking the gauges, instruments and controls of your vehicle so that it becomes "second nature". Anytime you drive an unfamiliar vehicle perform this drill before driving.

THE DASH PANEL:
Check the indicators before starting out. Make sure they are functioning. Know what they mean. Read your owner's manual if you are not sure. When purchasing a new vehicle, ask the salesperson for a copy of the owner's manual for your model while you wait for delivery; get a head start.

THE CONTROLS:
Get accustomed to the position and feel of the controls at slow speeds before venturing into heavy traffic. Don't take it for granted; your safety depends on it.

TEST A - WRITE "T" BESIDE STATEMENTS THAT ARE TRUE AND "F" BESIDE THOSE THAT ARE FALSE.

_____ **1.** The alternator warning light indicates the intensity of electrical current.

_____ **2.** The brake light only illuminates when the parking brake is applied.

_____ **3.** The oil pressure light indicates abnormal engine oil pressure.

_____ **4.** The temperature gauge indicates the temperature of engine coolant.

_____ **5.** The hazard signal switch activates the turn signals in both directions.

_____ **6.** The trip odometer (an option on some vehicles) indicates engine RPM.

_____ **7.** The tachometer indicates the vehicle speed in miles per hour.

_____ **8.** The rheostat allows the driver to change the intensity of the headlights.

_____ **9.** The horn should only be used to communicate with your friends.

_____ **10.** The START ignition switch position activates only the starter motor.

_____ **11.** The clutch safety switch prevents starting unless the clutch is depressed.

_____ **12.** The parking brake should be released prior to shifting into gear.

_____ **13.** If the service brakes fail, apply the parking brake in one motion.

_____ **14.** A shifter lock mechanism prevents shifting until the brake is depressed.

_____ **15.** A vehicle (automatic transmission) can start either in park or in neutral.

_____ **16.** The reverse position automatically activates the *back-up* lights.

_____ **17.** First gear is the most economical gear for city driving.

_____ **18.** A driving compartment drill should be performed each time prior to driving.

_____ **19.** A standard transmission shifts automatically to the appropriate gear.

_____ **20.** Overdrive (automatic) or fifth gear (standard) are the most economical gears for cruising at freeway speeds.

TODAY'S HANDBOOK PLUS WORKBOOK

*Check your comprehension and mastery of the contents of this chapter by completing the corresponding exercise that is found in the complement to the **TODAY'S HANDBOOK PLUS**:*

TODAY'S HANDBOOK PLUS WORKBOOK

Complete the exercise on Pages 52 to 57. If necessary, review the chapter when uncertain of an answer and refer to your instructor for further guidance.

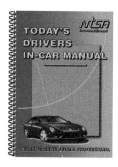

TODAY'S DRIVERS IN-CAR MANUAL

*Before any in-car session, prepare yourself and facilitate the development of proper driving skills and habits by reading the corresponding lesson in the complement to the **TODAY'S HANDBOOK PLUS**:*

TODAY'S DRIVERS IN-CAR MANUAL

Your instructor will evaluate your progress in the manual. Licensed parents or guardians should supplement your practice by following the manual procedures and coordinating with your in-car instructor.

Basic Maneuvers

Once you have acquired the correct approach to the vehicle, pre-driving and "driving compart-ment drill" habits, the real challenge begins.The driving task becomes more complicated. To build a proper house, you first must lay a solid foundation. Similarly, in driving, you have established the basics. Now it is necessary to build upon this base, one step at a time, mastering each new technique before proceeding to the next level.

Initially it's a challenge just to enter the flow of traffic, drive in a straight line, gain proficiency in the handling of the steering wheel, the accelerator pedal, the brake pedal, and then return your vehicle to a parked position.

At first, these basic maneuvers will require your total concentration. With time and practice, you'll be able to perform them easily and with confidence.

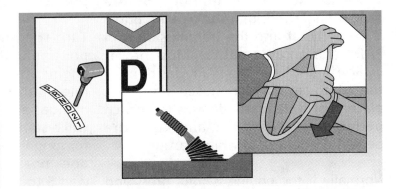

AFTER COMPLETING THIS CHAPTER, THE STUDENT MUST BE ABLE TO UNDERSTAND, DESCRIBE AND PERFORM:

- pre-drive and starting procedures.
- steering input as well as brake and accelerator pedal control tasks.
- the basic procedures for entering, following, backing and exiting traffic.

BASIC MANEUVERS:
To drive a vehicle in the HTS requires that you plan each maneuver, check that it can be performed safely, signal your intentions, and then proceed to actually execute the maneuver cautiously and with skill.

The sequence of actions for any maneuver will benefit by being sub-divided into three stages: ASSESS, PREPARE, and EXECUTE.

ASSESS:
At this stage, even though you should be aware of the traffic environment, examine the situation for signs and road markings, check the mirrors and blind spot, and decide whether to perform the maneuver.

PREPARE:
Having decided, signal your intentions and recheck the mirrors and blind spot to ensure that you can proceed to the final stage.

EXECUTE:
This stage involves using the controls of the vehicle to perform the actual maneuver: the steering wheel, the accelerator or the brake. As you execute the maneuver, look where you want to go, guiding your vehicle. When complete, verify the turn signal is no longer activated.

Throughout the explanation of any maneuvers in this text, this APE stage system will be applied.

Starting the Engine

Before starting any vehicle, you must have performed all the basics. The key is already in the ignition. Before proceeding, check that the parking brake is properly set and the transmission is in PARK (for an automatic). Most newer vehicles must be in the PARK position for the key to have been removed in the first place. For a standard, depress the clutch pedal, select NEUTRAL and keep the pedal fully depressed while starting.

Normally if the engine is cold, press and release the accelerator pedal to reset the electronic command module (**ECM**).

Turn the key in the ignition switch to the ON position. Verify the gauges and the indicator lights. (Diesel engines: wait for the GLOW PLUG light to go off before proceeding.)

Turn the ignition switch to the START position and listen to the sound of the engine; the moment the noise changes, release the switch. (Check your owner's manual as to the use of the gas pedal while starting.) Never engage the starter for longer than 10 seconds; if the engine does not start, release the switch and wait 5 to 10 seconds, then try again. (For a standard, release the clutch pedal once the engine starts.)

With the engine running, re-check the indicator lights and gauges. They should

STARTING THE ENGINE :
AUTOMATIC

STANDARD

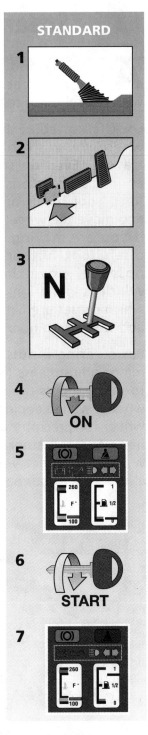

indicate normal operation (lights off). The brake light remains lit because the parking brake is still applied.

IN COLD WEATHER
Activate the parking lights (5-10 seconds) before starting to "prime" the electrical production in the battery.

Keep the accelerator pedal slightly depressed while cranking the engine to facilitate starting. Allow the engine to warm up for 30 seconds to ensure oil circulation before starting off.

Drive slowly at first to improve oil circulation and the initial lubrication of bearings, gears and other moving components. To enter heavy traffic immediately, extend the warm-up time slightly to permit the engine to reach operating temperature.

A FLOODED ENGINE
The starter sounds normal, but the engine doesn't start. The odor of gasoline permeates the passenger compartment. An excess of gasoline in the engine prevents combustion.

To start the engine, depress the gas pedal fully and maintain this position even if the first attempt fails. Turn the ignition switch to "START" for 5 to 10 seconds; release if it does not start. Try again. As soon as it does start, ease up on the accelerator quickly.

This procedure will work on all gas engines (check the owner's manual).

Steering and Visual Tracking

As mentioned earlier, grip the steering wheel firmly at 9 and 3 with your thumbs resting on the wheel.

Look far ahead at the center of the lane where you wish to travel (the path of travel). Even on straight roads, small course corrections will be necessary. Keep your hands on the steering wheel and move the wheel and hands together. If you are moving the steering wheel often, look further ahead. As much as possible, move the wheel while the vehicle is in motion; avoid "dry steering" which causes premature wear of the tires and steering components.

For steering inputs ranging from very minor adjustments (one to two degrees) to major inputs (up to a half turn of the wheel), while keeping both hands on the wheel for precision adjustments, use the hand-to-hand steering technique. This will also protect you from any risk of injury from the air bag, if it should deploy.

HAND-TO-HAND (PUSH / PULL) STEERING

If turning through a slight curve, both hands will typically retain their original grip on the wheel, making only slight finger or wrist adjustments to maintain path of travel. However, when moving through a turn, the hands may move up to 165 degrees (neither hand moving past the 6 or 12 o'clock positions).

Hand-to-hand involves moving the wheel with a sliding hand movement, one hand at a time. **When steering right for example**, move both hands and the wheel from the neutral position. As the right hand nears the six o'clock position and more steering input is required, slide it back to the normal position. Continue steering and slide the left hand to its normal position. Reverse the process to straighten. Do not let the wheel slip through the fingers to straighten, and both hands are always on the wheel to make adjustments.

"HAND-TO-HAND" STEERING TECHNIQUE

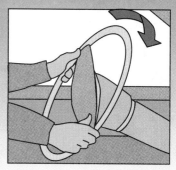

Alternating back and forth in this manner retains firm steering control by one hand while permitting smooth steering movement and maintains a sense of the neutral position at all times. This technique is ideal for precision maneuvers as it helps to prevent any oversteering or understeering.

HAND-OVER-HAND STEERING

Hand-over-hand is particularly well suited when speed of the steering input is critical, such as skid recovery (oversteer), or when maneuvering in a space with limited sightlines (shopping center perpendicular parking). Quick movements of the hands are recommended on entry, with smooth, slower inputs when returning the wheel while completing the maneuver.

TO TURN RIGHT
From the normal driving position, both hands turn the steering wheel to the right. When the right hand reaches the four o'clock position, release it and continue turning the wheel with the left hand. The right hand crosses over the left arm to grasp the wheel at the twelve o'clock position. Continue turning with the right hand while the left returns to the normal starting position. In extremely tight maneuvers, you may have to repeat these steps to turn the wheel sufficiently.

TO RETURN STRAIGHT
At slow speeds as well as in evasive or emergency maneuvers, return the steering by hand using the same technique. When turning 90 degrees, you may allow the steering wheel to slide through your grip on the wheel while accelerating gently. Be prepared to intervene to correct the final direction of the vehicle. The wheels will straighten with respect to your vehicle, not in relation to the direction you wish to travel.

EVASIVE ACTION STEERING

In evasive maneuvers, the steering input required is rapid and more abrupt than in normal steering maneuvers. To achieve

9

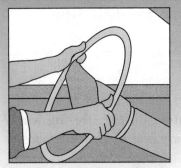

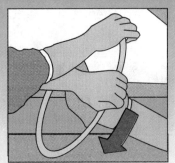

"HAND-OVER-HAND" STEERING TECHNIQUE

this from the basic steering position, the thumbs should be hooked on the steering wheel. A quick steering motion in either direction until the arms touch will permit a 180° steering input (below 45 mph). (Above this speed, a 90° movement and thrust acceleration will suffice.)

The resulting front wheel movement and change to the suspension settings will cause the front of the vehicle to move into the next lane. An immediate counter-steering motion to arm touch in the opposite direction (360°) will bring the rear of the vehicle into the next lane in a stable manner. A steering movement back to the neutral position will stabilize the vehicle and maintain the new lane position.

This type of steering input is utilized in rapid evasive maneuvers and permits a maximum of steering input without moving either hand from the original position on the wheel. It also continually provides good information about how to achieve the neutral steering position.

This rapid change of direction is not a normal steering input and **should be practiced with an instructor** in order to gain proficiency, skill, and confidence.

ONE HAND STEERING

This technique is reserved for backing maneuvers, where a change of seating position will require one hand steering input. In reverse, a smaller steering input is required to change direction. When more input is required, hand-over-hand should be used.

TIMING OF STEERING INPUT

All vehicles lag somewhat in responding to steering input. The greater the speed of the vehicle, the longer the distance traveled will become. For this reason, the driver must search ahead in order to have time to evaluate the driving scene and still input the steering correction or movement prior to the point where the vehicle must change direction.

The amount of steering lag varies from one vehicle to another. Timing must be learned through experience, with the application of lead time, and refined by practice on any particular vehicle. Continuous practice of the steering techniques is vital for optimum control of any vehicle. The basic hand position offers the driver maximum steering input while both hands are on the wheel.

SAFETY TIPS

Due to changes in steering ratios and the effort required to turn the wheel, recommendations relative to hand position on the steering wheel have become more flexible. Due to possible air bag deployment, lower positions are advisable.

Entering Traffic

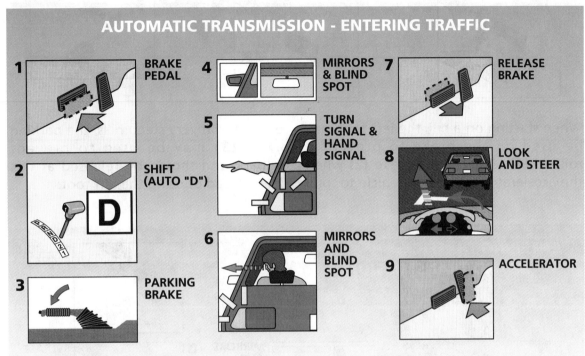

AUTOMATIC TRANSMISSION - ENTERING TRAFFIC

1 BRAKE PEDAL

2 SHIFT (AUTO "D") **D**

3 PARKING BRAKE

4 MIRRORS & BLIND SPOT

5 TURN SIGNAL & HAND SIGNAL

6 MIRRORS AND BLIND SPOT

7 RELEASE BRAKE

8 LOOK AND STEER

9 ACCELERATOR

AUTOMATIC TRANSMISSION

The engine is already running as described earlier, depress the brake pedal **(1)** and maintain it in this position (make sure the pedal feels firm).

Move the selector lever to the "D" position **(2)**. (You should already know the correct procedure for your vehicle) Release the parking brake **(3)**.

ASSESS:

- Make sure there is sufficient space to enter traffic.
- Check in the mirrors and toward the blind spot **(4)**.

PREPARE:

- Activate your turn signal, if there is any doubt as to the signal being seen, use a hand signal as well **(5)**.
- Re-check in your mirrors and toward the blind spot **(6)**.

EXECUTE:

- Release the brake pedal while looking towards your intended path **(7)**.
- Turn the steering as needed **(8)**.
- Begin to depress the gas pedal gently and increase your speed as required **(9)**.

STARTING ON AN UPHILL SLOPE (AUTOMATIC)

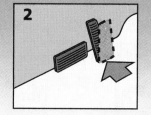

When starting on a hill, the left foot may be used on the brake to prevent a rollback **(1)**. Release the brake **(2)** when the accelerator causes the vehicle to pull forward. On very steep hills, the parking brake **(3)** may be used to prevent rollback and should be released at this time instead of using the left foot.

ENTERING TRAFFIC : STANDARD TRANSMISSION

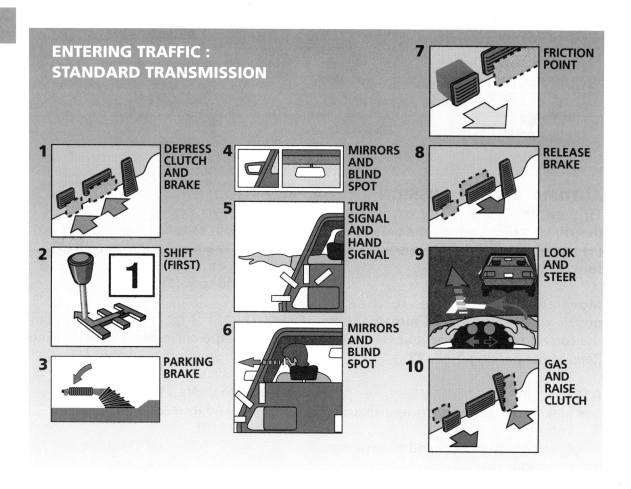

1. DEPRESS CLUTCH AND BRAKE
2. SHIFT (FIRST)
3. PARKING BRAKE
4. MIRRORS AND BLIND SPOT
5. TURN SIGNAL AND HAND SIGNAL
6. MIRRORS AND BLIND SPOT
7. FRICTION POINT
8. RELEASE BRAKE
9. LOOK AND STEER
10. GAS AND RAISE CLUTCH

STANDARD TRANSMISSION

The procedure is similar. Depress the clutch pedal completely and put the gear shift lever in first; apply the brake pedal firmly and then release the parking brake.

ASSESS and **PREPARE** as for the automatic transmission. **(1 to 6)**

EXECUTE:
- Raise the clutch pedal to the friction point (engine r.p.m. slows slightly) **(7)**.
- Release the brake **(8)**.
- Look towards your intended path of travel **(9)**.
- Lightly apply the gas while **(10)** raising the clutch pedal smoothly.
- Steer as needed.

STARTING ON A STEEP UPHILL SLOPE (STANDARD)

This technique is effective in all situations except the steepest of hills. In those cases, the parking brake **(1)** may be left engaged until the vehicle begins to pull forward **(2)** then release the parking brake **(3)** thus preventing any rollback.

9-D Acceleration and Braking

AUTOMATIC TRANSMISSION

You have put your vehicle in motion as per the steps explained earlier. Now to drive the automobile.

The speed of your vehicle is controlled by the pressure your right foot exerts on the accelerator or gas pedal. Keep your heel on the floor and depress the pedal with the "ball" of your foot. The vehicle reaction will depend on engine size, the power train, the road surface, and the weight of the vehicle. To develop a "feel" for driving, sense the change in body position (as you do when someone else is driving) and adjust your pressure on the gas pedal accordingly.

To increase your speed, depress the pedal gradually and adjust the pressure by the vehicle reaction. Always change your speed smoothly, this saves fuel and unnecessary "wear and tear" on the power train components.

MAINTAINING SPEED

Once you attain the desired speed (check your speedometer), ease up slightly and the vehicle will maintain this speed. If you ease up too much, the vehicle will begin to decrease in speed. With practice you should be able to cruise at the same speed effortlessly. Remember that any change in the inclination of the road will require an adjustment of the pressure on the accelerator pedal.

The automatic transmission will shift to the appropriate gear as you drive, whether accelerating or slowing. By looking far ahead, you may avoid having to use the brakes; releasing the gas and slowing gradually, the situation may change, and you may return to your cruising speed without stopping.

PLANNING YOUR STOP

When necessary to slow the vehicle, **tap the brake pedal** slightly **(1)**; this lights up the brake lights on the rear of your vehicle announcing your intentions. **Check the rear view mirror (2)**. **Re-apply the brake pedal** firmly **(3)**, reduce your speed in relation to the space available:

- Always plan to stop earlier than the intended location. You can always ease up on the brake later rather than run out of space. Just before coming to a full stop, decrease the pressure slightly **(4)** in order to stop smoothly. If it is possible in your vehicle, keep your heel on the floor while applying pressure to the brake pedal.

- To remain stopped, maintain pressure on the brake pedal.

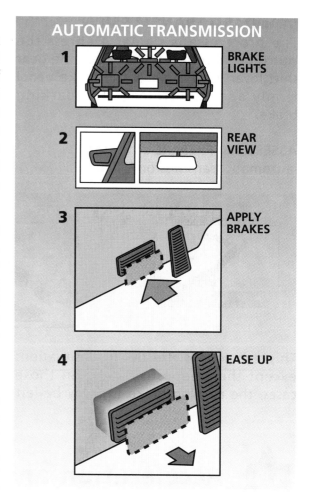

When safe to resume, release the brake and gradually depress the accelerator.

THE STANDARD TRANSMISSION

In these vehicles, you must manually shift into the appropriate gear as the speed changes. Automobile transmissions may have from 3 to 6 forward speeds (gear-ratios) as well as reverse. (Trucks may have even more gears.) Most modern vehicles have the gear shift lever on the floor (some are on the steering column).

Remember the clutch pedal must be depressed completely to start the engine, to shift gears , and to come to a full stop.

To begin, practice shifting into each gear with the vehicle stopped. Depress the clutch pedal completely, use the hand position illustrated for each gear and shift without looking at your hand.
Practice shifting down through the gears as well.

Once you master the shifting technique, you must accustom yourself to using the clutch pedal with the left foot and the brake pedal and the accelerator with the right foot. Choose a quiet area on level ground. Start the engine. Keep the clutch depressed (1). Shift into first (2). Release the parking brake (3).

Rest your right foot on the gas pedal (4) without applying any pressure on the accelerator throughout this maneuver. Raise the clutch pedal slowly until you reach the friction point (5). (The engine idle speed will decrease and the vehicle will try to move) Pause. Then slowly raise the clutch pedal (6) until the vehicle rolls smoothly. Release the clutch and place your left foot on the footrest (7). Allow the vehicle to roll several

9

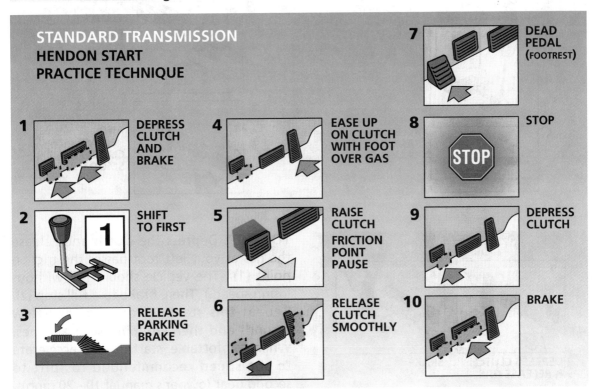

STANDARD TRANSMISSION
HENDON START
PRACTICE TECHNIQUE

7 DEAD PEDAL (FOOTREST)

1 DEPRESS CLUTCH AND BRAKE

2 SHIFT TO FIRST

3 RELEASE PARKING BRAKE

4 EASE UP ON CLUTCH WITH FOOT OVER GAS

5 RAISE CLUTCH FRICTION POINT PAUSE

6 RELEASE CLUTCH SMOOTHLY

8 STOP

9 DEPRESS CLUTCH

10 BRAKE

seconds, then depress the clutch pedal **(9)** and apply the brakes **(10)** to stop.

Practice this maneuver until you can move the vehicle smoothly and you are comfortable with the pedals. This will be useful for starting on slippery or icy surfaces and for "inching out" at intersections to check the traffic; however, this will be a little too slow for normal starting.

In normal starting, raise the clutch to the friction point, pause **(E)**, apply a slight pressure on the accelerator to raise the engine idle speed, then smoothly raise the clutch **(F)** while increasing pressure on the accelerator.

The HENDON START practice technique comes into play with the addition of the accelerator pedal.

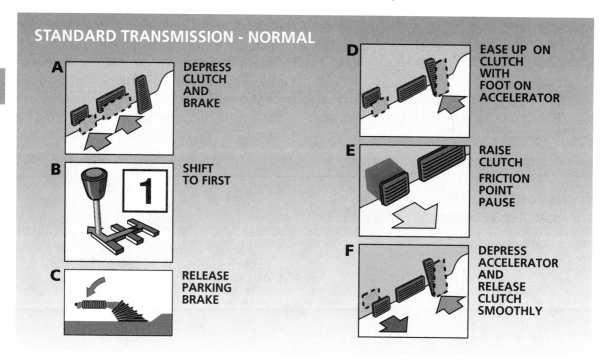

STANDARD TRANSMISSION - NORMAL

A — DEPRESS CLUTCH AND BRAKE
B — SHIFT TO FIRST — 1
C — RELEASE PARKING BRAKE

D — EASE UP ON CLUTCH WITH FOOT ON ACCELERATOR
E — RAISE CLUTCH FRICTION POINT PAUSE
F — DEPRESS ACCELERATOR AND RELEASE CLUTCH SMOOTHLY

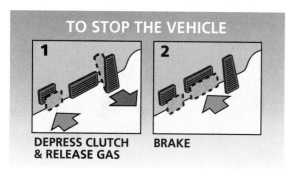

TO STOP THE VEHICLE

1 — DEPRESS CLUTCH & RELEASE GAS
2 — BRAKE

TO STOP: Depress the clutch and release the gas as your left foot passes the friction point **(1)**. (The vehicle should roll without losing speed.) Then, brake to a full stop **(2)**. Repeat this starting, driving for a few seconds and then stopping several times. When comfortable, start off and accelerate to the speed recommended to shift to second gear (owner's manual 10 - 20 mph).

TO UPSHIFT: Depress the clutch, release the gas as practiced, then shift to second gear. Raise the clutch smoothly and apply pressure to the accelerator as you pass the friction point. (Your vehicle should roll then accelerate without any hesitation)

To shift to the higher gears follow the same procedure. Listen to the sound of the engine so that soon, you will be able to "sense" when to shift without glancing at the speedometer as often.

Notice that the standard responds more exactly to the accelerator pedal than does the automatic. For this reason you can control your speed more easily with the gas pedal. When necessary to slow your vehicle quickly, release the accelerator and tap the brake pedal **(1)** then apply it. When you reduce speed below a speed range for the present gear, downshift.

TO DOWNSHIFT: Depress the clutch **(2)** and select the correct gear with the gear shift lever **(3)**. Ease up on the clutch while pressing on the brake **(4)** if you intend to continue slowing. Otherwise, if you wish to accelerate, as you ease up on the clutch, press on the gas pedal gently **(5)**.

You must downshift before turning corners, before climbing steep hills, before descending steep hills, and at anytime that the drone of the motor signals the need for more power. Be careful when downshifting not to over-rev the engine.

TO STOP: brake as for the automatic; however, make sure to depress the clutch as you slow to a stop. Even better, depress the clutch and shift to second gear as you

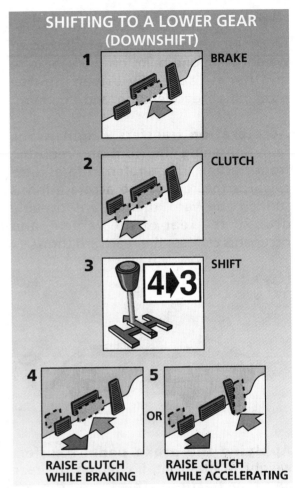

SHIFTING TO A LOWER GEAR (DOWNSHIFT)

1 BRAKE

2 CLUTCH

3 SHIFT 4▶3

4 5 OR

RAISE CLUTCH WHILE BRAKING

RAISE CLUTCH WHILE ACCELERATING

approach a blockage in traffic that requires you to stop; then if the situation changes, you can accelerate from a very slow speed as long as you did not come to a full stop.

Once you stop for any extended time, shift to neutral and release the clutch. Maintain pressure on the brake pedal.

With practice and experience, you will drive a standard with ease and confidence. At first, leave extra space and aim higher than usual, in order to avoid unnecessary anxiety and shifting, or sudden maneuvers.

WEIGHT TRANSFER

The transfer of the concentration of weight from one point on the vehicle to another is caused by driver inputs - acceleration, deceleration, and steering.

Acceleration transfers weight to the rear, lightening the front and reducing front traction. This is referred to as pitch towards the rear. If the acceleration is sudden and hard, there is a noticeable drop of the rear of the vehicle, and occupants can feel the rearward thrust.

Steering input transfers weight from one side of the vehicle to the other, in relation to which way you turn.

Steering input weight transfer is referred to as roll. The weight or mass shift is related to the speed of the vehicle, the traction available, and the amount of steering input. Occupants may or may not feel the forward movement toward the corner of the vehicle opposite the turn. When you steer toward the right, the vehicle rolls to the left.

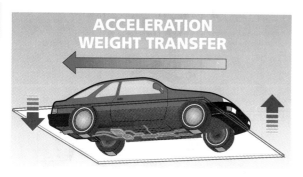

Applying the brake pedal transfers weight to the front, lightening the rear and rear traction. This is called pitch towards the front. If braking is hard, the hood drops, the rear rises, and occupants feel the forward movement.

Steering to the left transfers weight to the right (see below). The skill of the driver is to minimize weight transfer through precise movements of steering, smooth and progressive acceleration, and controlled braking.

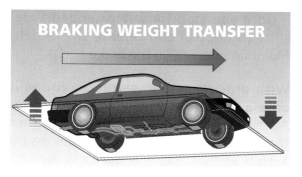

Reversing

Backing your vehicle requires visual tracking similar to driving forward, you must look where you wish to go in order to control the direction of your vehicle.

To back into a right turn, you must turn the top of the steering to the right. The front of the vehicle will however, swing in the opposite direction. The steering reaction is abrupt and requires less wheel movement to achieve the intended change of direction. You should carefully control your speed (move at "walking" speed, a "snail's pace") and steering while checking all around you.

BACKING STRAIGHT or INTO A RIGHT TURN (automatic transmission) you may, in most states, remove the safety belt to facilitate turning and looking to the rear.

ASSESS:
- Check in your mirrors.
- Check all around your vehicle.
- Are you permitted to reverse?
- Are there visual obstructions?
- **IS THE MANEUVER SAFE?**

BACKING STRAIGHT

PREPARE:
- Apply the brake.
- Shift the selector lever to (R) reverse (white back-up lights alert others).
- Release the parking brake (if it is engaged).
- Activate the turn signal (only if you are turning and it is not functioning).
- Recheck around your vehicle.
- Place your left hand at 12 o'clock on the steering wheel.
- Turn your torso and head to the right until you can target your path of travel **POT** (when backing straight, place the right arm across the top of the seat).

BACKING INTO A RIGHT TURN

EXECUTE:
- Ease up on the brake pedal to start reversing slowly (snail's pace).
- Maintain pressure as needed to control your speed.
- Glance frequently ahead and to the sides, while targeting your **POT**.
- When turning, check that the left front of your vehicle clears all obstructions.
- Apply the brake to stop.

9

In most cases, your vehicle will roll by releasing the brake; if necessary, gently press the accelerator to start the vehicle in motion. On uphill slopes you may have to use the gas to keep it moving. The situation can change very quickly. Move slowly to allow you time to check around your vehicle easily and often.

If you turned, begin straightening the wheel as you stop. Do not change position and look forward until after you have stopped.

BACKING INTO A LEFT TURN

BACKING INTO A LEFT TURN follow the same APE procedure except:

PREPARE:
- Place your right hand at 12 o'clock on the steering wheel.
- Turn your torso and head to the left until you target your path of travel.

While backing into a left turn, the right front of your vehicle will swing out; check that it will clear all obstructions while you turn. As well, your view to the right rear is limited in this position; include a glance to the right rear as you check ahead and to the sides.

For a standard transmission, follow the APE procedures described. To set your vehicle in motion, use the friction point. (Except on an uphill slope, when you will need to use the accelerator as well.) Ease up or depress the clutch pedal to control your speed. Cover the brake pedal, ready to stop.

9-F Leaving Traffic

To leave the traffic lane and park your vehicle, the simplest and safest method is to steer towards the curb from the lane beside the parked vehicles. This requires a large space, at least twice the length of your vehicle. Other ways to park will be discussed in Chapter 14.

ASSESS:
- Locate a parking space, while still paying attention to the traffic around you **(1)**
- Check for signs and pavement markings that govern parking.
- Check mirrors and blind spot.

IS THE MANEUVER SAFE?

PREPARE:
- Activate your turn signal **(2)** (when parking just after an intersection, wait until you enter it to signal).
- Tap your brake pedal, **(3)** then apply steady pressure to reduce your speed.
- Recheck your mirrors and blind spot before turning **(4)**.

EXECUTE:
- When the front of your vehicle reaches the space (front turn reference point), target your **POT** and steer towards the curb **(5)**.
- Continue slowing while steering to a stop parallel to the side of the road **(6)** (right side clearance reference point **(8)**).
- Within a foot of the curb in most jurisdictions.
- Make sure the turn signal is no longer activated.
- Make sure you are centered in the parking space **(7)**.

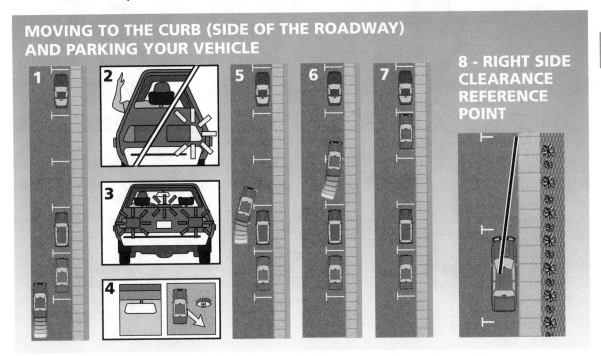

MOVING TO THE CURB (SIDE OF THE ROADWAY) AND PARKING YOUR VEHICLE

8 - RIGHT SIDE CLEARANCE REFERENCE POINT

9

EXITING THE VEHICLE

(Refer to the diagram on the next page - Page 9.18.) Once the vehicle is stopped **(1)** in the space, engage the parking brake **(2)**, ease up and re-apply the brake pedal to check the operation of the parking brake, then place the selector lever in PARK **(3)** (automatic) or shift into first or reverse **(3)** (standard- check owner's manual)

Release the brake pedal **(4)**. Turn off all accessories **(5)**, lights, comfort controls and close all windows. Turn the ignition switch to the lock position **(6)** and remove the key. Release the clutch pedal **(7)** (standard). Remove your safety belt. Check the left mirror and blind spot **(8)**. Use your right hand to unlock and open the door **(9)**, thus turning to check the traffic automatically. Exit carefully **(10)** and lock the door **(11)**. Walk toward the rear of your vehicle facing the traffic **(12)**.

These precautions concerning the doors and exiting should also apply to the passengers in your vehicle.

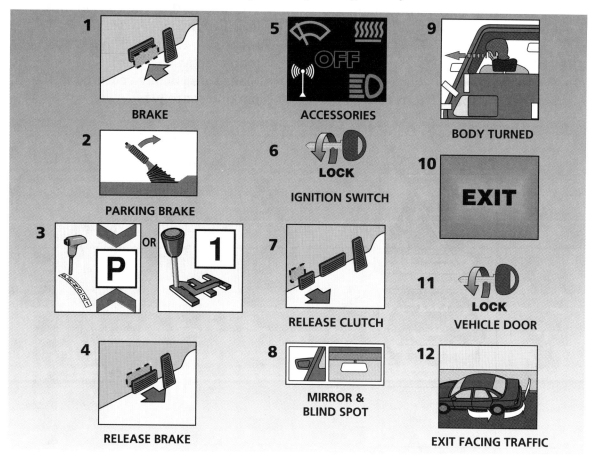

1 BRAKE

2 PARKING BRAKE

3 P OR 1

4 RELEASE BRAKE

5 ACCESSORIES

6 LOCK
IGNITION SWITCH

7 RELEASE CLUTCH

8 MIRROR & BLIND SPOT

9 BODY TURNED

10 EXIT

11 LOCK
VEHICLE DOOR

12 EXIT FACING TRAFFIC

SAFETY TIPS

Parking responsibility - choose a legal and safe parking space, apply the parking brake, stop the engine, turn the ignition switch to lock, remove the key, and when standing on a grade, turn the front wheels to the curb (or side of the road) when leaving your vehicle unattended. Never leave children unattended in a parked vehicle (Kaitlyn's Law - California)!

Visual Referencing

Most drivers learn the operating space for their vehicle by an involved trial and error process. Sometimes they guess right and at other times they err. It is always amusing to watch an experienced driver park a new vehicle for the first time.

As a novice, some means of improving this hit or miss system is strongly advised. A method of vehicle judgment and the space required. It is critical at the outset to base your decision on some fixed reference points that are based on experience. The more you practice applying these reference points in small operating spaces, the better your judgment will become. To take advantage of this technique, you must relate some part of the roadway to a particular part of your vehicle.

For example, when driving into a parking space alongside the curb, how can you tell how far the tires are from the edge of the curb? After attempting the maneuver and verifying the distance, you may come to realize that the center of the hood lines up with the curb. In future, you will be able to drive into the space and verify your position without having to climb out of the vehicle to see.

This same concept can be applied to most driving maneuvers and will assist you in gaining confidence and skill in proper fender judgment. This will remove anxiety in tight spaces and further assist you in proper decision-making for steering input (forward visual turning point and backing alignment, as two examples).

The problem that may arise is a tendency to stare at these reference points with your central conic vision. The proper technique is to use your fringe vision which allows you to see a wider area without the clear focusing ability of your central vision. This develops a spatial relationship. You will not have to stare and will thereby free your central vision to search and target space and area changes in the driving scene while your fringe vision accurately guides the vehicle on its intended path of travel.

You will also benefit any time you drive a different vehicle (a van where the driver seating position is above the front wheels, for example). After checking a few reference points, there will be a rapid transfer of learned referencing to any other vehicle you might drive.

SAFETY TIPS

Visual referencing facilitates vehicle operation and control of space! Once learned on any vehicle there will be an easy transference to any other vehicle you may drive, even though the referencing points will not be exactly the same!

Review

TERMS TO REMEMBER - WRITE A SHORT DEFINITION FOR THE FOLLOWING :

- Assess
- Prepare
- Execute
- Glow plug

- Choke
- Flooded engine
- Dry steering
- Hand-over-hand

- Friction point
- Rollback
- Hendon start
- Downshift

SUMMARY

Apply the APE system to every maneuver. Practice starting (automatic or standard) and setting your vehicle in motion. Always drive with both hands on the wheel for maximum control. Aim high into your path of travel. Use the accelerator and brake smoothly to drive more comfortably and save fuel and brakes. Practice hand-over-hand steering. When reversing, assume the correct position and look where you wish to go. Remember to check all around your vehicle as you move slowly. Practice exiting your vehicle properly

TEST A - WRITE "T" BESIDE STATEMENTS THAT ARE TRUE AND "F" BESIDE THOSE THAT ARE FALSE.

_____ **1.** The PREPARE stage involves signaling intentions and re-checking traffic.

_____ **2.** To start an engine, turn the ignition switch directly to the START position.

_____ **3.** Once the engine is running, check the indicator lights and gauges.

_____ **4.** In cold weather, always allow the engine to reach operating temperature.

_____ **5.** To start a flooded engine, depress and hold the gas pedal while cranking.

_____ **6.** Turning the steering wheel when a vehicle is not moving will not cause any adverse problems for the vehicle components.

_____ **7.** Release the parking brake after shifting the transmission into gear.

_____ **8.** Always accelerate smoothly to save fuel and wear of vehicle components.

_____ **9.** To reduce speed or stop, always tap the brake pedal before applying it.

_____ **10.** After applying the brake pedal firmly, always check the rear-view mirror.

_____ **11.** The clutch pedal must be depressed only when you stop the vehicle.

_____ **12.** When reversing, use the mirrors to guide the vehicle.

_____ **13.** The speed of the vehicle when reversing should be as slow as possible.

_____ **14.** Body position (reversing) should be the same for all backing maneuvers.

_____ **15.** The simplest and safest parking maneuver is to drive into a large space.

_____ **16.** Intending to park on the other side of an intersection, communicate your intention by activating the turn signal prior to the intersection.

_____ **17.** Preparing to park, re-check the mirrors and blind spot just prior to turning into the parking space.

_____ **18.** Once stopped (automatic), shift the selector lever into PARK.

_____ **19.** Turn off all accessories prior to turning the ignition switch to LOCK.

_____ **20.** Always exit the vehicle from the passenger side of the vehicle.

TODAY'S HANDBOOK PLUS WORKBOOK

Check your comprehension and mastery of the contents of this chapter by completing the corresponding exercise that is found in the complement to the TODAY'S HANDBOOK PLUS:

TODAY'S HANDBOOK PLUS WORKBOOK

Complete the exercise on Pages 58 to 62. If necessary, review the chapter when uncertain of an answer and refer to your instructor for further guidance.

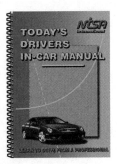

TODAY'S DRIVERS IN-CAR MANUAL

Before any in-car session, prepare yourself and facilitate the development of proper driving skills and habits by reading the corresponding lesson in the complement to the TODAY'S HANDBOOK PLUS:

TODAY'S DRIVERS IN-CAR MANUAL

Your instructor will evaluate your progress in the manual. Licensed parents or guardians should supplement your practice by following the manual procedures and coordinating with your in-car instructor.

Student notes

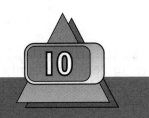

Defensive Driving

The only thing that may interest you is the freedom and pleasure that a driver's license will grant you. There is, however, another side to driving. In addition to the complex task of vehicle control, you must share the road with others and the many responsibilities this entails.

Many people drive from point A to point B without becoming involved in a collision. This does not mean that they are capable and defensive drivers; it may simply mean that they were fortunate. Most are "passive" drivers. They wait for things to happen and then they react; hopefully in time.

This chapter will outline a defensive driving system that will allow you to develop a "proactive" approach to driving, an early warning system intended to avoid potential conflicts before they materialize. A method to prevent collisions in spite of unfavorable conditions and the mistakes of others.

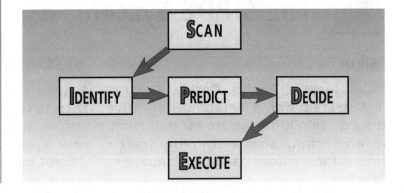

AFTER COMPLETING THIS CHAPTER, THE STUDENT MUST BE ABLE TO DEMONSTRATE A BASIC UNDERSTANDING OF:

- the SIPDE system and its strategic value.
- the management of space and time to minimize risk.
- adapting vehicle speed and position to potential hazards in the HTS.

The Attitude

It is improper to drive an unfamiliar vehicle that is mechanically defective in in the H.T.S. The attitude inherent in the defensive driver is that there is a correct manner to proceed. This applies to the vehicle, the task of driving, and the driver.

The vehicle must be in good mechanical condition, properly maintained, and adapted to the needs of environmental conditions. It can be dangerous to drive with something as "minor" as an empty windshield washer reservoir. The defensive driver ensures himself that all of the vehicle's systems are operational and ready to perform their function should the need arise.

The task of driving requires familiarity with the vehicle. Refer to "The Driving Compartment Drill" in Chapter 8 and the "Pre-Driving Protocol" in Chapter 7. The defensive driver will take the time necessary before starting out when driving an unfamiliar vehicle.

The driver must also know his or her own mental and physical state. You should consider it improper to drive when any factor that will negatively affect your ability to drive is present. **Even if it be over-tiredness.**

In short, the attitude of the defensive driver is **"I am ready to drive correctly".**

The SIPDE System

SIPDE

(**S**can, **I**dentify, **P**redict, **D**ecide, **E**xecute) is a strategy for developing defensive driving skills. It is a system for gathering, interpreting, and acting on traffic information before dangerous situations develop.

The "Active" driver, using this system, should not have to swerve, slam on the brakes, or take any other emergency evasive maneuver while driving.

S - SCAN

Actively scan the roadway a distance of 12 to 15 seconds ahead: looking for signs, signals, and potential problems. **Keep your eyes moving.** (Refer to Selective Vision-Chapter 4.) Develop a pattern to your visual search. Include the rear-view and side mirrors, as well as the dash. Check ahead from one side of the road to the other. You will have a complete traffic picture around you. By **aiming high** and **keeping your eyes moving,** you will center your vehicle in your lane on straight roads and in curves. At intersections, the scan should include cross traffic as far as possible before and as you enter the intersection.

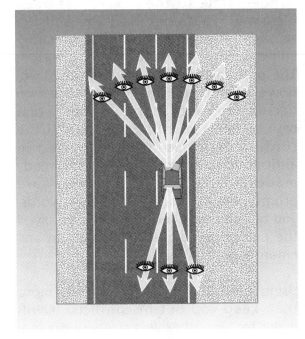

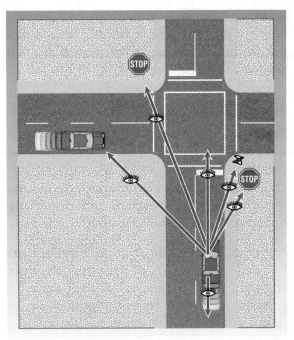

seconds before you will reach the identified hazard.

I - IDENTIFY

From all the information your eyes are scanning, you must select the critical data. The signs, signals, hazards and problems identified that require a decision on your part: your selective seeing ability.

Focus on other vehicles, pedestrians, animals, stationary and moving objects, and traffic devices that may affect your path of travel. You are in motion; you are getting closer to what you have identified. If you were scanning far enough ahead, you still have 8 to 10

P - PREDICT

Ask yourself: "What if...?" What is the "worst case scenario" for each of the identified items? You need to predict two levels - "What is the most probable?" and the "Worst case scenario". You need to know in advance what the potential paths of travel are, the timing of relative hazard movements, where and how collisions could occur, etc.

You must expect the **UNEXPECTED**. Be prepared for sudden movements of other road users. **Make sure they see you!** The use of the horn and/or flashing the high beams are effective means of getting attention. **Make "eye to eye" contact!**

Another road user looking at you, knows you are present, and is not likely to enter your path of travel. You are now 6-8 seconds from the hazard.

D - DECIDE

You must decide what you are going to do to minimize your risk. While predicting the two levels of danger from the upcoming situation, you communicated your presence and hopefully obtained "eye to eye" contact.

Now you must adapt to the potential hazard. Your path of travel and your speed are the two main aspects of control available to you. Reduction of speed will give you more time before you reach the hazard. The situation can change in this extra time. Reduced speed will lower the force of impact should a collision occur. A change of lane will create a larger "space cushion" between you and the hazard.

Decide on two levels - "What evasive maneuver will I employ?" **Leave yourself an out.** "Where will I go?" or "What will I do?" You are still 4-6 seconds away from the hazard.

E - EXECUTE

Immediately, execute stage one. Change your path of travel or your speed or both. You have minimized the probability of danger. Time to the hazard has been increased. Space between you and the hazard, in case the "worst case scenario" still develops, has also been increased. The probable danger has been reduced; however, you still have your stage two decision to execute should the "worst case scenario" occur; your "out" if the conflict develops. You have acted in anticipation and your decision is already made for your "out". You are programmed for action. In other words, you have already decided and have saved the normal decision-making time in any emergency situation.

Using the SIPDE procedure can do more than keep you out of conflicts. It will make for smoother, less stressful driving. You will make early course corrections and speed adjustments to avoid disruptions. You will avoid having to perform evasive emergency maneuvers. You will **ACTIVELY** control your vehicle in the HTS.

Managing Time and Space

The SIPDE approach is a tactical early warning and resolution system to keep you out of trouble. It enables you to control time and space. By scanning far ahead you have control of time; now let us take a further look at space.

SPACE AREAS

While in motion, there are six areas that surround your vehicle as well as the blind zone, see diagram below.

SCAN - you must constantly scan these areas for the ever-changing traffic situation. Scan for whether the areas are **open** (clear of any other road users), **closed** (occupied by others), or **changing** (about to be occupied). This will indicate if you may use an area as a path of travel and if your line of sight is clear.

IDENTIFY - What risk does the situation present? To what space area can you move to reduce the risk? Which are open?

EVALUATION OF THE SPACE AREAS

The areas of concern (space areas) can present one of the following conditions:

OPEN SPACE AREA: There is a space or area available to operate your vehicle without any restrictions to your line of sight or path of travel. No road users occupy the space and nothing impedes your line of sight through the area.

CLOSED SPACE AREA: The space area is not available for your path of travel because it is presently occupied by another road user or, of equal importance, your line of sight is restricted. You are unable to determine what the situation is.

CHANGING SPACE AREA: There is a space or area available to operate your vehicle at present, but some other road user is about to occupy the space area or your line of sight is about to be restricted. It is in the process of becoming a closed space area. It could also be a closed space area that is about to become worsened by an additional factor coming into play.

EXECUTE - without losing vehicle balance, move your vehicle to the area or lane position that reduces risk. Adjust speed to further minimize risk.

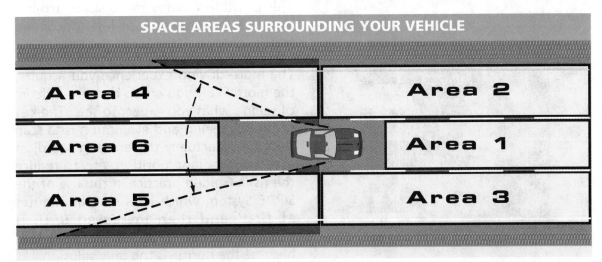

SPACE AREAS SURROUNDING YOUR VEHICLE

Area 4 Area 2 Area 6 Area 1 Area 5 Area 3

LANE POSITION

What do we mean by change lane position? Since a lane of traffic is wider than a passenger vehicle, you must realize that it is possible to occupy more than one position in any lane without encroaching on the lanes beside you. The advantage to this concept is that it affords the proactive driver the opportunity of leaving a greater distance (more space, SIPDE system) on one side of the vehicle without changing lanes.

LANE POSITION 1

While driving, if you center your vehicle in your lane of travel, you are occupying **lane position 1** (lane center-position). In this position, you have approximately 2 to 3 feet on both sides of your vehicle (depending on the type of roadway).

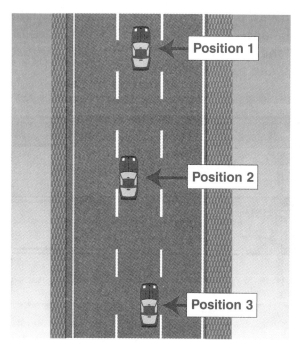

This indicates that in your judgment there is no hazard on either side of your vehicle that requires you to adapt your space to minimize a potential risk.

LANE POSITION 2

When you position your vehicle near the line on the left side of your lane, you are occupying **lane position 2** (lane left-position). In this lane position, you have approximately 4 to 6 feet of space to the right of your vehicle (contingent on road).

This position would be utilized to create more space from a potential hazard on the right or when preparing to turn left.

LANE POSITION 3

Positioning your vehicle near the right edge of your lane or near the curb will leave approximately 4 to 6 feet on the left side of your vehicle (subject to the type of roadway). This is referred to as **lane position 3** (lane right-position).

This position creates more space from a potential hazard on your left (oncoming traffic, potential danger in the left lane).

The more driving experience you acquire, the more likely you are to become a victim of seeing what you expect to see. The key to proper seeing and evaluation is to scan for what is actually present and to adjust speed, space, lane position, etc. to reduce the risk. Guided practice in the use of the SIPDE System which lasts several minutes at first, and then increased until it becomes a habit - practiced decisions that become the norm - is the only solution.

THE DANGER ZONE

A danger zone is present both in front and behind your vehicle. In front of you, a space in which it is impossible to stop; likewise behind you, the vehicle trailing yours has a certain distance in which it cannot stop. The length of these is related to many factors: speed, road conditions, the vehicle's mechanical condition, the tires, as well as the driver's condition.

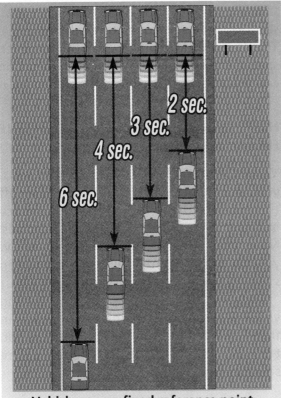

Vehicle passes fixed reference point
(the sign, in this case),
count one thousand and one,
one thousand and two, etc.

Your vehicle should reach the sign,
after you say two, three, four, etc.
(depending on the desired interval).

In ideal conditions (at city speeds), your danger zone dictates a **two second** *minimum* **following distance**. Don't be deceived, you cannot stop in 2 seconds at most driving speeds. This presupposes that the preceding vehicle requires the same distance to stop. **As your speed increases, 3 seconds would be advisable.**

FOLLOWING TIME INTERVALS

What is the correct time interval? The absolute minimum following distance in ideal urban driving conditions should be the "**TWO SECOND RULE**"; however, you should consider several factors before determining what you should use while driving in the HTS. *Many jurisdictions now suggest a minimum 4 SECOND RULE FOR ALL DRIVERS.*

Taking into account **a novice driver's level of experience**, the time lag in steering input, the time to react once the decision is made, the time to apply the brake pedal, as well as the **distance traveled (vehicle speed)**, you should conclude the following:

2 SECOND TIME INTERVAL
Provides the driver time to steer and avoid a hazard at all listed speeds on a dry surface, and to apply the brake to prevent a collision **at speeds under 30 mph.**

3 SECOND TIME INTERVAL
Permits the driver to steer and avoid a hazard at all listed speeds on a dry surface, and to apply the brake to prevent a collision **at speeds up to 45 mph.**

10

4 SECOND TIME INTERVAL
Permits the driver to steer and avoid a hazard on a dry surface, or *to apply the brake, to prevent a collision up to 70 mph - THE NEW SUGGESTED MINIMUM.*

6 SECOND TIME INTERVAL
Permits the driver to maintain control **in most adverse driving conditions.**

Lengthen this following time taking into consideration the following factors:
- your **speed** (or reduce your speed),
- the **road conditions** (friction/traction),
- the **weather conditions** (visibility),
- the **density of traffic**, and
- your **level of previous experience with the existing conditions**.

As a novice driver, you should always add one second to the time interval that would be appropriate to the driving conditions. In ideal urban conditions, you should apply a **"THREE SECOND RULE."**

Your strategy is to keep this space clear in front and behind you. When anything or anyone infringes on this space, action on your part is needed. How can you keep this space clear?

VEHICLES AHEAD
To control your front space area, you must control your following distance (interval). The absolute minimum of 2 seconds, preferably more, is within your control, by adjusting the speed of your vehicle. As a novice driver, because of your lack of driving experience, 3 seconds is the recommended minimum.

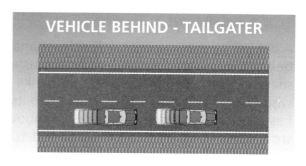
VEHICLE BEHIND - TAILGATER

VEHICLES BEHIND
You must keep a minimum interval behind your vehicle to ensure that a trailing vehicle will not crash into you, should the need to stop suddenly occur. This is more difficult to control; however, speed, change of lane, or communication can achieve your goal (but, it isn't easy).

HOW CAN YOU PREVENT SOMEONE FROM "TAILGATING"?

YOU CANNOT! But when it happens, you must react. **DON'T PANIC!** Ease off the accelerator gently. Allow your space in front to increase to at least 4 seconds. Now, you have space in front to allow you to brake gently even in a sudden stop situation. This will give your "tailgater" space to stop without hitting you. Moreover, with this large space in front, the "tailgater" will be encouraged to pass you and thus alleviate the situation behind you.

On a multi-lane roadway, a lane change would be an appropriate way to reduce the risk from a "tailgater". If the rear turn signals are amber colored, activating the hazard lights will also alert the tailgater, leaving no doubt as to your message.

RISK-REDUCTION CONCEPTS

To help manage time and space, in your decision making always consider these three basic concepts:

A-) MINIMIZE: reduce the risk from any one hazard by increasing time - reduce your speed; by increasing your space cushion - change lanes; and by communicating your presence - horn, high beams or hazard lights.

B-) SEPARATE: take each hazard one at a time, if at all possible. When multiple problems appear ahead, manage your time and space to separate them. This will make a difficult situation easier.

C-) COMPROMISE: when a number of hazards cannot be separated, weigh the dangers relatively. Leave more space from the most dangerous hazard without unnecessary risk from the others.

Adapting to the H.T.S.

In theory, defensive driving sounds logical. What happens when you enter rush hour traffic? Accelerate and blend with expressway traffic? **The defensive driver applies the SIPDE tactical approach in all driving situations and at all times.** Momentary lapses lead to surprises. Surprises while driving become emergency conflicts.

In the city, the visual search pattern and selective seeing will permit you to anticipate hazards. Space and time management will maintain the margin of safety needed to stay out of trouble. Remember rapid, sudden changes in speed or direction will put you in conflict with other road users, especially the **PASSIVE** type. Your early warning system gives you the edge. Your speed and direction corrections are done early and gently. Chapter 15 will discuss the urban environment and specific applications.

On rural roads and expressways, the increased speed of your vehicle and the environment changes the driving task. The tactical system adapts to these situations also. Because of the higher speeds, your eye lead time, which was calculated in seconds, focuses a greater distance ahead. The following distance, also calculated in seconds, is longer. Two seconds at 55 mph is almost double the distance at city speeds.

In adverse driving situations, whether the problem is road conditions, weather conditions, or visual conditions, you must adapt your time and space management to acquire a longer trailing distance. **At least four to six seconds is recommended.** Combinations of these conditions may necessitate even longer trailing distances. If, as a novice driver, conditions appear extreme, the decision not to drive at all may be wise and necessary.

10

Review

TERMS TO REMEMBER - WRITE A SHORT DEFINITION FOR EACH OF THE FOLLOWING :

- "ACTIVE" driver
- "Worst case scenario"
- Scan
- Identify
- Predict

- Decide
- Execute
- Path of travel
- 2-second rule
- Danger zone

- "Eye to eye contact"
- Tailgater
- Minimize
- Separate
- Compromise

SUMMARY

THE ATTITUDE:
The defensive driver makes sure the vehicle, his/her familiarity with it, and his/her physical and mental state are in the proper condition to drive.

THE STRATEGY:
The "ACTIVE" approach - aim high and scan the driving environment, "read" the traffic, identify potential hazards, predict the possible situations that may develop,

decide what to do in the event of any of these problems and execute decisions early while in readiness to act further.

THE APPLICATION:
Manage your "visibility", "time" and "space" to minimize the risk. Keep space to avoid the need for rapid evasive maneuvers and at the same time provide an "out". Adapt the strategy to any and all driving scenarios.

TEST A - APPLY THE CONCEPTS OF THE SIPDE STRATEGY TO THE FOLLOWING SCENARIOS

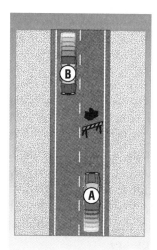

1. **You are driving Vehicle A approaching a closed portion of the road. Vehicle B is traveling in an oncoming direction.**

    a) How can you separate these hazards?

    b) What factors will affect your decision?

    c) How should you proceed safely?

    _____

    _____

    _____

    _____

    _____

    _____

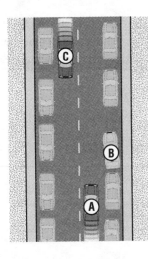

2) You are traveling in Vehicle A on a street with parked cars. Vehicle B has a driver behind the steering wheel. Vehicle C is approaching in an oncoming direction.
   a) What are the potential hazards?
   b) What would be the "worst case scenario"?
   c) How can you minimize the risks?
   d) What would be your final solution?

_____

_____

_____

_____

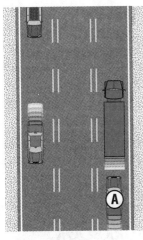

3) You are driving Vehicle A following a slow-moving heavy vehicle in the right lane on a three lane highway. There is a long line of traffic in the oncoming lane.
   a) What are the potential hazards?
   b) What is the "worst case scenario"?
   c) What should you do immediately?
   d) What is the final solution?

_____

_____

_____

_____

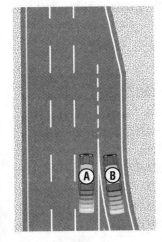

4) You are driving Vehicle A on an expressway. Vehicle B is on the acceleration lane signaling a merge onto the road.
   a) What conflicts could occur?
   b) What should you do?
   c) What factors will affect your decision?
   d) How could you avoid such a situation?

_____

_____

_____

_____

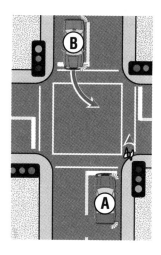

5. You are driving Vehicle A intending to turn right at the intersection. The signal light facing you is green. A pedestrian is just starting to cross the intersection. Vehicle B is signaling a left turn.

   a) How can you separate these hazards?

   b) How should you proceed safely?

   _____

   _____

   _____

   _____

   _____

Student notes

_____

_____

_____

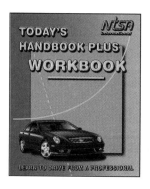

TODAY'S HANDBOOK PLUS WORKBOOK

*Check your comprehension and mastery of the contents of this chapter by completing the corresponding exercise that is found in the complement to the **TODAY'S HANDBOOK PLUS**:*

TODAY'S HANDBOOK PLUS WORKBOOK

Complete the exercise on Pages 63 to 66. If necessary, review the chapter when uncertain of an answer and refer to your instructor for further guidance.

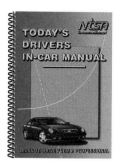

TODAY'S DRIVERS IN-CAR MANUAL

*Before any in-car session, prepare yourself and facilitate the development of proper driving skills and habits by reading the corresponding lesson in the complement to the **TODAY'S HANDBOOK PLUS**:*

TODAY'S DRIVERS IN-CAR MANUAL

Your instructor will evaluate your progress in the manual. Licensed parents or guardians should supplement your practice by following the manual procedures and coordinating with your in-car instructor.

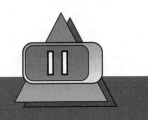

The Laws of Physics

As a passenger, you have observed the effect of natural laws on vehicle performance. Sudden acceleration or braking maneuvers have pushed you backwards or forwards in your seat. While turning a corner, you have felt the sensation of leaning towards the outside of the curve. You may have felt a minor skid on slippery pavement.

While riding a bicycle on a downgrade, you have experienced the increased acceleration that may have been exhilarating but required an extremely long braking distance. Conversely, riding uphill required extra exertion and selecting a lower gear.

All of these situations illustrate the laws of physics acting upon a vehicle in motion. As you become a driver, you must be aware of these forces and adapt your driving so that the natural forces will not adversely affect the control of your vehicle.

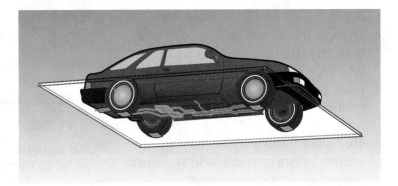

AFTER COMPLETING THIS CHAPTER, THE STUDENT MUST UNDERSTAND THE LAWS OF PHYSICS AS THEY APPLY TO THE DRIVING TASK WITH RESPECT TO:

- friction and vehicle control.
- gravity and vehicle balance.
- kinetic energy and its impact on inertia and force of impact.

Friction

Friction is the resistance to motion between two objects in contact with each other. This resistance to slipping between the four patches of rubber and the road surface, produces the TRACTION that is used to control your vehicle.

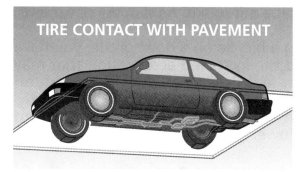

TIRE CONTACT WITH PAVEMENT

These four traction points are used to:
- **put your vehicle in motion**
  push the accelerator and the drive wheels turn against the pavement to move the vehicle forward or backward.

- **change the direction of your vehicle**
  turn the steering and the front wheels turn. They rub against the road causing the vehicle to change direction.

- **stop your vehicle**
  apply the brake pedal and the brake system slows the four tires. They react against the pavement slowing the vehicle.

The amount of traction produced is limited even when all the factors are ideal. When driving, you must avoid dividing the available traction. When you brake in a straight line, you can use all the available traction for braking. If, however, you brake and steer or accelerate and steer, you divide the available traction. If the requirements of traction exceed the amount available; then, the vehicle will skid.

THE FACTORS AFFECTING TRACTION

TIRES: Tires are designed with grooved surfaces called treads. These are designed to channel water, snow, etc. through the grooves and keep the rubber in contact with the road. Different tread patterns are intended for special uses such as snow tires.

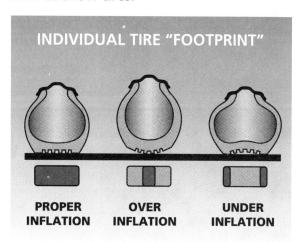

INDIVIDUAL TIRE "FOOTPRINT"

| PROPER INFLATION | OVER INFLATION | UNDER INFLATION |

As the tire wears the rubber tread thins and eventually becomes smooth (bald tire). The best traction is produced when the treads are in good condition.

Tire inflation is also very important. As shown in the diagram, properly inflated tires produce the largest "footprint" with the pavement; therefore giving the best traction. (See Chapter 20 for complete details on tires and tire maintenance.)

FRICTION FACTORS	TYPES OF SURFACE
0.9	Smooth dry asphalt
0.70	Average dry pavement
0.60	Wet asphalt-based concrete
0.50	Dry or wet gravel
0.40	Wet concrete, wet and oily gravel
0.35	Average damp pavement and melted ice
0.20	Muddy and frozen asphalt
0.05	Ice

THE ROAD SURFACE: The best traction is available on smooth dry pavement. Any variation and the friction factor diminishes accordingly. Refer to the chart, the starting point is a friction factor of 1; excellent tires stopped on a perfectly smooth surface.

SPEED: The speed at which you drive also decreases traction. As speed increases, distortions in the tire shape reduce the surface area touching the pavement. The increased air flow under the vehicle as your speed rises tends to reduce the pressure exerted by the weight of the vehicle on the tires.

Both of these factors cause a decrease in traction as the speed of your vehicle increases.

MECHANICAL CONDITION: The wheel alignment, the suspension, and the steering will reduce traction when not in proper operating condition. (See Chapter 20 for more complete details.) One example: the shock absorbers are intended to keep the tires in contact with the pavement. When in poor condition, the tires tend to skip on the pavement, causing loss of contact and premature "spotty" wear of the treads.

Gravity

The invisible force that pulls objects to the center of the earth is called **GRAVITY.** This force gives objects their weight and keeps them in contact with the ground. Without gravity a vehicle could not accelerate, brake or steer. In certain situations, uphill and downhill, you must compensate for this force acting upon the vehicle.

DRIVING UPHILL: The force of gravity will slow your vehicle; the steeper the grade, the greater the affect. Thus, as you approach a hill, you must choose the

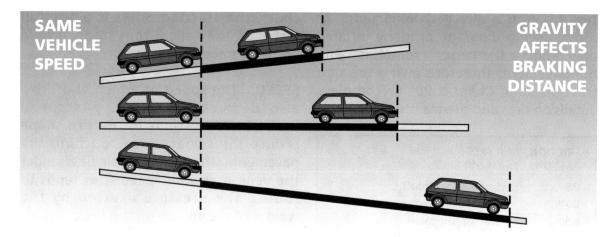

appropriate gear that will provide the necessary climbing power. In a standard, downshift; in an automatic, select a lower gear by pressing the accelerator sharply (kickdown) on a short grade or by moving the selector lever to a lower gear on a longer grade. (Second gear at 25 to 40 mph; first gear at 15 to 25 mph.) Try to avoid shifting on the hill. While going uphill, maintain your speed by increasing pressure on the gas pedal.

As you near the crest, ease up on the accelerator and keep to the right side of your lane until you can see far ahead again. When you return to a level surface select DRIVE in the automatic or shift to the appropriate gear in the standard.

Remember if you have to stop on the upgrade, your stopping distance will be much shorter. Be prepared to ease up on the brake to stop in the correct place.

DRIVING DOWNHILL: The opposite is true. The force of gravity will cause your speed to increase. The braking distance will be much longer. When you approach the downgrade, (signs will warn of the hill, length and steepness) check the brakes by applying a slight pressure. If the hill is steep, shift to a lower gear in keeping with the appropriate speed required. As you descend the slope, release the accelerator to take advantage of the engine compression for braking power. If necessary, apply the brakes as well, gently and intermittently. Increase the following distance and, if you must stop, prepare yourself by braking earlier and much more firmly than normal.

Your vehicle's **CENTER OF GRAVITY** is the point around which all of its weight is balanced. Most modern automobiles have a very low center of gravity; this gives them excellent road-handling characteristics. Pick-up trucks, jeeps, four wheel drive vehicles, and cars with rooftop carriers tend to have higher centers of gravity. This must be taken into consideration otherwise braking and steering conditions can become dangerous in these vehicles.

Kinetic Energy

Any body in motion acquires KINETIC ENERGY or momentum. (The word kinetic is derived from the Greek word meaning "to move") The formula for calculating this energy is kinetic energy equals one-half the mass (weight of the object) times the velocity (speed) squared.

$$KE = 1/2\ M\ V^2$$

Increase in MASS (weight) proportionally increases the kinetic energy of an object.

SPEED increases kinetic energy by the square of the number of times speed is increased.

This acquired kinetic energy comes into play in all aspects of driving. To stop, you must dissipate the kinetic energy by braking (Chapter 12) or by hitting another object (force of impact).

To steer, you must overcome the momentum (inertia) of the vehicle in order to change direction.

The most important factor in kinetic energy is your speed. First of all, a small change in speed has a **tremendous effect** on kinetic energy. Secondly, this factor is **under your control**. Slow your vehicle, reduce the speed in half and the kinetic energy acting on your vehicle is only one quarter of what it was before braking.

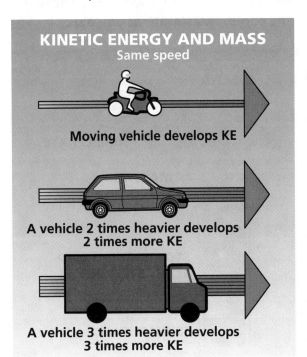

KINETIC ENERGY AND MASS
Same speed
Moving vehicle develops KE
A vehicle 2 times heavier develops 2 times more KE
A vehicle 3 times heavier develops 3 times more KE

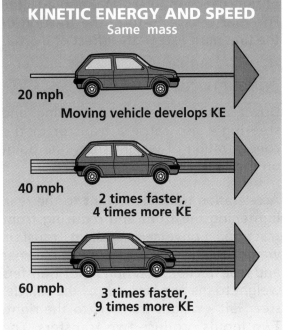

KINETIC ENERGY AND SPEED
Same mass
20 mph — Moving vehicle develops KE
40 mph — 2 times faster, 4 times more KE
60 mph — 3 times faster, 9 times more KE

Inertia

Sir Isaac Newton, the British scientist, stated three laws dealing with motion. The first law is called the **LAW OF INERTIA**. The law states, in part:

> A body at rest tends to remain at rest. (static inertia)
>
> A body in motion will continue in a straight line unless some force acts upon it. (dynamic inertia)

Vehicle control (and occupants) are affected by inertia. You have felt the effect of acceleration, of deceleration and of the vehicle turning a corner. The more kinetic energy the vehicle and the occupants accumulate the greater the effect of inertia. In a curve, the sharpness of the change of direction is also a factor. For your vehicle to turn, the traction of the tires must exceed the effect of inertia.

WEIGHT TRANSFER

Driver inputs - acceleration, braking, and steering - also cause a transfer of the concentration of weight from one point on the vehicle to another (Chapter 9).

Acceleration transfers weight to the rear, lightening the front and reducing front traction. Conversely, braking transfers weight to the front, lightening the rear and rear traction. Steering input transfers weight to the opposite side of the vehicle; steer left - weight transfers to the right. Two inputs produce two transfers. The driver must minimize weight transfer or utilize it to increase vehicle control.

TO TAKE A CURVE PROPERLY

You have no control over the sharpness of the curve or the weight of your vehicle; **You do have control of your speed.** If you brake on a curve, you divide up the available traction that is needed to steer. As well you further upset vehicle balance (two inputs - two weight transfers) that is already reacting to the effect of inertia.

Nearing curves, **reduce speed**, respect suggested speeds, check the sharpness of the curve, and verify the slant (sideways slope) of the road. **Maintain speed on the curve. Accelerate as you exit.**

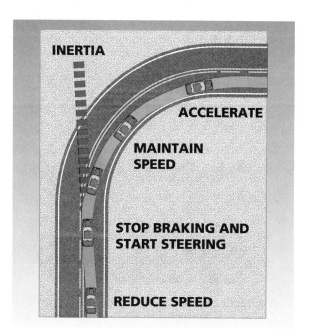

INERTIA

ACCELERATE

MAINTAIN SPEED

STOP BRAKING AND START STEERING

REDUCE SPEED

A FLAT ROAD has no slope and will not assist the vehicle to negotiate the curve.

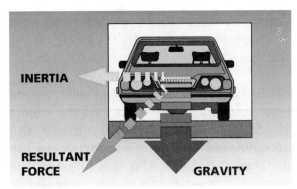

A BANKED CURVE has a higher edge on the outside of the curve and slopes down to the inside. The vehicle will lean toward the inside of the curve (similar to riding a bicycle); inertial energy partly pushes the tires into the pavement increasing traction. This allows you to negotiate the curve safely at a higher speed.

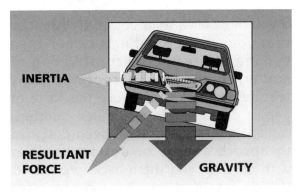

A CROWNED ROAD is higher at the center and slopes down to both sides. Approaching a right curve, this slope is similar to the banked curve; in a left turn, (see below) it is very dangerous and should be negotiated at very slow speeds.

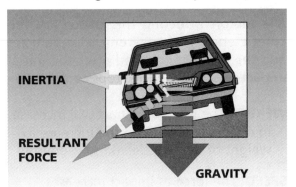

On vehicles with a higher center of gravity, special caution must be exercised on curves. Reduce speed. Remember it is better to enter more slowly, you can always accelerate gradually. If you enter too fast, a loss of control will be inevitable.

The dead pedal (footrest) should be used to brace yourself on curves or during sudden maneuvers to maintain a proper seating position, rather than relying on the seat belt or hanging on to the steering wheel "for dear life". This technique will permit you to maintain steering control in any driving situation.

SAFETY TIPS

The natural forces that act upon your vehicle do not require a police officer to ensure that they are obeyed. They are always in force. Disregard them and the result will be a loss of vehicle control and a potential collision. The driver needs to be aware of the laws of physics and act in good time to maintain control of the vehicle.

Force of Impact

The force with which a moving vehicle collides with an object or another moving vehicle is called the **FORCE OF IMPACT**.

The factors affecting this force are the kinetic energy of the vehicle or vehicles and the distance traveled after the initial impact until the vehicle stops completely.

WEIGHT: The force of impact will increase in direct proportion to the increase in weight of the vehicle . (kinetic energy)

SPEED: The force of impact increases exponentially by the square of the number of times speed is increased. (kinetic energy)

DISTANCE: The force of impact dissipates in relation to the square of the distance traveled after the initial contact.

When a collision is unavoidable, slow your speed as much as possible to reduce the force of impact dramatically and follow these basic concepts.

AVOID HEAD-ON COLLISIONS at all costs. The speed of the oncoming vehicle adds to your own speed. If you are both traveling at 30 mph, the force of impact

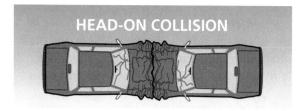

HEAD-ON COLLISION

would be equal to an impact at 60 mph (double the speed = 4 times the kinetic energy and thus 4 times the force of impact).

STEER TOWARDS OBJECTS that will offer the least resistance on impact. As the object yields on impact, it will absorb the accumulated energy in proportion to the distance it "gives". This will diminish the amount of energy your vehicle must absorb and increase your chance of avoiding injury.

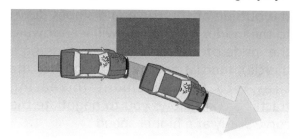

If you must hit a solid object, try to hit so that your vehicle deflects rather than striking it directly. The construction of modern highways incorporates many features designed to reduce the force of impact. Guard rails, sand-filled canisters, cement barriers, etc. have been designed to absorb energy or deflect vehicles without throwing them back into traffic. Vehicle manufacturers have incorporated many energy absorbing features and passenger restraint systems to protect the occupants (Chapter 13). Engineers have done their utmost to make driving safer and should a collision occur, to reduce the chance of injury.

Only the DRIVER can avoid collisions.

Review

TERMS TO REMEMBER - WRITE A SHORT DEFINITION FOR THE FOLLOWING :

- Friction
- Traction
- Tire footprint
- Gravity

- Center of gravity
- Kinetic energy
- Momentum
- Inertia

- Banked road
- Crowned road
- Force of impact

SUMMARY

Gravity keeps the tires in contact with the road providing the traction to control your vehicle. This traction is limited by the tires, the road surface, speed and other factors. Avoid dividing the available traction by steering and braking at the same time. Foresight can control the effects of gravity on braking distance and speed on hills. Kinetic energy and inertia affect braking distance, force of impact and the stability of your vehicle in curves. Know the physical forces that affect your driving and you will maintain control of your vehicle.

TEST A - WRITE "T" BESIDE STATEMENTS THAT ARE TRUE AND "F" BESIDE THOSE THAT ARE FALSE.

_____ **1.** Different tire treads are designed for specific road conditions.

_____ **2.** All road surfaces provide the same traction.

_____ **3.** The mechanical condition of the vehicle does not affect the road holding ability (traction) of any vehicle.

_____ **4.** Gravity has no effect on a vehicle when it is traveling on a level road.

_____ **5.** The higher the center of gravity of a vehicle, the more stable the vehicle will be.

_____ **6.** Kinetic energy increases proportionally with an increase in mass.

_____ **7.** A banked curve is the safest.

_____ **8.** Braking while rounding a curve is the best method for reducing speed.

_____ **9.** Force of impact is not related to the speed of the vehicle.

_____ **10.** When a collision seems inevitable, steer towards the nearest solid object in order to reduce the force of impact.

Student notes

_____
_____
_____
_____
_____
_____
_____
_____
_____
_____
_____
_____
_____
_____
_____
_____
_____
_____
_____

TODAY'S HANDBOOK PLUS WORKBOOK

Check your comprehension and mastery of the contents of this chapter by completing the corresponding exercise that is found in the complement to the **TODAY'S HANDBOOK PLUS**:

TODAY'S HANDBOOK PLUS WORKBOOK

Complete the exercise on Pages 67 to 72. If necessary, review the chapter when uncertain of an answer and refer to your instructor for further guidance.

Stopping Distances

Total stopping distance is a lot longer than most novice drivers realize. IT IS NOT POSSIBLE TO STOP "ON A DIME". From the moment a hazard appears on the roadway ahead until you bring your vehicle to a complete stop, time will pass and your vehicle is in motion. It will cover a certain distance. The length of that distance is directly related to many factors.

In the last chapter on the laws of physics, you studied some of these factors. Kinetic energy, the energy of motion, is a major factor in the actual distance needed to stop your vehicle once the brakes are applied.

In this chapter, you will examine all the factors as well as how to adapt your driving to these factors. You will learn the different braking techniques and advancements in modern brake technology.

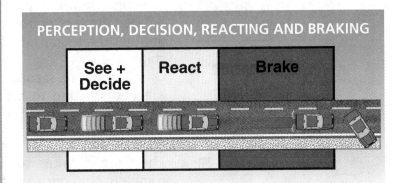

PERCEPTION, DECISION, REACTING AND BRAKING

| See + Decide | React | Brake |

AFTER COMPLETING THIS CHAPTER, THE STUDENT MUST BE ABLE TO UNDERSTAND, IDENTIFY AND BE PREPARED TO APPLY OR ADAPT TO:

- the factors in total stopping time and distance.
- the various braking techniques.
- the ABS brake system and the use thereof.

Time and Distances

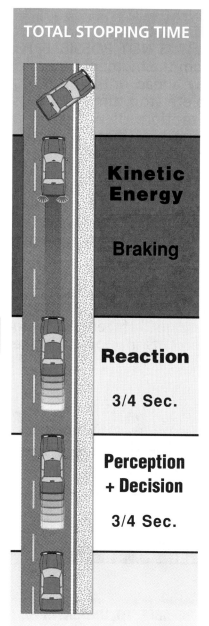

TOTAL STOPPING TIME

Kinetic Energy

Braking

Reaction

3/4 Sec.

Perception + Decision

3/4 Sec.

TOTAL STOPPING TIME consists of the entire time from the moment a hazard appears ahead until you bring your vehicle to a complete stop. It can be subdivided into:

Perception time:

The time it takes you to spot the danger. This depends on your mental and physical state, your experience, your eye lead time (how far ahead you scan the road), and how quickly you identify the hazard (SCAN - IDENTIFY). In poor visual conditions, reduce your speed so that you compensate for your shorter eye lead time. (At slower speeds it will take more time to reach the hazard)

Decision making time:

The time it takes you to PREDICT and DECIDE what to do. Your experience, physical and mental state, as well as the attention you give to the driving task will all affect how much time will elapse. If all the factors are at their best, three quarters of a second will elapse for the perception and decision making stages.

Reaction time:

The time it takes you to EXECUTE your decision. Release the accelerator and apply the brakes. At best, another three quarters of a second will elapse for this stage.

One and a half seconds in total time and only now are you starting to brake. This total can be much longer depending on the driver.

Braking time:

The time it takes for your vehicle to come to a complete stop once the brakes are applied. This time is related to your experience and skill in braking, the kinetic energy of your vehicle, the mechanical condition of your vehicle, and the road conditions.

Let's translate this elapsed time into distances.

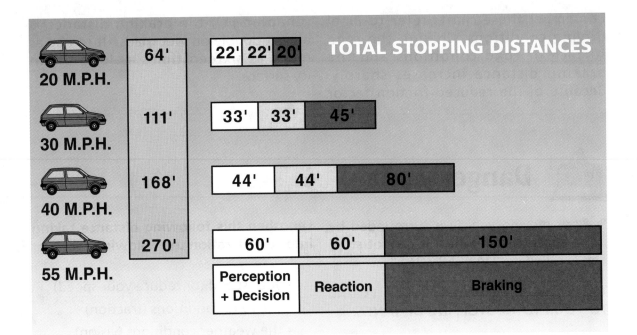

TOTAL STOPPING DISTANCES

20 M.P.H.	64'	22' 22' 20'
30 M.P.H.	111'	33' 33' 45'
40 M.P.H.	168'	44' 44' 80'
55 M.P.H.	270'	60' 60' 150'
		Perception + Decision / Reaction / Braking

TOTAL STOPPING DISTANCE is the distance your vehicle will travel from the moment the hazard appears ahead until your vehicle comes to a complete stop.

Look at the chart. Compare the total stopping distance at 20 mph to what it becomes as the speed increases.

Compare the braking distances (the distance your vehicle travels from the time the brakes are applied until it stops) at 20 mph and 40 mph. The speed is doubled. The braking distance ... ? This is a result of kinetic energy as it applies to braking distance. Look at the chart below for a comparison of braking distance and speed.

12

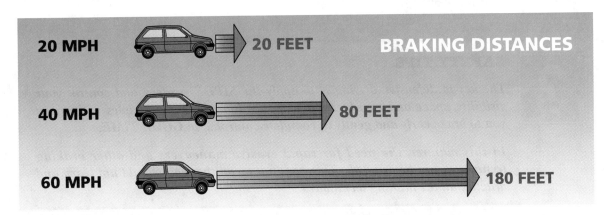

BRAKING DISTANCES

20 MPH	20 FEET
40 MPH	80 FEET
60 MPH	180 FEET

Remember these charts refer to ideal driving conditions. Change the road surface or road conditions and the braking distance increases sharply. Because of the reduced friction factor (Chapter 11), the braking distance is almost double on wet roads. It can be as much as sixteen times as long on an icy surface.

Danger Zone

Your moving vehicle is surrounded by a space within which it cannot stop. This is called its **"DANGER ZONE"**.

THE SPACE IN FRONT OF YOU IS EQUAL TO YOUR TOTAL STOPPING DISTANCE.

THE SPACE BEHIND YOU IS EQUAL TO THE TOTAL STOPPING DISTANCE OF THE VEHICLE FOLLOWING YOU.

To protect yourself, always maintain a **"SAFETY CUSHION"** around your vehicle. (Chapter 10) By utilizing the **"TWO SECOND RULE"** as a minimum, you leave a 1/2 second margin of safety from the preceding vehicle. (You require one and a half seconds to start braking.)

Lengthen this following distance taking into consideration the following factors:

- your speed (or reduce your speed)
- the road conditions (traction)
- the weather conditions (vision)
- the density of traffic
- your level of experience in this particular driving environment

Apply these same concepts to the space behind you. When another vehicle encroaches on your safety cushion (tailgater - Chapter 10), react accordingly.

SAFETY TIPS

The key to defensive driving is to apply the SIPDE strategy and control your visibility, space and speed. Proper application of these principles will permit you to brake early and gently in complete control... in GOOD TIME.

In this manner, the need for rapid evasive maneuvers and other braking techniques can be avoided. This does not mean that you should not learn and practice all the braking techniques.

Braking Techniques

To bring your vehicle to a stop in complete safety regardless of the many factors involved, there are several techniques to master.

BRAKING IN "GOOD TIME"
The first and the best method is to constantly monitor your speed, space, and driving conditions. Then you can brake with a steady pressure on the brake as normal; braking in "GOOD TIME."

This method will keep you out of trouble though it requires a long braking distance. To succeed, this technique is based on the driver - YOU must think ahead, apply the SIPDE strategy, and drive defensively.

THRESHOLD BRAKING:
This method involves applying the brake pedal more firmly, just to the point prior to "locking the wheels". Shift to neutral (depress the clutch pedal - standard transmission) to remove the unbalancing effect of the drive wheels and the differential. If the wheels lock, ease up slightly adjusting the pressure to apply as hard as you can without lock-up. As your vehicle slows to a stop, ease up gradually. To master this technique requires practice and skill. The advantages are:

- the braking distance is shorter
- you maintain your steering control
- the tires wear evenly and avoid skidding

The problem with this method is that road surfaces are rarely smooth. On wet, icy, or uneven pavement, the "lock-up point" will vary while you are braking. It requires considerable skill to maintain full braking without skidding.

"PUMPING THE BRAKE PEDAL"
This method involves applying the brake pedal completely (locking the wheels), then releasing the brake sufficiently to permit wheel rotation. Then re-applying the brake pedal again. These actions are repeated until your vehicle comes to a standstill. Shifting to neutral (depressing the clutch pedal - standard transmission) at the start of the pumping action will again remove any unbalancing effect from the power train.

This technique permits control of the steering; however, the braking distance is not as short as threshold braking.

"LOCKING THE BRAKES"
This method is not a normal stopping technique. It is intended to be used in EMERGENCY SITUATIONS ONLY; when it is a choice between a collision or stopping. The braking distance is the shortest; however, you lose steering control.

APPLY THE BRAKES SUDDENLY AND FULLY.

The immediate result is continuous braking action. The tires are skidding. Your vehicle may rotate on its axis while stopping in a straight line. **This is not a normal stopping method.**

12

ABS Brakes (Anti-lock Braking System)

One of the greatest recent advancements in modern automotive technology is the "ABS BRAKE SYSTEM".

This system assists the driver; allowing you to perform an emergency stop while retaining steering control. You apply the brakes fully. The onboard computer controls the brake pressure at each wheel; cycling from locked to slightly rolling in a pumping-like action many times a second.

The result is continuous braking action, under control while maintaining steering control. The vehicle will not rotate on its axis! You do not have to modulate the pressure on the brake pedal.

SLAM AND HOLD THE BRAKE!

The result will be:
- The system will look after you
- Remember, you can still steer

Brake as hard as you can, look where you want to go, steer where you want to go - you will reduce speed rapidly and still change direction.

REMEMBER, BRAKE AND STEER!

If you purchase a vehicle with ABS, you should practice emergency stops to learn the technique required to take full advantage of the system.

Most drivers, who are not familiar with the technology, *defeat the system by easing off the pedal* when the pedal begins to pulsate, or because of the noise the system produces when it is activated. Other drivers defeat the system by attempting to pump the brake pedal out of habit.

Don't think you can drive faster because your vehicle is equipped with ABS. It does not produce a shorter braking distance!

SAFETY TIPS

Many insurance companies offer special premium reductions for vehicles that are factory-equipped with the ABS brake system because of the tremendous advantages of this system in avoiding collisions during emergency maneuvers when used properly.

Most automotive manufacturers are including the system as standard equipment on many of their models. When you purchase a vehicle, this is an item you MUST CONSIDER. If it is not included on the model of your choice, order it as an option. If it is not available as an option, choose another make or model that has an ABS system.

Check the owner's manual for any special service requirements.

Review

TERMS TO REMEMBER - WRITE A SHORT DEFINITION FOR THE FOLLOWING :

- Perception time
- Decision making time
- Reaction time
- Braking time

- Total stopping distance
- Danger zone
- Safety cushion
- ABS brakes

- Braking in "good time"
- Threshold braking
- Pumping the brakes
- Locking the brakes

SUMMARY

It is impossible to stop a vehicle in motion instantly. Before you come to a complete stop, a certain distance will be required. The length of this distance depends on:

- **THE DRIVER:**
  Physical / Mental state
  Eye lead time
  Driving experience
  Reaction time
  Skill

- **THE VEHICLE:**
  Kinetic energy
  - mass (weight)
  - velocity (speed)
  Mechanical condition
  - brakes / tires / suspension

- **THE ROADWAY:**
  Traction conditions
  - friction
  - type of surface
  The slope (gravity)
  - downhill / uphill

TEST A - IDENTIFY THE FOLLOWING STATEMENTS AS TRUE OR FALSE.

_____ **1)** Perception and decision making time are the same for all drivers.

_____ **2)** Reaction time, the time to actually execute the maneuver decided upon, will require at least three quarters of a second

_____ **3)** Braking time, the time that elapses from the moment the brake is applied until the vehicle comes to a complete stop, only varies with vehicle speed.

_____ **4)** Total stopping distance includes the distance traveled while seeing, deciding and reacting as well as the distance required to stop the vehicle.

_____ **5)** If the stopping distance at 20 mph is 20 feet, the stopping distance, all other factors remaining the same, at 60 mph would be 180 feet.

_____ **6)** The "SAFETY CUSHION" equals the distance needed to stop the vehicle.

_____ **7)** The driver who tailgates, follows your vehicle too closely, is creating a hazardous situation for you as well as for himself.

_____ **8)** Applying the brake pedal suddenly and fully, "LOCKING THE BRAKES", is a normal braking technique and is used in most stopping situations.

_____ **9)** Shifting to NEUTRAL (depressing the clutch) before braking, increases control because it removes the unbalancing effect of the differential/power train.

_____ **10)** Braking in "GOOD TIME" requires the driver to constantly monitor speed, space and driving conditions in order to stop the vehicle safely.

TEST B - MATCH THE DESCRIPTIONS IN COLUMN B TO THE ITEMS IN COLUMN A

COLUMN A

_____ **A)** Danger zone

_____ **B)** Perception time

_____ **C)** Reaction time

_____ **D)** Following distance

_____ **E)** Safety cushion

_____ **F)** Braking in good time

_____ **G)** Threshold braking

_____ **H)** Intermittent braking

_____ **I)** Locking the brakes

COLUMN B

1) The distance a vehicle travels while you see a hazard and decide what to do.

2) Plan ahead, adapt to the environment, and keep pace to brake gently in all circumstances.

3) Emergency stop, applying the brakes just before the locking point.

4) The space surrounding the vehicle in which it cannot stop.

5) Emergency stop, shift to neutral and pump the brake pedal.

6) The distance the vehicle travels while you execute your decision.

7) Emergency stop, shift to neutral and depress the brake pedal suddenly and completely.

8) The minimum distance that must be kept from the preceding vehicle in order to avoid becoming involved in collisions.

9) The space in front of your vehicle allowing for perception and reaction time as well as a margin for safety.

TODAY'S HANDBOOK PLUS WORKBOOK

*Check your comprehension and mastery of the contents of this chapter by completing the corresponding exercise that is found in the complement to the **TODAY'S HANDBOOK PLUS**:*

TODAY'S HANDBOOK PLUS WORKBOOK

Complete the exercise on Pages 73 to 76. If necessary, review the chapter when uncertain of an answer and refer to your instructor for further guidance.

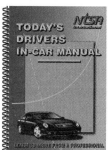

TODAY'S DRIVERS IN-CAR MANUAL

*Before any in-car session, prepare yourself and facilitate the development of proper driving skills and habits by reading the corresponding lesson in the complement to the **TODAY'S HANDBOOK PLUS**:*

TODAY'S DRIVERS IN-CAR MANUAL

Your instructor will evaluate your progress in the manual. Licensed parents or guardians should supplement your practice by following the manual procedures and coordinating with your in-car instructor.

Safety Technology

Engineers are responsible for improving vehicles, highway design, and traffic control systems. Today's automobiles are safer, more efficient, and more comfortable to drive than ever before.

In the event of a collision, the interior has been designed with a padded dash, head restraints, controls that are recessed or break away, a collapsible steering column, and shatter-proof windshields. The vehicle has energy-absorbing bumpers to minimize low speed impacts. The front and rear sections are designed to crush. Beams reinforce the side doors to reduce the possible effect on the passenger compartment in crashes.

The single most effective safety device during a collision is the safety belt!!

AFTER COMPLETING THIS CHAPTER, THE STUDENT MUST DEMONSTRATE COMPLETE COMPREHENSION OF THE IMPORTANCE AND PROPER USAGE OF:

- **safety belts.**
- **air bags.**
- **child restraints.**

Restraint Systems

When a vehicle is involved in a collision, three impacts occur in rapid succession.

- The **vehicle collides** with another vehicle or object.
- The **occupants collide** with the interior of the vehicle.
- The **interior organs collide** with the interior of the body cavity.

You have already seen how engineers design the vehicle to absorb impacts and how you as the driver can minimize the force of impact during a collision.

In a crash at 30 mph, the impact on an occupant of the vehicle is equal to falling from a three story building. The force of impact equals 35 TIMES YOUR BODY WEIGHT.

The brain and other interior organs strike the interior of the skull and body cavity with this tremendous force when the exterior of the body collides and stops instantly.

To minimize the consequences of these two impacts, the occupants should be protected by RESTRAINT DEVICES. These are designed to keep them in their seats and to cushion the stopping motion. They prevent the second impact. At the same time they slow the forward motion (effect of inertia) and bring the occupants to a stop more gradually (impact distance).

Safety Belts

A safety belt that the occupant must attach or buckle is called an ACTIVE RESTRAINT device.

The lap portion of this belt is designed to keep you in your seat. It should be adjusted to fit snugly low across your hips below the stomach.

The shoulder portion prevents your head and torso from striking the interior of the passenger compartment. It should pass over the shoulder and cross your chest diagonally with a minimum of slack. Your clenched fist should barely fit between the belt and your chest, if the belt does not adjust automatically.

NEVER ATTACH THE SAFETY BELT IF IT IS TWISTED!

NEVER WEAR THE BELT LOOSELY OR IMPROPERLY!

In either case, you will defeat the proper operation of the safety belt.
The result may be a more serious injury if a collision were to happen.

During a collision, the combined action of the lap and shoulder belt will maintain your seating position, cushion the impact, and distribute the force over your shoulders, hips and rib cage.

Seat belts have been proven effective in reducing the probability of serious injury by 40 percent and increasing the chance of survival by 60 percent. As a result, the majority of states have passed legislation that requires the wearing of safety belts and all states require the use of child restraints by law.

PASSIVE RESTRAINT DEVICES do not require the occupant to fasten or buckle these protective devices. Many vehicles are equipped with passive seat belts that are attached to the door and to the floor; they automatically fasten when the door is closed. This safety belt provides the same protection to the occupant.

13

SAFETY TIPS

The National Highway Traffic Safety Administration (NHTSA) estimates that 226,567 lives were saved by safety belts from 1975 through 2006. 15,383 lives in 2006. In 2006, if all occupants (over age 4) had worn safety belts, an additional 5,441 lives could have been saved! NHTSA - DOT HS 810 807
In 2006, 51% of passenger car occupants and 72% of light truck occupants involved in fatal crashes were unrestrained. NHTSA - DOT HS 810 807

Air Bags

The air bag is another passive restraint device. It can be installed in the center of the steering wheel for the driver and in the dash for other front seat passengers.

The concept is to reduce the speed of the occupant to zero, with little or no damage, by cushioning the force of impact and distributing it over a wider surface of the torso. The air bag has the space between the occupant and the steering wheel (or dash) and a fraction of a second in which to work.

A sensor causes the air bags to inflate instantly in any frontal collision over 10 to 15 mph. The inflation system ignites a solid propellant producing a large volume of nitrogen gas - the air bag bursts from its storage site at over 200 mph (faster than the blink of an eye)! A second later, the gas dissipates through tiny holes in the bag and it deflates. (This whole process occurs in only one/twenty-fifth of a second.) A powdery substance may be released along with the air bag - it is cornstarch or talcum powder which manufacturers use to keep the bag pliable and lubricated while in storage

AIR BAGS DO NOT REPLACE SAFETY BELTS! THEY COMPLEMENT THEM!
- Used together, they reduce the probability of a fatality by 70 %.
- The air bag alone - only 35 %.
- The seat belt alone - 60 %.

CAUTION: **Passenger side air bags can cause harm to children in any child restraint attached to the front seat!** The safest position for passengers (especially children) is the back seat!

THE RISKS
It didn't take long to learn that the force of an air bag deploying can hurt those who are too close (the risk zone is the first 2 to 3 inches of inflation). "Too close" can occur when an occupant, typically unbelted or leaning out of position, is thrown forward just before the crash impact (the period known as pre-crash braking) to within a few inches of, or directly on top of, the rapidly accelerating air bag. In 1997, "*depowered*" air bags were introduced to reduce the danger.

By 1999, all new passenger vehicles and light trucks were required to have driver and passenger air bags (a deactivation switch was optional).

A third generation air bag is being phased in from 2003 until 2005. These "*advanced*" frontal air bags are designed to meet the needs of the occupant in a variety of specific crash situations. They automatically determine if, and with what level of power, the driver and/or the passenger air bag will inflate.

The appropriate level of power is based upon sensor inputs that can typically detect (1) occupant size, (2) seat position, (3) seat belt use, and (4) crash severity - some systems use the occupant's distance from the air bag as well.

Vehicles with advanced frontal air bags are required to have:
- warning labels with the phrase "EVEN WITH ADVANCED AIR BAGS" on the

sun visors for both the driver and passenger seating positions.

⚠ WARNING
EVEN WITH ADVANCED AIR BAGS
- Children can be killed or seriously injured by the air bag
- The back seat is the safest place for children
- Never put a rear-facing child seat in the front
- Always use seat belts and child restraints
- See owner's manual for more information about air bags

- an indicator light with the phrase "PASSENGER AIR BAG OFF" or "PASS AIR BAG OFF." When illuminated, this indicator light informs you that the passenger air bag has been turned off (suppressed) by the advanced air bag system and therefore will not deploy.
- a complete explanation of the system in the owner's manual.

SIDE AIR BAGS

In recent years, side air bags to protect the driver and the passengers when involved in a side-impact collision have

13

SAFETY TIPS

The advantages of air bags are such that many insurance companies are already offering significant premium reductions for vehicles that are equipped with air bags. Moreover, new vehicles are including air bag systems as standard equipment on many models. When purchasing your next vehicle, this option should be a factor in your choice of vehicle. Make sure that they are included on the model you choose whether as standard equipment or as an option.

The National Highway Traffic Safety Administration (NHTSA) estimates that 2,796 lives were saved by air bags in 2006 (22,466 lives between 1987 and 2006). DOT HS 810 807

been introduced. The problem with this type of collision is that both the time factor (between the vehicle crash and the occupant being struck) and the space available (between the initial crash and the occupant) are very small compared to frontal impacts (also, the danger in two vehicle crashes where an SUV or mini-van crashes into the side of a passenger car). The side air bag must perform within very tiny constraints.

There are essentially three types:
- **Curtain** - an air bag descends from the roof of the vehicle to protect the heads of occupants in both the front and rear seats;

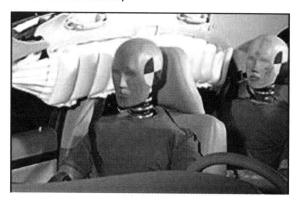

- **Inflatable tube** - a tubular air bag attached to the roof deploys to protect the head along with separate side air

bags in the doors designed for the torso; and

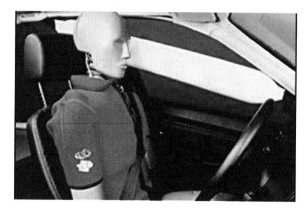

- **Torso/head combination** - combination air bags deploy from the vehicle seats, or sometimes from the doors, to protect both the head and torso.

Air bags have been designed and installed on some vehicles since the mid-1990s. Since 1997, the Insurance Institute for Highway Safety in the United States has been testing vehicles with various side air bag designs. Overall effectiveness in real-world crashes has been estimated at - *45% fatality reduction for drivers of cars with head-protecting side air bags*. In 2006, 40% of vehicle models offered side air bags as standard equipment and 26% offered them as an option.

SAFETY TIPS

Approximately 25% of passenger vehicle occupant fatalities occur in side impact collisions every year. Head injuries are the leading cause. Side air bags - offering head protection (curtain and inflatable tube types) - reduce the risk of death by 45% - Insurance Institute for Highway Safety.
Make sure your next vehicle is equipped with side air bags!

Child Restraints

I t is extremely dangerous to ride in a moving vehicle while holding a child on your lap. Rather than protecting them, you are putting them at risk!

In a collision, the child will continue forward (kinetic energy - inertia) and the force required to stop this motion is beyond human capability.

**IF YOU LOVE THEM, PROTECT THEM!
PUT THEM IN A CHILD RESTRAINT!
IT`S THE LAW IN ALL STATES!**

Children should be secured in a device appropriate to their size and age. These child restraints should be properly installed in accordance with the seat manufacturer's recommendations.

THE INFANT SEAT

This restraint is intended for children weighing less than 20 lbs. The child is cushioned by the seat on all sides. At this age, the child's head is larger and heavier than the rest of his/her body. The seat should be positioned facing the rear with the child firmly secured to the seat which is then attached to the vehicle using the safety belt.

Check on your child without turning around. Make sure that you do this by glancing in the rear-view mirror and returning your eyes to the road ahead in between glances. Do not permit yourself to become distracted.

If any situation arises where your infant requires attention. STOP THE VEHICLE. In a safe manner of course, then care for your child. ***Do not put yourself and your infant at risk.***

THE TODDLER SEAT

This seat is designed for children ranging from 20 to 40 lbs. who have now become more active. This seat requires a quasi-permanent installation and is best attached to the rear seat. Secure the toddler seat using the seat belt and in keeping with the recommendations of the manufacturer of the restraint. Your child should be facing forward and securely buckled into the toddler seat.

Accustom yourself to conversing with your child without taking your eyes off the road. Check by using the mirror.

13

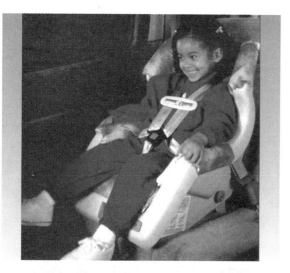

As previously mentioned, park your vehicle if you must offer physical assistance. The control of your children will become easier as they mature; the use of the seats and eventually the safety belt will have become second nature.

PRE-SCHOOLERS

Children weighing 40 to 50 lbs. are too big for the usual child restraint and yet they are not quite large enough to use the regular safety belts, especially the shoulder belt. You may often see parents allowing children to stand just behind the front seats in order to see the road.

You can imagine what will happen in a collision.

There are a variety of booster seats available which raise the child while incorporating the safety belt. This raises him/her to a sufficient height that the shoulder belt may also be used.

Engineers have also designed a shoulder harness that is adjustable, the height of the shoulder attachment can be raised or lowered to accommodate children.

SAFETY TIPS

In 2006, 361 children under age 5 were passenger vehicle occupant fatalities. An estimated 32% (109) were totally unrestrained. Six children (14 and under) were killed and 732 were injured every day in motor vehicle crashes. HS 810 931

Protect your children! Make sure they are properly restrained in a properly installed, age-appropriate child restraint that is attached to the back seat (or wearing a safety belt seated in the back when they outgrow the restraints).

A Few Facts

Safety belts properly used, help keep you behind the wheel in control of your vehicle in sudden maneuvers.

Seat belts help keep passengers in their seats in sudden maneuvers and therefore prevent them from hindering the driver.

MYTH! Pregnant women should not wear seat belts. **FACT:** They should wear them. Properly worn over the hips and across the chest, the belt will restrain the mother without harming the fetus. *The most common cause of fetal fatalities in collisions is the death of the mother.*

25 percent of traffic fatalities occur when occupants are thrown from their vehicles. *The risk of death is 5 times greater in such cases.*

The fear of being trapped by the safety belt in a burning or sinking vehicle is a false fear. The use of the safety belt increases the likelihood that you will be conscious and able to escape.

50 percent of all collisions occur within a 5 mile radius of your home. All the more reason to use the safety belt even on short, close to home trips.

60 percent of all collisions occur at speeds below 30 mph. What better time to be wearing a safety belt?

SAFETY BELTS WHEN WORN PROPERLY:
- reduce the risk of injury by 50%
- reduce the risk of death by 60%

IN CONJUNCTION WITH AIR BAGS:
- REDUCE THE RISK OF DEATH BY 70%

13

Safety Technology

The safety engineers are responsible for many improvements in vehicle and highway design that have created a safer environment for today's drivers.

HIGHWAY DESIGN IMPROVEMENTS

Among the safety features that are being designed into roadways, there are:
- wider, clearly marked lanes,
- wider and clear highway shoulders,
- rumble strips at the road edge to alert drivers (drowsiness),
- Potts dots or other lane markers that can be felt or reflect at night,
- elimination of grade intersections,
- new design median barriers that minimize vehicles rebounding into traffic,

- break away sign support posts,
- new design guard rails that reduce penetration of guardrail into vehicle,
- crash attenuators such as vinyl liquid or sand filled drums in front of barriers or cement columns,
- protected left and right turn bays,
- collector/distributor lanes on high speed, high density highways to separate slower moving entering/exiting traffic from the through movement traffic flow, and also,
- electronic message signs to alert drivers to problems ahead.

VEHICLE CONTROL ADVANCEMENTS

In recent years, a wide variety of vehicle improvements have been introduced to increase the stability of vehicle handling and to improve the construction of the vehicle, and as a consequence, have contributed to improved occupant safety.

ABS (Anti-lock Braking System)
This system is composed of a computer controller, sensors at each wheel to determine if the wheel is about to lock, and the capability of regulating the brake torque at the wheel. Most ABS systems control the brake torque at each of the front wheels independently, but some control only the rear wheels independently, whereas others control the rear wheels as a pair.

In some cases, the ABS controls only the rear wheels (RWAL, which is found on pick-up trucks and larger trucks).

The concept is that the system monitors the vehicle wheel speeds, and then regulates the brake force to control the slip between the tire and the road surface. By avoiding wheel lock, vehicle stability is improved and the driver retains the ability to steer.

TRACTION CONTROL SYSTEMS (TCS)
There are a variety of TCS systems. Any time a tire is given more torque than it can transfer to the road, the tire loses traction and spins (hard acceleration). To prevent this on vehicles with ABS, the TCS applies the brake at that wheel. This slows the tire, preventing wheelspin.

The TCS can also reduce engine speed and torque, if braking alone is not sufficient. In that case, the ABS/TCS control module signals the engine control module (ECM). It then retards the spark and reduces the amount of fuel delivered by the fuel injectors to stop wheelspin.

By controlling wheelspin, the vehicle stability, steerability, and acceleration are improved. Also, engine torque can be transferred through the differential from one drive wheel to the other. This can improve vehicle mobility and acceleration on surfaces which have non-uniform frictions. The system may disable when brake temperature rises excessively.

ACTIVE YAW CONTROL SYSTEMS (AYC)
All AYC systems include ABS and apply on the two front, or on all four wheels, and may, or may not, have the ability to control the engine speed and torque.

Active Yaw Control Systems use various sensors (typically wheel speed sensors, steering angle sensors, yaw rate sensors, and accelerometers) to monitor the dynamic state of the vehicle and the driver's commands. They then apply the brakes individually (and adjust engine torque) to adjust the rotational movement and correct the path of the vehicle to the driver's intended path. These systems improve the stability of the vehicle, the driver's control of the vehicle, and correct understeer and oversteer.

SUSPENSION STABILITY SYSTEMS

On many new vehicles, the suspension system is active. It can adjust to road conditions, vehicle balance, vehicle speed, and body roll. Various sensors send information to the ECM, which then sends signals to the hydraulic actuators (these replace springs and shocks) to raise or lower the wheel, stiffen or soften the ride, etc. All of these actions occur almost instantly, and go unnoticed by the driver. The concept is to keep the vehicle level while each tire pushes against the road surface with a constant force, despite weight shifts during cornering, hard acceleration, and hard braking.

ACTIVE STEERING CONTROL

Controlled steering systems have the ability to adjust the steered angle (steering input) or the camber angle (wheel alignment) of the wheels to influence the longitudinal and lateral forces of each tire. This system improves the stability of the vehicle and the driver's control of the vehicle while steering.

VEHICLE CONSTRUCTION IMPROVEMENTS

Engineers have redesigned the automobile with a padded dash, controls that are recessed or break away, a collapsible steering column, side impact beams, and energy-absorbing bumpers.

CRUMPLE ZONES

Certain segments of the vehicle, in front of and behind the passenger area, were designed to collapse while the passenger compartment remained intact. Other segments were constructed to spread the force of impact over a wider area. Both of these were intended to reduce the risk of penetration into the passenger seating area. Side impact beams and air bags were an extension of this concept.

IMPROVED DOOR SECURITY

Door fasteners used to resemble those found in the interior of the typical home, and generally flew open in a crash. Improvements have been engineered so that locks and door latches stay closed under the most severe conditions and impacts.

WINDSHIELDS

With the advent of tempered glass, as required by national safety standards, facial disfigurement associated with partial ejection through laminated glass has literally been eliminated.

HEADLIGHTS

In the past 15 years, headlights have undergone dramatic improvement in terms of level of illumination, focus, and reliability.

13

Review

13-F

TERMS TO REMEMBER - WRITE A SHORT DEFINITION FOR EACH OF THE FOLLOWING :

- Seat belt
- Active restraint
- Torso
- Passive restraint
- Air bags
- Infant seat
- Toddler seat
- Pre-schoolers seat

RESUME

Engineers are responsible for continual improvements in highway design, traffic control systems and vehicle construction. All of these are useless unless you, the driver, take advantage of them. When purchasing your next vehicle, make new safety technology one of the factors that determines which vehicle you choose to buy.

TEST A - WRITE A "T" FOR TRUE OR AN "F" FOR FALSE IN THE SPACES PROVIDED.

_____ 1. Collisions occur most frequently far from home.

_____ 2. In a vehicle equipped with air bags, the driver and passengers do not need to buckle up the seat belts.

_____ 3. Pregnant women should wear their seat belts as the best protection for themselves and their unborn children.

_____ 4. How you wear the seat belt does not matter, as long as you buckle up.

_____ 5. Children weighing less than 20 lbs. should be restrained in a toddler's seat.

_____ 6. A booster seat is intended for children weighing 40 to 55 lbs.

_____ 7. The safest position for children in any vehicle is buckled in an appropriate restraint system attached to the front seat.

_____ 8. Safety belts reduce the risk of death in a collision by 60%.

TODAY'S HANDBOOK PLUS WORKBOOK

Check your comprehension and mastery of the contents of this chapter by completing the corresponding exercise that is found in the complement to the TODAY'S HANDBOOK PLUS:

TODAY'S HANDBOOK PLUS WORKBOOK

Complete the exercise on Pages 77 to 79. If necessary, review the chapter when uncertain of an answer and refer to your instructor for further guidance.

14

Driving Techniques

Drivers require good driving techniques that are second nature. Initially, concentrate and master the basic skills; develop a strategy and visual skills to adapt to the environments you will encounter when driving in the city, the country, and expressways. Each present special problems.

City driving has congested streets, intersections, road users of all kinds, as well as a multitude of signs and signals. INFORMATION OVERLOAD!

Open scenery and low volume of traffic present an idyllic picture in country driving. This can be deceiving. Higher speeds, hidden crossings, pavement variations, hills, curves, etc. are all potential hazards.

On expressways, speeds are high. There are no stop signs, no intersections, and interchanges are few and far apart. There are fewer maneuvers to perform; they are usually more dangerous.

14

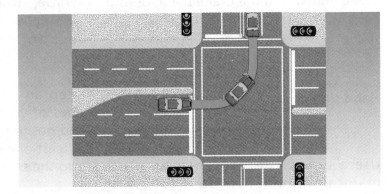

AFTER COMPLETING THIS CHAPTER, THE STUDENT MUST BE ABLE TO RECOGNIZE, EVALUATE AND RESPOND TO CHANGES IN THE DRIVING ENVIRONMENT:

- **while applying the SIPDE system and proper vehicle control.**
- **while maneuvering using appropriate risk-reduction techniques.**
- **with respect to the basic maneuvers.**

14-A Basic Rules

COMMUNICATION

Signal your presence and what you intend to do. Sharing the road in any environment requires that others can see you and that they know your intentions. COMMUNICATE. (Despite a signal to go from another road user, you must still check traffic - you are the one responsible for your safety.) Use the tools at your disposal early and intelligently.

Headlights: turn them on while driving, flash the high beams to communicate your presence

Turn signals: activate early to warn of turns or lane changes (avoid causing confusion)

Hazard lights: activate to warn of risk and abnormal situations

Brake lights: tap the brake pedal before applying the brakes

Horn: tap to attract other road users attention (eye-to-eye contact)

Hand signals: to warn of intentions and communicate right-of-way (Chapter 2).

Use a timed interval (Chapter 10) to maintain a minimum safe following distance. Increase this distance whenever possible particularly when driving conditions are not ideal, when following large vehicles that block your field of vision or when following a motorcycle.

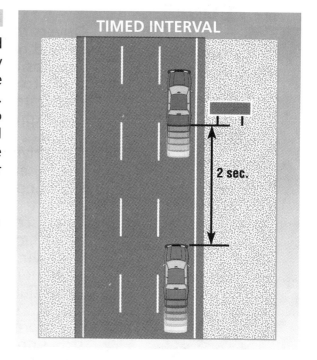

TIMED INTERVAL

2 sec.

Maintain an equal space behind your vehicle. If a following vehicle tailgates, ease up on the accelerator and increase your following distance. Look for a chance to change lanes.

Keep an "out", an open space, to the sides of your vehicle. Adjust your speed and position in traffic to keep a space on at least one side so that you could swerve into the space to avoid a hazard.

When driving in the lane beside parked vehicles, maintain the widest margin of space possible. Position your vehicle in the left portion of your lane to leave extra space (lane-left position reference).

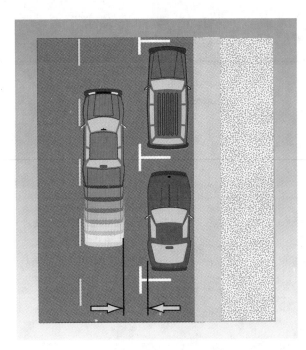

When you stop behind another vehicle, maintain a distance of at least one half a car length. You should be able to see the rear tires touching the roadway over the top of the hoodline.

This space will enable you:
- to change lanes if the lane is blocked, the vehicle stalls, or a rear-end collision is imminent

- to leave the vehicle ahead space to maneuver should the driver wish to reverse
- to avoid a roll back as the vehicle tries to advance up the slope
- to avoid carbon monoxide and hot exhaust emissions from having an adverse effect on you or your vehicle.

RIGHT-OF-WAY

It is important to understand that the right-of-way is something that must be given to you. The law specifies who must yield to whom; it never states who HAS the right-of-way. Moreover, situations are not always clear-cut. When in doubt, extend the courtesy of yielding to a vehicle with which you are in conflict. The law provides rules to go by, but people create the helpful "courteous" environment (Chapter 3).

MANEUVERS

Each maneuver should be performed applying the APE system (Chapter 9). The system sequence is **ASSESS**, **PREPARE**, and **EXECUTE**.

ASSESS: Scan the situation for signs and road markings, check the mirrors and blind spot, and decide whether to perform the maneuver.

PREPARE: Having decided, signal your intentions and recheck the mirrors and your blind spot to ensure that you can proceed in complete safety.

14

EXECUTE: Perform the maneuver, looking where you want to go and guiding your vehicle. When complete, make sure your turn signal is no longer activated.

CHANGING LANES

To alter your lane position, you must perform a lane change; whether to avoid an obstacle, pass another vehicle, prepare for a turn, leave the roadway, or merely to increase space from a potential hazard. Whatever the reason, plan ahead and use the APE system.

ASSESS:
- Check ahead in your lane and the lane you want to enter **(1a)** (space, speed, obstacles).
- Is the maneuver permitted?
- Check mirrors **(1b)** and blind spot **(1c)** (space and speed).

IS THIS MANEUVER SAFE?

PREPARE:
- Signal your intention by activating your turn signal (hand signal) **(2a)**.
- Recheck traffic ahead **(2b)**.
- Recheck the mirrors **(2c)** and in the blind spot **(2d)**. (Standard- shift to the appropriate gear.)

EXECUTE:
- Aim high at the center of the intended lane **(3a)**.
- Adjust speed **(3b)** (accelerate if the traffic permits).

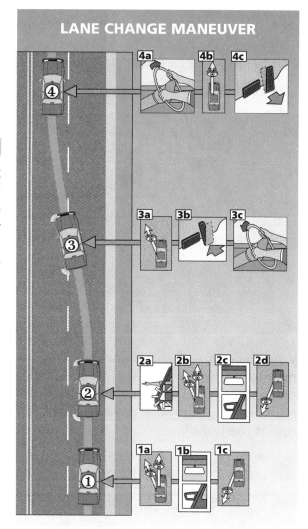

LANE CHANGE MANEUVER

- Steer gently **(3c)** (ease into lane).
- Center your vehicle in the lane **(4a)** by aiming far ahead **(4b)**.
- Readjust your speed to the flow of traffic **(4c)**.
- Cancel the turn signal.

When changing lanes on multi-lane roadways, be sure to check your blind spot across the entire roadway.

14

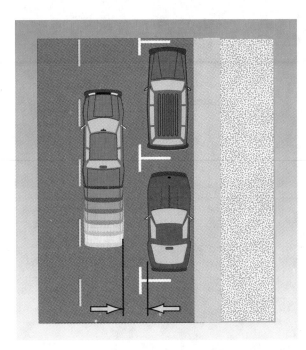

When you stop behind another vehicle, maintain a distance of at least one half a car length. You should be able to see the rear tires touching the roadway over the top of the hoodline.

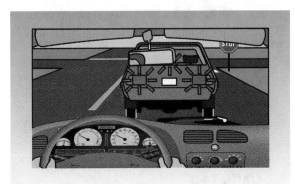

This space will enable you:
- to change lanes if the lane is blocked, the vehicle stalls, or a rear-end collision is imminent

- to leave the vehicle ahead space to maneuver should the driver wish to reverse
- to avoid a roll back as the vehicle tries to advance up the slope
- to avoid carbon monoxide and hot exhaust emissions from having an adverse effect on you or your vehicle.

RIGHT-OF-WAY

It is important to understand that the right-of-way is something that must be given to you. The law specifies who must yield to whom; it never states who HAS the right-of-way. Moreover, situations are not always clear-cut. When in doubt, extend the courtesy of yielding to a vehicle with which you are in conflict. The law provides rules to go by, but people create the helpful "courteous" environment (Chapter 3).

MANEUVERS

Each maneuver should be performed applying the APE system (Chapter 9). The system sequence is **ASSESS**, **PREPARE**, and **EXECUTE**.

ASSESS: Scan the situation for signs and road markings, check the mirrors and blind spot, and decide whether to perform the maneuver.

PREPARE: Having decided, signal your intentions and recheck the mirrors and your blind spot to ensure that you can proceed in complete safety.

14

EXECUTE: Perform the maneuver, looking where you want to go and guiding your vehicle. When complete, make sure your turn signal is no longer activated.

CHANGING LANES

To alter your lane position, you must perform a lane change; whether to avoid an obstacle, pass another vehicle, prepare for a turn, leave the roadway, or merely to increase space from a potential hazard. Whatever the reason, plan ahead and use the APE system.

ASSESS:
- Check ahead in your lane and the lane you want to enter **(1a)** (space, speed, obstacles).
- Is the maneuver permitted?
- Check mirrors **(1b)** and blind spot **(1c)** (space and speed).

IS THIS MANEUVER SAFE?

PREPARE:
- Signal your intention by activating your turn signal (hand signal) **(2a)**.
- Recheck traffic ahead **(2b)**.
- Recheck the mirrors **(2c)** and in the blind spot **(2d)**. (Standard- shift to the appropriate gear.)

EXECUTE:
- Aim high at the center of the intended lane **(3a)**.
- Adjust speed **(3b)** (accelerate if the traffic permits).

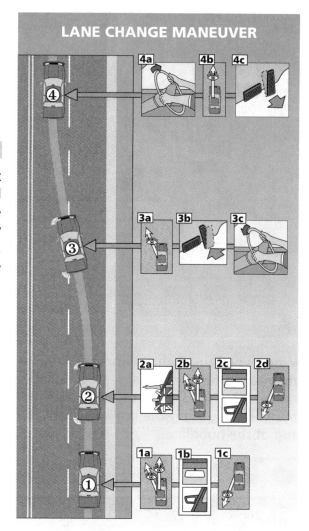

LANE CHANGE MANEUVER

- Steer gently **(3c)** (ease into lane).
- Center your vehicle in the lane **(4a)** by aiming far ahead **(4b)**.
- Readjust your speed to the flow of traffic **(4c)**.
- Cancel the turn signal.

When changing lanes on multi-lane roadways, be sure to check your blind spot across the entire roadway.

14

Intersections

When two roadways meet, other road users may want to use the same space at the same time as you do. This may present a hazard, the risk of a collision.

Most collisions involving pedestrians, motorcycles, or bicycles with motorized vehicles occur at intersections.

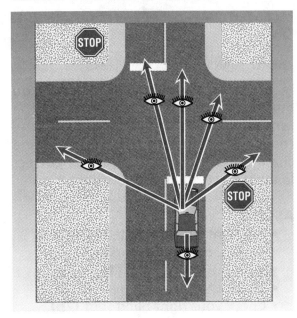

Scan the intersection to identify the situation. Controlled intersections (traffic lights or stop signs at all approaches), partially controlled (one roadway has stop signs), or uncontrolled intersections-each present different levels of danger. Check the traffic behind you.

If you are not required to stop, ease off the accelerator, cover the brake, and scan left, center, right and left again before entering the intersection. Reduce speed if your vision is blocked by large parked vehicles, trees, snow banks, etc.

BUS CREATES BLIND INTERSECTION

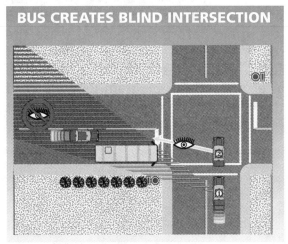

Pay special attention to the presence of pedestrians, especially children, the visually or physically impaired, or senior citizens. **Yield** to any vehicle or pedestrian already engaged in the intersection. **Do not enter the intersection** unless you can cross and exit in complete safety.

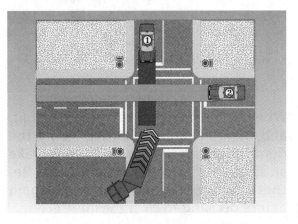

14

When required to stop, tap the brake, check the rear-view mirror, and then apply the brake pedal. Make a smooth stop before the stop line, the crosswalk, or the edge of the crossroad (front stop reference).

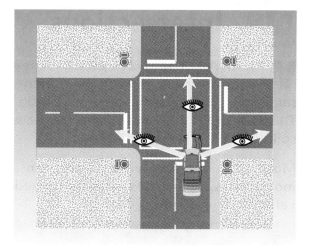

At a traffic light, wait for the green signal then check left, center, right and left again before proceeding - **use the count of three technique**. Be aware of road users that might enter the intersection late (diagram below). Yield to pedestrians and vehicles that have not yet cleared the intersection.

RIGHT TURNS

In order to perform a right turn, you must first position your vehicle in the lane closest to the right side of the roadway. This means completing a lane change maneuver (if not in the correct lane) at least 200 feet prior to the turn.

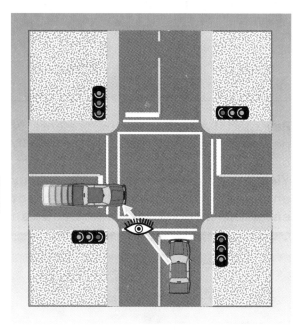

ASSESS:
- Is a right turn permitted **(1)** (signs, signals, pavement markings)?
- Scan the intersection **(1)**.
- Check the rear-view mirrors **(2a)**.
- Check your right blind spot **(2b)**.

IS THIS MANEUVER SAFE?

PREPARE:
- Activate the right turn signal **(3a)**.
- Tap the brake then reduce speed **(3b)** (standard- downshift to second gear.)
- Move to the right in your lane **(3)** (3 to 5 feet from the curb).
- Re-scan the intersection **(4a)**.
- Re-check in the mirrors **(4b)** and in

When at a stop, check left, center, right, and then left again (**LCR&L**). Apply the right-of-way rules. Ease up on the brake and advance into the intersection. Re-check left, center, right, and left again before deciding to cross the intersection.

the blind spot **(4c)**.

EXECUTE:
- Once the front wheels reach the curve of the curb **(5)** (turning reference).
- Look through the turn (along the intended path).
- Steer hand over hand **(5a)** (following the intended path).
- Release the brake **(5b)**.
- Aim ahead into the right lane.
- Accelerate gently **(5c)**.
- Target your path of travel **(6a)**.
- Straighten the steering **(6)**.
- Accelerate smoothly to normal speed **(6b)**.
- Check the turn signal.

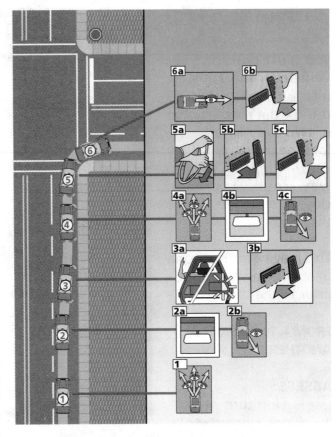

When performing a right turn from a stop, begin turning the steering wheel (as explained above) as you advance into the intersection to check traffic. When the way is clear, accelerate gently while steering hand-over-hand.

MULTIPLE RIGHT TURN LANES
If there is more than one lane designated for right turns by signs or pavement markings, you should exit and then enter the corresponding lane on the new roadway (right lane to right lane, or second lane to second lane). *Be alert for drivers that may cross or drift out of their lane as they turn in this situation.* To reduce the risk, avoid turning alongside another vehicle (keep your vehicle ahead of or behind it in the adjacent lane).

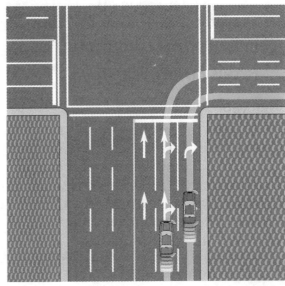

14

LEFT TURNS

To perform a left turn, you must position your vehicle in the furthest left lane that you may use on the roadway (on a two-way road, the lane nearest the yellow center line; on a one-way road, the lane closest to the left side of the road).

This may necessitate one or more lane changes prior to the turn.

FROM A TWO-WAY TO ANOTHER TWO-WAY

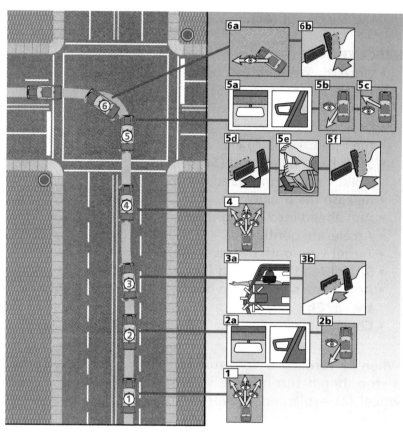

ASSESS:
- Is a left turn legal (signs, signals, etc.)?
- Scan the intersection **(1)**.
- Check the rear-view mirrors **(2a)**.
- Check your left blind spot **(2b)**.

IS THIS MANEUVER SAFE?

PREPARE:
- Activate the left turn signal **(3a)**.
- Tap the brake then reduce speed **(3b)** (standard- downshift to second gear).
- Advance until the front of your vehicle nears the center **(4 to 5)**.
- Scan the intersection and the oncoming traffic **(4 to 5)**.
  STOP WITH YOUR TIRES STRAIGHT IF PEDESTRIANS OR ONCOMING

TRAFFIC IMPEDE THE TURN
(Standard- shift to first gear)
- Check mirrors **(5a)** and blind spot **(5b)**.

EXECUTE:
- Aim at the center of the intended lane **(5c)**.
- Release the brake pedal **(5d)**.
- Steer hand over hand **(5e)** (following the intended path).
- Accelerate smoothly **(5f)**.
- Aim ahead into the left lane **(6a)**.
- Straighten the steering
- Accelerate to normal speed **(6b)**.
- Check the turn signal is off.

As soon as possible after straightening in the left lane, perform a lane change to the right (if a lane is available to the right) to move out of the passing lane. The passing lane should be left clear whenever possible.

MULTIPLE LEFT TURN LANES
If there is more than one lane designated for left turns by signs or pavement markings (often a left turn bay and another lane), you should exit and then enter the corresponding lane on the new roadway. *Be alert for drivers that may cross or drift out of their lane as they turn in this situation.* To reduce the risk, avoid turning alongside another vehicle (keep your vehicle ahead of or behind it in the adjacent lane).

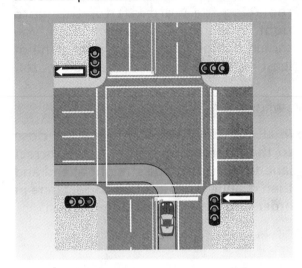

turn when the front of your vehicle reaches the crosswalk. Otherwise follow the same procedures.

FROM A ONE-WAY TO A TWO-WAY
On a one-way street, you must position your vehicle in the lane closest to the left side of the road in order to turn left. Change lanes into this lane at least 150 to 200 feet prior to the turn. Follow the same procedures as for a two-way to a two-way left turn.

14

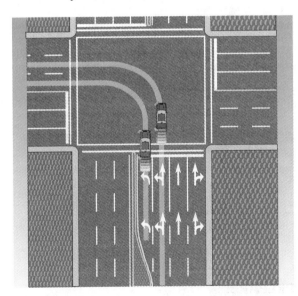

FROM A TWO-WAY TO A ONE-WAY
The lane that you intend to enter is the one beside the curb. Stop or begin the

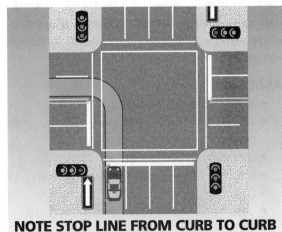

NOTE STOP LINE FROM CURB TO CURB ON A ONE-WAY STREET

FROM A ONE-WAY TO ANOTHER ONE-WAY

Follow the procedures for a right turn replacing the word left for the word right. When the turn is completed, you should change lanes to the right (lane of least resistance and your intended route).

WRONG LANE FOR TURN

In all turning situations, if you are close to the intersection and in the incorrect lane to turn, continue straight ahead and then change lanes into the correct lane in order to turn at the next intersection!

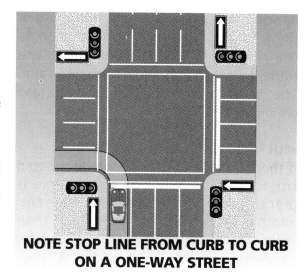

NOTE STOP LINE FROM CURB TO CURB ON A ONE-WAY STREET

Turning About

U-TURNS

Though a relatively simple and quick way to turnabout, a U-turn requires a wide roadway and is illegal in some places. In urban areas, a turn around the block would be preferable.

ASSESS:
- Is a U-turn permitted?
- Are you near hills, curves, or intersections?
- Is the road wide enough?
- Do you have a clear view 500 feet in both directions?
- Will you interfere with traffic (both directions, pedestrians)?

IS A U-TURN SAFE TO PERFORM?

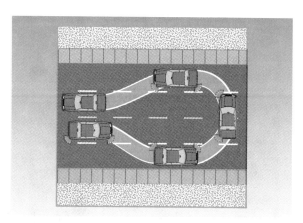

PREPARE:
- Perform a lane change to the right side of the road.
- Stop your vehicle.
- Activate the left turn signal.

14

- Recheck the oncoming traffic.
- Recheck mirrors and blind spot.

EXECUTE:
- Release the brake pedal.
- Steer left rapidly (hand-over-hand).
- Accelerate gently.
- Aim at your intended lane.
- Allow the wheel to slip through your grip to straighten (be ready to correct).
- Accelerate to normal speed.
- Check the traffic.

THREE-POINT TURNS

You can perform a three-point turn in a variety of ways: by heading or backing into a driveway on the right or left, or turning on the roadway. Backing across a lane of traffic or reversing into a lane of traffic can be very hazardous and should be avoided. In most circumstances, it is preferable to back into a driveway so that your forward field of vision takes in the whole roadway as you prepare to re-enter traffic.

BACKING INTO A DRIVEWAY ON THE RIGHT

ASSESS:
- Do you have a clear view?
- Is there traffic behind you?
- Is the driveway clear?
- Will you interfere with traffic (both directions, pedestrians)?

IS THIS 3-POINT TURN SAFE?

PREPARE:
- Tap the brake pedal.
- Perform the steps for a right lane

USING A DRIVEWAY ON THE RIGHT

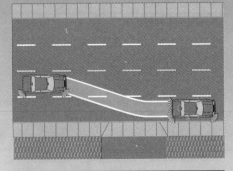

change in complete safety.
- Stop your vehicle about 3 feet from the curb with the rear just beyond the driveway.
- Check mirror and blind spot.
- Shift to (R)everse.
- Check the traffic all around your vehicle.
- Place your left hand at the 12 o'clock position and the right hand at the 5 o'clock position (backing into a right turn position - Chapter 9).
- Look over your right shoulder toward the right rear.

EXECUTE:
- Ease up on the brake (clutch to friction point - standard).
- Reverse slowly (press gently on the accelerator to start the vehicle

14

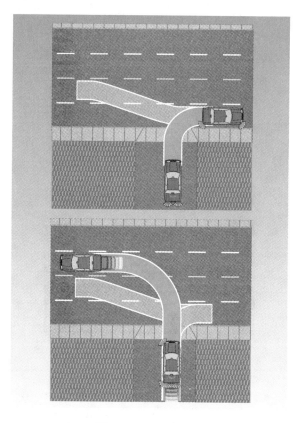

USING A DRIVEWAY ON THE LEFT

moving, if necessary).
- Aim at the center of the driveway.
- Turn the steering sharply.
- Re-check traffic to the left.
- As you enter the driveway, countersteer to straighten in the center of the driveway.
- Stop when the front of your vehicle clears the sidewalk.
- Shift to (D)rive (1st gear - standard).
- Activate the left turn signal.
- Advance slowly to check traffic (pedestrians and other road users - yield if close enough to constitute a hazard - stop at sidewalk).
- Advance into the street and perform a left turn safely.

DRIVING INTO A DRIVEWAY ON YOUR LEFT

ASSESS:
- Check the same items as previously.
- Check the driveway for hedges and other objects that may obstruct your vision when you reverse into the roadway.

IS THIS 3-POINT TURN SAFE?

PREPARE:
- Activate your left turn signal.
- Check the driveway.
- Proceed as for a left turn.

EXECUTE:
- Aim at the center of the driveway.
- Steer sharply, advance slowly.
- As you enter the driveway, countersteer to straighten in the center of the driveway.

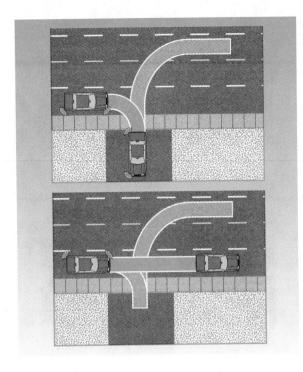

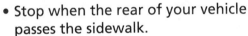

- Stop when the rear of your vehicle passes the sidewalk.
- Shift to (R)everse.
- Activate your right turn signal.
- Check to the left, right and behind your vehicle.
- Assume the position for backing into a right turn (Chapter 9).
- Reverse slowly, glancing around your vehicle (traffic, left front clearance).
- Steer toward the nearest lane.
- Entering the first lane of traffic, countersteer to straighten your vehicle in the lane and then stop
- Shift to (D)rive (1st - standard)
- Activate the left turn signal.
- Check mirrors and blind spot.
- Aim down the roadway.
- Accelerate to normal speed and cancel the turn signal.

3-POINT TURN ON THE ROADWAY

This maneuver puts you at more of a risk and should be performed only if the street is too narrow, there are no driveways available, you cannot drive around the block, you have excellent visibility, and the traffic is very light.

ASSESS:

DO YOU HAVE ANY OTHER OPTION? IS THE MANEUVER SAFE?

PREPARE:
- Perform a right lane change, and then stop your vehicle near the right edge of the roadway.
- Activate the left turn signal.
- Check the oncoming traffic.
- Check the left mirror and blind spot.

14

EXECUTE:
- Advance slowly and steer sharply.
- As you approach the opposite curb, countersteer and then stop.
- Activate the right turn signal.
- Shift to (R)everse.
- Check the traffic in all directions.
- Assume the position for backing into a right turn (Chapter 9).
- Reverse slowly, steering right sharply.
- Prior to stopping, countersteer to straighten.
- Shift to (D)rive (1st - standard)
- Activate the right turn signal.
- Check traffic all around your vehicle.
- Aim at your intended path of travel.
- Accelerate to normal speed.
- Check the rear-view mirror.
- Verify the turn signal is off.

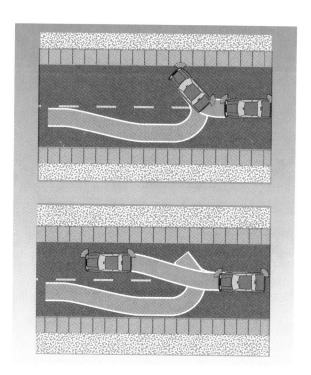

SAFETY TIPS

In any high-risk or high-density of traffic environment, driving around the block would be a much safer means of turning about.

Parking

Though not a dangerous maneuver because of the slow speed, parking requires excellent control of your speed (walking speed) and steering (smaller movements) as well as accurate judgment of space. This does not mean that there is no risk. Far too many collisions occur in parking situations. Checking the traffic constantly while maneuvering will diminish the danger. Choosing to park your vehicle, whenever possible, so that you may drive into and/or out of the parking space, rather than reversing, will also diminish the risk.

Practice the different types of this essential task so that you may perform diagonal, perpendicular and parallel parking maneuvers easily, safely and with confidence.

DIAGONAL PARKING

ASSESS:
- Locate a space on your right.
- Check for parking signs.
- Check the oncoming traffic.
- Check the rear-view mirrors and right blind spot.
- Check the position of the vehicles on both sides of the space.
- Be alert to the possible movement of any parked vehicles or pedestrians.

CAN YOU PARK SAFELY?

PREPARE:
- Activate the right turn signal.
- Tap the brake pedal.
- Move to the left to leave about a car width from the parked vehicles.
- Reduce speed until you can see into the parking space.
- Recheck your mirrors and blind spot.

EXECUTE:
- Aim into the center of the space.
- Steer sharply while rolling slowly.
- Glance to check your clearance on either side.
- Countersteer to straighten your vehicle into the center of the space.
- Reduce speed.
- Stop when your vehicle is straight and in line with the other parked vehicles (if properly parked).
- Follow the procedures to exit the vehicle (Chapter 9).

To diagonal park on the left, keep on your side and follow the same procedures substituting left for right.

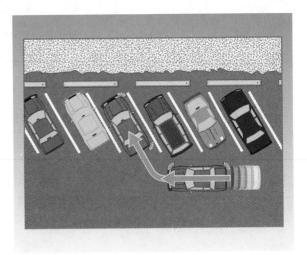

LEAVING A DIAGONAL PARKING SPACE

ASSESS:
- Check the position of the front tires as you approach your vehicle.
- Check the flow of traffic

IS BACKING INTO TRAFFIC SAFE?

PREPARE:
- Follow your normal pre-driving protocol (Chapter 8).
- Start the engine (Chapter 9).
- Apply the (service) brake pedal.
- Shift to (R)everse.
- Activate the right turn signal.
- Release the parking brake.
- Re-check to the left, right and to the rear.
- Assume the position for backing into a right turn (Chapter 9).

EXECUTE:
- Ease off the brake pedal (clutch to friction point -standard), a gentle pressure on the accelerator may be

14

BACKING OUT OF A DIAGONAL PARKING SPACE

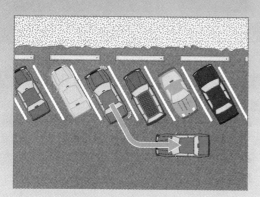

- When the front of your vehicle passes the rear of the vehicle on your left (fender clearance), look to the right rear and turn sharply in that direction.
- Re-check traffic and glance to the left rear to check your clearance.
- Just before stopping, countersteer to straighten the wheels.
- Stop, shift to (D)rive (1st - standard).
- Activate the left turn signal.
- Check the traffic in both directions.
- Accelerate to normal speed.
- Cancel the turn signal manually.

DRIVING INTO A PERPENDICULAR SPACE

It is easier and safer to drive into a space on the left. Ideally, choose a space that permits you to drive forwards when you must leave so that you can avoid backing your vehicle into traffic.

ASSESS:

- Choose an available parking space on your left.
- Check traffic (pedestrians as well) in both directions and your left blind spot.
- Check the position of the vehicles on both sides of the space.
- Be alert to the possible movement of any parked vehicles.

IS A TURN INTO THE SPACE SAFE?

PREPARE:

- Activate the left turn signal.
- Tap the brake pedal.

required to initiate movement.
- Reverse slowly and turn the wheel slightly (1/4 turn of the wheel).
- Recheck traffic to the left and right.

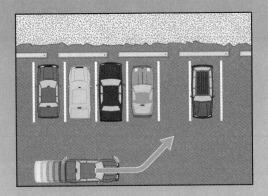

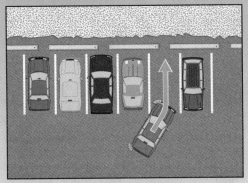

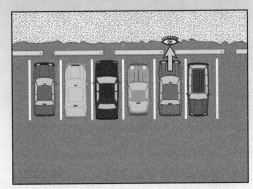

- Move to the right slightly to leave as much space as possible from the vehicles on the left.
- Reduce speed until you can see into the parking space.
- Recheck your mirrors and blind spot.

EXECUTE:
- Aim at the center of the space.
- Steer sharply to the left.
- Maintain a slow speed.
- Glance to check the clearance from the vehicles on both sides.
- Countersteer to straighten into the center of the space.
- Stop when your vehicle is aligned with the other parked vehicles (if properly parked).
- Follow the procedures for exiting your vehicle (Chapter 9).

BACKING INTO A PERPENDICULAR SPACE

It is easier and safer to back into a space on your right. Leaving the space will be performed driving forwards into traffic which is also safer.

ASSESS:
- Locate a space on your right.
- Check the oncoming traffic.
- Check the rear-view mirrors and right blind spot.
- Check the position of the vehicles on both sides of the space.
- Be alert to the possible movement of any parked vehicles.

IS BACKING INTO THE SPACE SAFE?

PREPARE:
- Activate the right turn signal.
- Tap the brake pedal.
- Move to the left to leave about a car width from the parked vehicles.
- Reduce speed and stop when the rear of your vehicle is lined up with

14

the center of the vehicle parked after the space (rear turning reference).
- Shift to (R)everse.
- Recheck your mirrors and blind spot.
- Assume the position for backing into a right turn (Chapter 9).

EXECUTE:
- Ease off the brake (clutch to friction point - standard).
- A gentle pressure on the accelerator may be needed to initiate movement.
- Aim at the center of the space.
- Steer sharply to the right.
- Recheck traffic.
- Glance to check clearance on both sides of the space.
- Countersteer to straighten into the center of the space.
- Stop when your vehicle is aligned with the other vehicles (if properly parked).
- Check the space on both sides, you may have to advance straight ahead and back into the space again to center your vehicle.
- Follow the procedures for exiting the vehicle (Chapter 9).

LEAVING A PERPENDICULAR SPACE

If you positioned your vehicle properly, you will drive forward out of the space. When you must back out of the space, follow the procedures for backing out of a diagonal parking space.

ASSESS:
- Check the position of the front tires as you approach (Chapter 7).

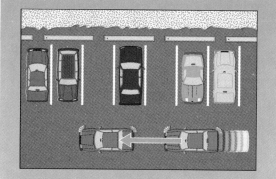

BACK INTO A PERPENDICULAR SPACE

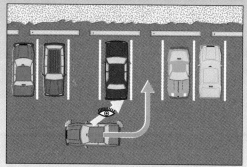

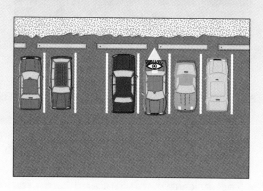

14

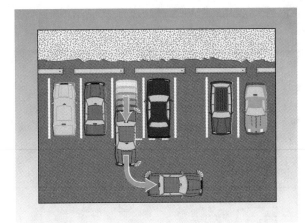

- Check the flow of traffic (including pedestrians, bikes).

IS DRIVING INTO TRAFFIC SAFE?

PREPARE:
- Follow your normal pre-driving protocol (Chapter 7).
- Start the engine (Chapter 9).
- Apply the service brake.
- Shift to (D)rive (1st gear - standard).
- Activate the left turn signal.
- Release the parking brake.
- Re-check for any road users to the left and right.

EXECUTE:
- Ease off the brake pedal (clutch to friction point - standard), a gentle pressure on the accelerator may be required to initiate movement.
- Advance slowly straight ahead.
- Re-check traffic to the left and right.
- When your body passes the end of the vehicle on your left, perform a left turn.
- Accelerate to normal speed.

The ability to perform this maneuver is essential when parking in a crowded urban environment. Look for a space one and a half times the length of your vehicle on the right side of the roadway. It is possible to park in a smaller space; however, it is not recommended.

ASSESS:
- Locate a parking space.
- Make sure the space is legal (sign, driveway, fire hydrant, etc.).
- Is the space large enough?
- Are you in the correct lane?
- Check oncoming traffic.
- Check mirrors and blind spot.

IS THE MANEUVER SAFE?

PREPARE:
- Tap the brake pedal **(1)**.
- Activate the right turn signal.
- Re-check mirrors and blind spot.
- Reduce speed.
- Stop beside the vehicle ahead of the chosen parking space **(2)** (parallel to the curb, 3 feet away from the other vehicle, back bumpers in line).
- Shift to (R)everse
- Re-check oncoming traffic / left mirror.
- Assume the position for backing into a right turn.

EXECUTE:
- Ease off the brake pedal (clutch to friction point - standard), a gentle pressure on the accelerator may be required to initiate movement.
- Reverse slowly - walking speed (on

14

slopes, the brake or the accelerator may be required).

- Turn the steering wheel sharply.
- When you reach **(3)** the proper angle (30° to 45° with the curb or in line with the front right corner of the vehicle behind) countersteer to straighten.
- Control your speed (speed tends to increase as you straighten).
- When your right front corner clears the vehicle ahead **(4)**, look back and steer left rapidly.
- Just prior to stopping, countersteer to straighten.
- Stop without touching the vehicle behind **(5)**.
- Shift to drive (1st gear - standard).
- Advance slowly **(6)** (straightening and positioning your vehicle in the center of the space).
- Follow the procedures to exit.

This maneuver requires practice to perform comfortably, confidently and safely.

When parallel parking on the left side of the street (one-way street), follow the same procedures, but assume the position for backing into a left turn at the outset, and then turn the wheel in the opposite direction (though this is still towards the curb).

When you reach the proper angle and are ready to straighten the wheels, change position to assume the position for backing into a right turn. Remain in this position until the end of the parking maneuver; remember to glance forward to check the front fender clearance.

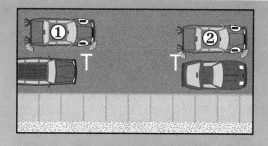

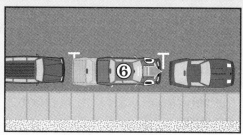

PARKING ON A HILL

Parking your vehicle on a hill has already been explained in each of the parking maneuvers. However, the final position of your vehicle before exiting requires some explanation.

The front tires must be turned in such a manner as to cause the vehicle to roll out of traffic or against the curb should the vehicle move (parking brake/transmission lock slips).

When parking downhill, whether or not there is a curb, the tires should be turned toward the near side of the road.

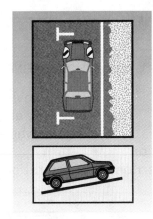

When parking uphill without a curb, the tires should be turned toward the near side of the road.

When parking uphill with a curb, the tires should be turned away from the near side of the road (preferably resting against the curb).

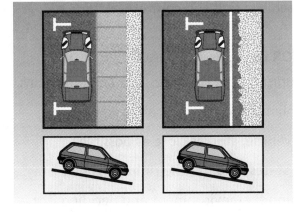

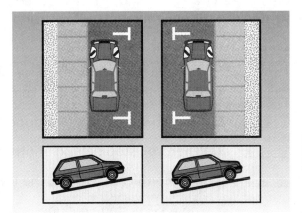

14

SAFETY TIPS

Parking responsibility - choose a legal and safe parking space, apply the parking brake, stop the engine, turn the ignition switch to lock, remove the key, and when standing on a grade, turn the front wheels to the curb (or side of the road) when leaving your vehicle unattended. The vehicle doors should be locked. Never leave children (or pets) unattended in a parked vehicle (Kaitlyn's Law - California)!

Review

TERMS TO REMEMBER - WRITE A SHORT DEFINITION FOR EACH OF THE FOLLOWING :

- Communicate
- Keep an "out"
- APE system
- Controlled intersection
- Uncontrolled intersection

- Urban environment
- Highway environment
- Expressway environment
- U-turn
- Acceleration lane

- 3 point turn
- Velocitization
- Diagonal park
- Perpendicular park
- Parallel park

SUMMARY

Apply the APE system to all driving maneuvers in order to perform them safely and properly: right turns, left turns and lane changes. Adapt the SIPDE strategy to all environments while using selective seeing to identify the important data.

Parking, in all its forms, is a complex maneuver that requires practice to achieve skill and comfort.

TEST A - WRITE A "T" FOR TRUE OR AN "F" FOR FALSE IN THE SPACES PROVIDED.

_____ **1.** Sharing the road requires communication of your presence and intentions.

_____ **2.** The two second rule is a good following distance in all conditions.

_____ **3.** When you stop behind another vehicle, stop as close as possible.

_____ **4.** In all conflict situations, the law states who has the right-of-way.

_____ **5.** The ASSESS stage includes scanning the environment and deciding if the maneuver is safe to perform.

_____ **6.** To change lanes, the first step is to signal your intention.

_____ **7.** Most collisions involving pedestrians and cyclists occur at intersections.

_____ **8.** When a traffic signal light changes to green, check left, center, right and then left again before proceeding.

_____ **9.** To turn right, position your vehicle in the lane closest to the right.

_____ **10.** If there is more than one lane designated for right turns, you should exit and then enter the corresponding lane on the new roadway.

_____ **11.** To turn left, position your vehicle in the lane beside the left sidewalk.

_____ **12.** In multiple left turn lane situations, you should turn alongside another vehicle in order to reduce the risk of a collision.

_____ **13.** When in the wrong lane for a turn, stop and wait for traffic, then turn.

_____ **14.** When turning left, target the lane closest to the right on the new road.

_____ **15.** Turning left onto a one-way street, target the lane closest to you.

_____ **16.** When turning about, the safest maneuver is to drive around the block.

_____ **17.** Turning about using a driveway, it is preferable to drive into the space.

_____ **18.** Parking maneuvers require a slow speed and accurate judgment.

_____ **19.** To parallel park safely, you should select a space one and a half times the length of your vehicle.

_____ **20.** When parking your vehicle on a downhill slope, the front tires should be turned towards the near side of the road.

TODAY'S HANDBOOK PLUS WORKBOOK

Check your comprehension and mastery of the contents of this chapter by completing the corresponding exercise that is found in the complement to the TODAY'S HANDBOOK PLUS:

TODAY'S HANDBOOK PLUS WORKBOOK

Complete the exercise on Pages 80 to 89. If necessary, review the chapter when uncertain of an answer and refer to your instructor for further guidance.

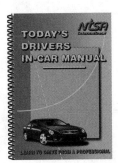

TODAY'S DRIVERS IN-CAR MANUAL

Before any in-car session, prepare yourself and facilitate the development of proper driving skills and habits by reading the corresponding lesson in the complement to the TODAY'S HANDBOOK PLUS:

TODAY'S DRIVERS IN-CAR MANUAL

Your instructor will evaluate your progress in the manual. Licensed parents or guardians should supplement your practice by following the manual procedures and coordinating with your in-car instructor.

Student notes

Urban/Rural Environment

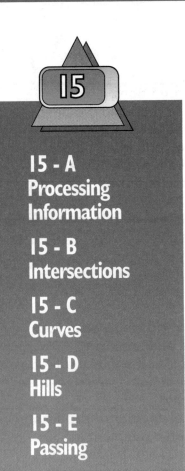
Having studied the SIPDE system and visual skills, you must now apply these same skills to interacting with other road users in complex and in higher speed driving conditions.

Intersections, curves, and hills present restrictions to your line of sight. You must adapt to the special problems they create.

Passing and being passed are usually high risk situations in two-way traffic environments. Applying the SIPDE system and cooperating with other road users to reduce the risk as much as possible is a must.

The nucleus of safety, however, is still the driver (attitude, physical and mental condition), his/her driving skills, and the level of their experience, as well as the application of the SIPDE system.

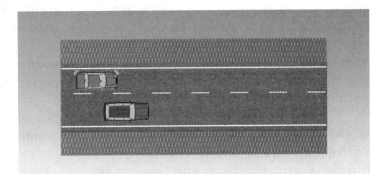

15

AFTER COMPLETING THIS CHAPTER, THE STUDENT MUST BE ABLE TO RECOGNIZE RISK AND APPLY RISK REDUCTION STRATEGIES TO:

- establish roadway position, vehicle speed, and communicate.
- approach intersections, curves, and hills.
- select and safely execute space / speed adjustments to pass a vehicle.
- possible hazards and corresponding solutions when being passed.

Processing Information

In order to process information, you must first gather the information by applying the SIPDE system.

The key to seeing what is actually there is to develop a pattern to your scan of the roadway. This will enable you to scan more quickly and more efficiently. It also, when performed often, will develop into a visual habit that will diminish the probability that you may miss something ("Officer, I never saw the car," a common refrain).

A suggested pattern would be to scan far ahead (20 to 30 seconds - area 1), then closer (12 to 15 seconds - area 1), a glance in the rear-view mirror (area 6, 4 and 5), under the mirror to space area 3 (8 seconds ahead), sweep to the left to return to area 1, and then area 2. Glance at the instrument panel (for speed and any gauges), and then start the entire pattern over again.

WHAT TO SCAN FOR

To be effective, when scanning the highway and traffic scene, you must search for what is actually present within certain parameters.

Roadway features to scan for:
- road and lane width,
- lane markings,
- roadway surfaces,
- shoulder conditions,
- slope of the road and shoulder,
- curb types and height,
- hills, curves, and intersections,
- areas of limited visibility, and
- structures adjacent to the roadway.

Signs, signals and markings to scan for:
- warning signs,
- regulatory signs,
- directional signs, and
- informational signs.

Motorized vehicles to scan for:
- cars, SUVs, and mini-vans,
- trucks, vans, and tractor-trailer rigs,
- buses, school buses, and mini-buses,
- motor homes,
- motorcycles and motorized scooters,
- construction equipment,
- farm vehicles and tractors, and
- other slow-moving equipment.

Non-motorized road users:
- pedestrians,
- bicyclists, skaters, and skateboarders.
- horse-drawn equipment, and
- animals.

At 25 to 30 seconds ahead, identify potential problems. At 12 to 15 seconds ahead, identify objects that require a change in speed or direction. At 12 to 15 seconds ahead, identify alternate paths of travel. At 4 to 8 seconds ahead, identify your stopping zone and following interval.

If everything is clear, you are fortunate. You occupy the enviable position of being the only vehicle on the road with no road users present in your environment.

Normally, you will have found other road users or line of sight closures (blocked sightlines) occupying some of the space areas surrounding your vehicle. Alter your pattern to search the opposing space areas. For example, if a road user is in space area 3 (see below), check space area 2, as well as area 4, and your left blind spot. Are they open, closed or changing areas?

DECIDE - Can you move your vehicle towards area 2 safely? Will this reduce a risk from area 3? Can this be done smoothly without upsetting your vehicle balance? Are there any other factors? Search again. Would a speed change suffice? Would a change of lane position reduce the risk sufficiently? When your evaluation is complete, **EXECUTE**.

DECISION-MAKING

This is just one simple example of visual searching (**SCAN/IDENTIFY**) and the steps to reach a decision (**PREDICT/DECIDE**) prior to reducing the risk (**EXECUTE**).

These same general principles must be applied continuously to all the possible driving situations that may arise. With practice and continued application, these concepts and procedures will become habits. This will not happen by itself. You must apply and practice them; hence, the initial need for guided practice with a professional instructor.

Often, the situation will be much more complex and will require the application of the principles mentioned in Chapter 10, **Minimize**, **Separate** and **Compromise**.

Whatever the situation, applying good visual searching, thinking ahead, and evaluating the situation carefully will lead to reduced-risk decision-making.

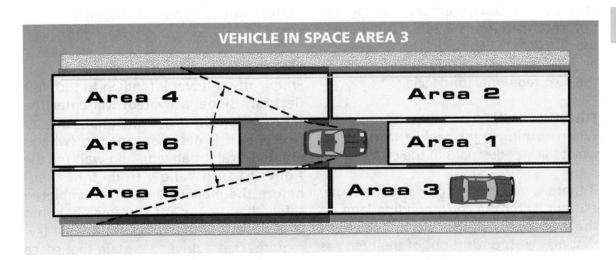

VEHICLE IN SPACE AREA 3

Area 4 | Area 2
Area 6 | Area 1
Area 5 | Area 3

15-B Intersections

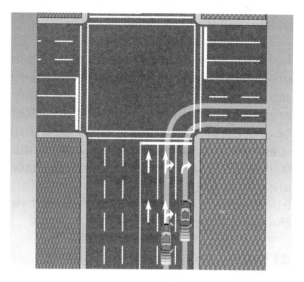

While the procedures for crossing or joining traffic traveling at higher speeds on multiple lane roadways are similar to those employed for basic intersection maneuvers, it is important to realize that the risk increases substantially.

SIGNALIZED INTERSECTIONS

Before entering an intersection controlled by traffic signals, check again for oncoming traffic signaling a left turn, for pedestrians, and for any cross traffic (make sure it is stopped).

Whether stopped first in line or in a line of vehicles at a red signal that changes to green (fresh green), use the count of three technique (count one, two, three before moving), and check traffic while doing so. This will provide some protection from drivers who fail to stop for a red light (transverse road), or drivers ahead who suddenly brake to a stop. Do not enter the intersection until there is space for your vehicle in the next block, or you may remain in the intersection on the next red signal (grid lock).

TURNING RIGHT

When turning right, yield the right-of-way to any pedestrians in the crosswalk.

If there is more than one right turn lane, exit and enter the corresponding lane on the new roadway. Be alert for drivers that may cross or drift out of their lane as

they turn in this situation. To reduce the risk, avoid turning alongside another vehicle (keep your vehicle ahead of or behind it in the adjacent lane).

Remember, when turning right on a red signal, you must first stop and yield the right-of-way to any vehicles, bicycles, or pedestrians in your intended path of travel.

LEFT TURNS

Frequently, a driver intending to turn left (left turn signal activated) will enter the intersection on a green signal, only to find that it is necessary to stop (wheels pointed straight ahead), and wait for the signal to turn yellow (sometimes red) before the maneuver can be completed safely. It is important to remember that prior to entering an intersection, the law requires that a driver ascertain that space is available in the street to be entered (left cross street, in this case). Failure to check before entering frequently results in being unable to clear the intersection, which may lead to a traffic citation for blocking traffic (grid lock).

If there is more than one left turn lane (often a left turn bay and another lane), turn and enter the corresponding lane on the new roadway. Be alert for drivers that may cross or drift out of their lane as they turn left in this situation. To reduce the risk, avoid turning alongside another vehicle (keep your vehicle ahead of or behind it in the adjacent lane).

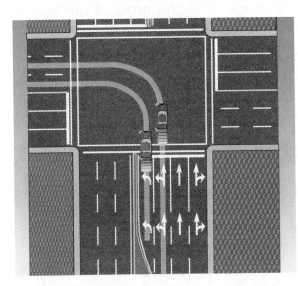

TIME / SPACE JUDGMENT

At intersections controlled by stop signs and yield signs, it is vital that you are able to judge the length of the gap in traffic that would be required to enter, to cross, or to join traffic safely. The width of the roadway, the time to perform the maneuver, and the speed of the traffic are the factors that must be taken into account.

Crossing a two-lane roadway (30 feet wide) at a brisk rate of acceleration requires a gap of at least six seconds. A vehicle approaching on the cross street at 30 mph will travel 264 feet (about one half a block) in that time. At 60 mph, the same vehicle would travel 528 feet. If the road is wider, the gap required would increase in proportion to the increased width.

When turning right into traffic traveling at 30 mph, a gap of eight or more seconds is required so that you can complete the maneuver and still leave the driver approaching from the left a following interval of 3 to 4 seconds. This works out to 352 feet. At 55 mph, a gap of eleven seconds (880 feet) is required.

To perform a left turn, the problem is more complex. You need to judge a gap of approximately three to four seconds in the traffic approaching from the left in order to cross the first half of the intersection safely. At the same time, for vehicles approaching from the right at 30 mph (the second half of the intersection), you will need a gap of 11 or more seconds (484 feet) to enter the left lane, accelerate to the speed of traffic, and still leave the approaching driver a following interval of 3 to 4 seconds. At 55 mph, 14 seconds (1,130 feet) would be required.

When turning left at or crossing a divided highway, it may be necessary to cross the first half of the intersection, and then stop to yield to the traffic on the second half, before completing your maneuver.

STOPPING

Anytime you prepare to stop, you should check the rear-view mirror, tap the brake pedal to flash the brake lights and alert drivers to the rear, and then apply the brake pedal to stop smoothly at least one car length from the stop line or the vehicle ahead. Focus your attention on the rear-view mirror until at least one other vehicle stops safely behind you, providing protection to the rear. You may then ease off the brake and roll up to the stop line (behind a vehicle, retain the safe distance).

STAGGERED STOP

When your vehicle is in the left lane or in a single lane situation, and there is no vehicle in front of you at an intersection, stop one half a car length before the line

in order to maintain control of your front space area. This staggered stop technique will eliminate the possibility of a vehicle turning left (from the right on the cross street) sideswiping your vehicle.

RIGHT TURN LANE SQUEEZE

Large trucks and buses often move to the left (partly or completely into the second lane) when preparing to make a right turn. This helps prevent the rear wheels from riding over the curb while turning right.

Always check the turn signals on the vehicle before moving into the lane (to the right of it) beside the sidewalk. Not being aware of this problem can lead to your being caught in a right turn squeeze (between the vehicle and the curb), which can result in vehicle damage. Leave the space open, follow behind it (in the lane near the curb), and then make your right turn after it has completed the turn.

RIGHT TURN LANE SQUEEZE

STAGGERED STOP - RED VEHICLE

SHARED LEFT TURN LANES

You may often hear the expression "center turn lane" used to describe the situation illustrated below. (Note the unique lane markings on the center lane - a solid and a broken yellow line on either side of the lane.) The usual term used on signs is the two-way turn lane. Either term refers to the same roadway variation which can be found in rural, highway, and many urban environments.

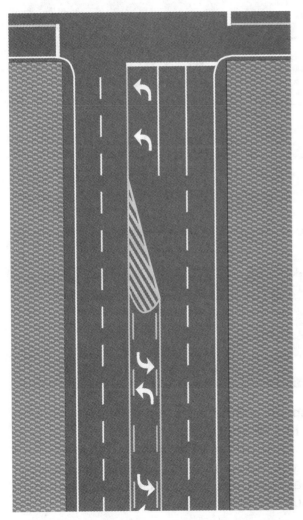

The center lane may be used to turn left for traffic in both directions, as well as by drivers turning left onto a congested street from alleys, driveways and parking lots **(not at intersections)** (they may turn into this lane and then wait for a gap to merge with traffic).

This presents one of the dangers of using this lane. Since traffic can enter from various directions to turn left, **you must check carefully before entering**. Is an oncoming vehicle about to enter the lane? Is any vehicle about to enter from a driveway on the left or on the right? Did a vehicle behind you enter the lane and is now overtaking you?

For your safety, yield the right-of-way to the lane to any vehicle that has already entered or is signaling the intention of entering the lane.

Once you are certain it is safe, signal, then check again prior to entering the lane. Do not drive in this lane for a long distance (200 to 300 feet would be a suggested maximum distance). Stop in the lane (with the front tires straight ahead) while waiting for a sufficient gap in oncoming traffic to complete your left turn maneuver.

At intersections, the ideal is the situation depicted in the diagram . The lane markings have changed to delineate a left turn bay (this is not always the case). You must check before entering the turning bay; other drivers may enter the lane too soon and illegally drive over the

15

zebra stripes (diagonal yellow lines) to enter the turn bay.

To use a shared left turn lane to enter a street from a driveway, you should:

- Signal a left turn and stop at the edge of the roadway.
- Check for drivers on your side of the road (to the left) waiting to turn left.
- Check for drivers approaching from the right (opposite side of the road) signaling or waiting to turn left.
- Check for a safe gap in traffic approaching from your left.
- If traffic is clear in both directions, enter the nearest through lane. Do not use the shared left turn lane.
- If there is a gap to your left but not to the right, turn into the shared left turn lane and then stop. Signal a right turn, wait for a gap in traffic, and then move into the nearest lane.

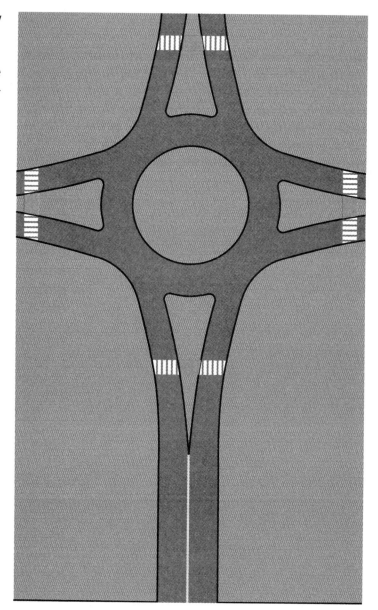

ROUNDABOUT INTERSECTIONS

This type of intersection is essentially a traffic circle with only one lane of traffic moving around the center island.

Reduce speed and be prepared to yield to vehicles already in the roundabout. When no traffic is approaching (or far enough away not to be a hazard), you may enter the roundabout (counter clockwise direction) and proceed. Remember to signal your intentions.

SAFETY TIPS

Roundabouts have been proven to reduce collisions without reducing the volume of traffic in the intersection. Pedestrians cross at pedestrian corridors prior to the intersection - thus removing one risk. Approaching drivers are directed along a curved path which lends itself to speed reduction, and must then yield to traffic in the roundabout. Once engaged, they must be given the right-of-way by any traffic approaching. When approaching and exiting, watch for pedestrians crossing at the pedestrian corridors.

RAILROAD GRADE CROSSINGS

The law requires obedience to a signal indicating the approach of a train. You must stop **within fifty (50) feet but not less than fifteen (15) feet from the nearest rail** (in most states) if:

- A clearly visible railroad signal warns of the approach of a train;

- A crossing gate is lowered or a human flagman warns of the approach or passage of a railroad train;

- The driver is required to stop by other law, a rule adopted under a statute, or an official traffic control device or signal;

- A train approaching within fifteen hundred (1,500) feet of the highway crossing emits a signal audible from such a distance, and such engine, by reason of its speed or nearness to such crossing, is an immediate hazard;

- An approaching train is plainly visible and in hazardous proximity to such crossing.

A person who fails to obey the law with respect to railroad grade crossings is subject to a fine.

The driver of a vehicle required to stop as provided by this law shall remain stopped until the driver is permitted to proceed and it is safe to proceed.

REMEMBER

The railroad tracks are private property. Trains can travel at very high speeds. Even at slow speeds, a train requires a very long distance to stop. A train can cross at any time. Combine these four concepts. **You will realize that safety at railroad crossings is your responsibility.**

ADVANCE WARNING

Don't take signs for granted. Reduce speed, search the controls at the crossing as well as the lines of sight. Turn off the radio, lower a window and listen for trains. Reduce speed further when a line of sight is closed in either direction.

SAFETY TIPS

Do not be fooled by the optical illusion – the train you see is closer and faster moving than you think! If you see a train approaching, wait for it to go by before you proceed across the tracks.

CROSSING CONTROLS

Most crossings only have a crossbuck posted. The rest have flashing signals, bells, crossing gates and on occasion, a stop sign or flagman, depending on the circumstances at the particular crossing. **The small tab under the crossbuck indicates the number of sets of rails.** Trains emit an audible signal 1,500 feet before reaching a crossing.

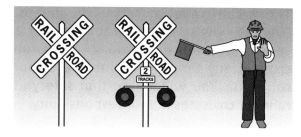

CROSSING SAFETY

Never pass as you near a crossing. (Prepare to stop behind a school bus, bus or vehicle transporting hazardous cargo, as they must stop at all times.) After a train passes, check for any additional trains before crossing. Make sure you can clear the tracks before starting to cross; never stop on the tracks. (Standard transmission - avoid shifting gears on the tracks.)

Trains cannot stop in time! You must protect yourself and your passengers at this high-risk intersection!

Additional safe driving driving procedures at railroad crossings are:

- If a crossing is marked only with a crossbuck - **reduce speed**, **look both ways**, and **listen** for the audible train whistle. If a train is approaching - **STOP**; if not, proceed only upon exercising due care.
- If red lights are flashing at the crossing - **STOP** and remain stopped until the train passes by and the lights stop flashing.
- If railroad crossing arms have been lowered - **STOP**, wait until the train has passed and the gates are raised.
- **Never stop on the tracks.** If your car stalls on the tracks and you cannot restart it (if no train is approaching), get out and try to push it off the tracks. If you cannot push it off the tracks, get help. **If a train is approaching,** get out quickly and get clear of the tracks. Run in the direction from which the train is approaching to avoid flying debris (staying clear of the tracks).
- **Be sure all tracks are clear** before you proceed across. There may be two or more sets of tracks (a tab under the crossbuck indicates the number of tracks). One train could be blocking the view of another (closed sightline) which could be approaching from either direction.

- Remember, trains do not and cannot stop at crossings - **they always have the right-of-way**. Even if the locomotive engineer sees you, a freight train moving at 55 miles per hour can take a mile or more to stop once the emergency brakes are applied (about 18 football fields!).
- Audible signals or whistles may be difficult to hear as you approach a crossing. You should **open your** window, **turn off your radio**, and listen carefully.
- **ALWAYS EXPECT A TRAIN!**
- If you encounter a railroad crossing signal problem, please call the 1-800 number (posted on or near the signal), your local police department, or county sheriffs' office. Each crossing has an identifying number. Please note the number and be ready to provide it when reporting a problem.

URBAN / RURAL COMPARISON

A city can be an exciting environment; however, crowded streets, heavy traffic, and a multitude of traffic signals can make driving a difficult challenge to the uninitiated. This is especially true for novice drivers.

Driving in rural areas is less hectic and more relaxing, however, you must adjust to higher speeds, a variety of road conditions, and traffic patterns. Accidents are fewer but more serious.

Characteristics to be wary of:
- a multitude of intersections
- rows of parked vehicles
- off-road parking
- school buses
- school and playground zones
- changing speed limits
- traffic jams
- numerous traffic signals
- city buses, delivery vehicles and other vehicles that stop frequently

Particular dangers:
- slow-moving vehicles
- oncoming vehicles especially large ones that produce air turbulence
- off-road vehicles
- crossings- animals, trucks, etc.
- railroad crossings
- wild animals
- hidden intersections
- winding roads and hills
- unpaved shoulders and no shoulders
- unpaved roads
- narrow bridges

15

SAFETY TIPS

In 2001, there were 22,736 fatal crashes (60 percent) in rural areas and 15,060 fatal crashes in urban areas. Head-on crashes make up 17 percent of rural fatal crashes (only 9 percent in urban areas). Rural fatalities have remained at approximately 25,000 per year since 1990; urban have declined by 18 percent.

Curves

On the open highway, the roads adapt to the environment. They are characterized by curves and hills that follow the lay of the land. In the same way, you must adapt your driving and apply the SIPDE system.

CURVES

The ideal technique for negotiating a curve requires thinking ahead. How sharp is the curve? Are there any warning signs? Is the road surface banked? What would be a safe speed? What transfer of weight may occur? What quality of traction do the tires have with the road surface?

All of these questions must be answered before reaching the curve. **SEARCH - EVALUATE** - then **EXECUTE**:

Reduce vehicle speed (braking and/or downshifting) in a straight line as you approach the curve (**1-2**).

Once you start to steer and enter the curve (**3-4**), apply a slight pressure on the accelerator to balance the vehicle (minimize weight transfer) and maintain speed. Target the center of the lane as far ahead as is possible and input smooth steering movement.

As soon as your line of sight extends down the straightaway, begin to unwind the steering to exit (**5-6**). Accelerate smoothly to return to normal speed.

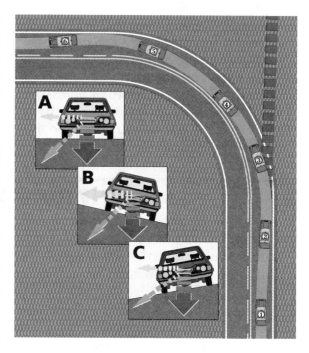

SPEED AND BRAKING

The slope of the road (**A**- flat, **B**- banked or **C**- crowned), the pavement, your line of sight, signs, sharpness of the curve, etc. are all factors. It is preferable to enter a curve more slowly, you can always accelerate. If you enter too fast, a loss of control will be inevitable.

HAZARDS

Oncoming vehicles that may cross the center line, a closed line of sight, and too much speed are hazards in every curve. Look ahead into the curve. Never brake on a curve! Braking puts extra stress on the front tires (weight transfers to one front corner); a blowout or loss of control could result.

Hills

On hills, gravity affects the movement of your vehicle - uphill reduces speed and shortens the braking distance; downhill increases speed and lengthens the braking distance. When it is quite steep, a warning sign may be posted.

SHIFTING GEARS
Uphill, shift to a lower gear (even with an automatic transmission) to make the engine turn faster and develop more power to climb more easily. Downhill, also shift to a lower gear (without pressing the accelerator), and the engine compression will help control the speed so that you will not have to press the brake pedal firmly and continuously.

VISIBILITY AND SPEED
Approaching the crest of the hill, your front line of sight is closed. Keep your vehicle positioned to the right in your lane (lane position 3), and ease off the accelerator until your line of sight allows you to see the other side of the hill (your lane and oncoming traffic). Expect the unexpected! Reduce speed in relation to your line of sight.

CLOSED LINE OF SIGHT

BRAKE FAILURE OR OVERHEATING
Uphill, the transmission and the engine are both working harder than normal, especially if you don't downshift. (On shorter hills, with an automatic transmission, the "kickdown" may suffice to climb without over-straining.) This excessive straining will cause both the engine and the transmission to overheat, and can lead to a breakdown.

Check the brakes by tapping on the brake pedal prior to any downgrade. If they malfunction, you can stop before gravity will increase the danger. Moreover, continuous braking on steep slopes (if you don't downshift) causes the brakes to heat up and brake "fade" may occur. Pressure on the brake pedal will not result in normal speed reduction.

ON THE DOWNGRADE
When driving down long, steep grades (6 degrees or greater), it is even more vital to control your vehicle's speed. Moreover, you should check your rear-view mirror about every five seconds for the presence of any large vehicles. Any rapidly approaching large vehicle, particularly one with white smoke billowing out from beneath it, is apt to be a runaway (brake loss due to overheating).

Do not try to outrun the vehicle. Instead, check carefully, and then pull off the road as far as possible to give the driver as much space as you can.

15

Passing

Passing is one of the most dangerous driving maneuvers. Before passing, you must decide whether it makes sense under the existing road, traffic and weather conditions. Your speed, the speed of the other vehicle, and the speed limit are major factors.

Whether or not passing is permitted by law, your line of sight, and the situation ahead are other items to be taken into consideration. **When the vehicle ahead is driving at least 10 mph slower** (than both your speed and the speed limit), and the maneuver can be performed safely and legally, you might come to the decision that you should pass.

GOOD JUDGMENT

Considering the multitude of factors involved, the passing driver requires good judgment (SCAN - EVALUATE) in order to assess the situation. The last thing you need is impatience; hasty decisions are rarely safe or accurate.

RAPID DECISION MAKING

When passing, an oncoming vehicle in the passing lane is closing the gap at a combined speed well over 100 mph.

You must mentally prepare an "out" - have predetermined options ready in case any "worst case scenario" develops - and be ready to implement them.

ASSESS
- Is passing permitted (pavement lines, no passing signs, hill, curve, intersection, bridge, etc.).
- Check the situation ahead in space areas 3, 1 and 2 (at right- signs, intersections at left- off-road vehicles, oncoming vehicles).
- Check your mirrors and left blind spot - space areas 4 and 6 (vehicles behind passing).

IS IT SAFE TO PASS?

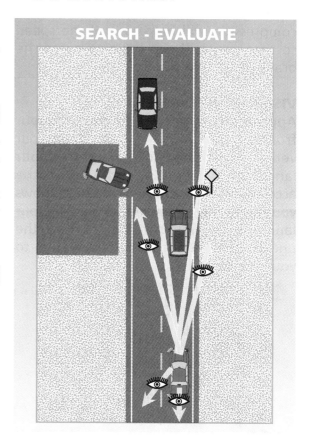

SEARCH - EVALUATE

PREPARE

- Activate the left turn signal.
- Signal your presence and intention to the driver ahead (honk or flash the high beams).
- Accelerate - running start (15 mph speed superiority) (automatic - kickdown; standard - select a gear that provides power to pass).
- Recheck the situation ahead in space areas 3, 1 and 2.
- Recheck the mirrors and the left blind spot (space areas 6 and 4).

EXECUTE

- Target and steer into the passing lane (lane change to the left).
- Occupy lane position 2 (lane-left position).
- Check the space ahead and behind (space areas 1 and 6).
- Glance at the left front tire of the vehicle you are about to pass (be prepared to abort at this point).
- Firmly maintain speed and lane position while moving by the vehicle.
- Check the rear-view mirror (both front tires of the vehicle you are passing should be visible).
- Activate the right turn signal.
- Check the right blind spot.
- Target and steer into the right lane (lane change right).
- Center your vehicle in the lane (lane position1, center-position).
- Cancel the turn signal.
- Maintain speed until you have a safe interval (space cushion) behind your vehicle then ease off the accelerator (return to normal cruising speed).

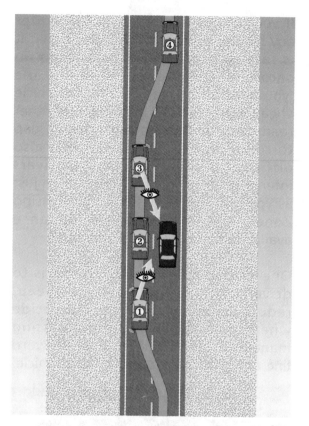

WHEN PASSING, NEVER PASS MORE THAN ONE VEHICLE AT A TIME!

HIGH RISK SITUATIONS

When you are driving on a two-way roadway and you are considering passing the vehicle ahead, there are several situations, though not technically illegal, that you should recognize and decide not to perform the maneuver.

If the vehicle ahead is driving at or near the speed limit, the distance and time required to complete the pass will be much longer than normal. The situation can change rapidly. **Don't pass.**

If your line of sight ahead is limited for any reason, you cannot determine that it is safe to pass. Never pass when an oncoming vehicle appears to be too close (you need a safe margin). If the vehicle ahead is preceded by a long line of other road users, you may not be given a gap to return to the right lane. It is also difficult to know what these drivers intend; they may plan to stop or turn just as you pull out to pass. A "No Passing Zone" ahead limits the distance available, it may not be long enough.

One of the most common errors is to drive right up to the vehicle ahead, reduce speed, and then try to decide whether or not to perform a passing maneuver. At this point, your forward line of sight is obstructed by the vehicle.

LOSS OF FOLLOWING DISTANCE

You have lost your minimum following distance (in case you have to brake for any reason), as well as any speed superiority (running start). In normal passing situations, all three of these help reduce the risk of a passing maneuver.

Instead, as you approach, move into lane position 2 (lane left-position) to see past the preceding vehicle. Evaluate the situation, and prepare to pass without reducing speed. Predict all possible scenarios and pre-plan responses.

If you decide to pass, move into the passing lane while increasing speed (speed differential, running start). The point of final decision (whether to abort or to proceed) must be just prior to reaching the rear of the preceding vehicle that you are about to pass.

Apply these concepts, as well as the steps for performing the passing maneuver outlined earlier, and you will learn to pass safely and quickly. Never forget to apply all of the concepts to any passing situation. Passing is one of the most dangerous maneuvers; only you can reduce the risk.

SAFETY TIPS

Head-on collisions, typically involving a passing maneuver, annually account for 8,000 fatalities. This is approximately 20% of all traffic fatalities. NHTSA While some crashes occur due to impatience or illegal actions, many result from a lack of knowledge regarding time/space gap requirements. You must learn to determine a safe passing gap at various speeds.

PASSING AND THE LAW

You may not pass another vehicle on the left side of a two-lane road or in the center lane of a three-lane road, unless the lane is clearly visible and is free of oncoming traffic for a sufficient distance to pass safely (without interfering with an oncoming vehicle or the vehicle overtaken).

Passing on the left is prohibited when:

- you must cross a solid yellow line;
- a "No-Passing" sign is posted or the triangular "No-Passing Zone" sign is posted on the left;
- approaching a hill or curve where your view ahead is obstructed;
- within 100 feet of a bridge, viaduct, or tunnel (except on a one-way road);

- oncoming traffic is too close; and also
- you cannot see ahead clearly.

PASSING ON THE RIGHT

On a one-way road or divided highway, passing other vehicles on either side is permitted. However, slower moving vehicles should keep to the right except when preparing to turn left.

It is legal to pass on the right of another vehicle waiting to turn left, provided it can be done in complete safety without leaving the pavement or traveled portion of the roadway. Crossing the white line that marks the right edge of the road onto the shoulder, even if the shoulder is paved, is illegal.

Being Passed

When another vehicle is passing you on the left, you must cooperate. Your safety depends on it.

You should:

- refrain from increasing speed;
- move to the right on audible signal;
- check for an "out" to the right; and
- be prepared to adjust speed.

If the passing driver suddenly decides not to do so (starts braking) because of an oncoming vehicle (see right), accelerate to help him/her re-enter the lane behind you. If he/she continues to complete the pass, apply the brakes to help him/her re-enter the lane in front of you. As a last resort, move onto the shoulder.

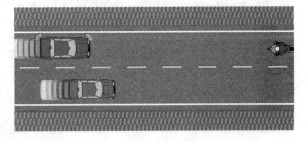

15

Review

I5-G

- Intersections
- Staggered stop
- Right turn lane squeeze

- Shared left turn lane
- Roundabout
- Banked curve

- Speed superiority
- Running start
- Out

SUMMARY

Apply the APE system to the urban and rural environments and all of the maneuvers performed to reduce the risk.

Passing and being passed are situations fraught with elevated risk. Protect yourself by making reduced-risk decisions.

WRITE A SHORT PARAGRAPH ANSWERING / EXPLAINING THE FOLLOWING.

1. What should you scan for in urban environments?
2. What is a roundabout and how should you proceed when approaching it?
3. Describe the correct procedures for negotiating a curve.
4. What extra precautions should you take approaching hills and downgrades?
5. Describe the correct procedures for safely passing a vehicle ahead of you.
6. What extra precautions should you take when being passed?

TODAY'S HANDBOOK PLUS WORKBOOK

Check your comprehension and mastery of the contents of this chapter by completing the corresponding exercise that is found in the complement to the TODAY'S HANDBOOK PLUS:

TODAY'S HANDBOOK PLUS WORKBOOK

Complete the exercise on Pages 90 to 93. If necessary, review the chapter when uncertain of an answer and refer to your instructor for further guidance.

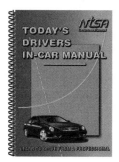

TODAY'S DRIVERS IN-CAR MANUAL

Before any in-car session, prepare yourself and facilitate the development of proper driving skills and habits by reading the corresponding lesson in the complement to the TODAY'S HANDBOOK PLUS:

TODAY'S DRIVERS IN-CAR MANUAL

Your instructor will evaluate your progress in the manual. Licensed parents or guardians should supplement your practice by following the manual procedures and coordinating with your in-car instructor.

Expressway Environment

Having acquired the strategy (the SIPDE system) and visual skills as they apply to the every day driving scene, you must now apply these same skills to interacting with other road users in the expressway environment.

It is important to understand the characteristics of expressways and to adapt your driving techniques to the higher speed environment. Special skills are required to safely enter the expressway using the various types of entrance ramps. Once you are traveling at speeds up to 70 mph, you must apply critical thinking, utilize problem-solving skills, as well as risk-reduction decision-making to the complex risk environment.

The presence of a wide variety of other road users will also require special adaptations. The level of experience of a novice driver must also be considered.

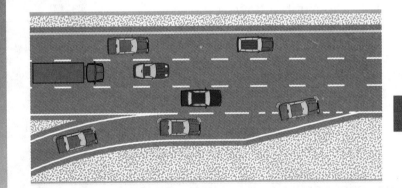

AFTER COMPLETING THIS CHAPTER, THE STUDENT MUST BE ABLE TO RECOGNIZE, EVALUATE, AND APPLY RISK-REDUCTION STRATEGIES TO :

- enter and exit the expressway.
- establish speed and lane position while interacting with other road users.
- travel on multi-lane roadways at speeds up to 70 miles per hour.
- adapt to the special expressway situations and high speed considerations.

Characteristics

Traveling on freeways, the normal traffic speed is higher than the urban or rural environment.

Drivers must adapt the SIPDE system to manage time, space and visibility in this controlled environment. Most multiple vehicle collisions occur on expressways due to vehicles following too closely or conflicts at entrances and exits.

CHARACTERISTICS
- Higher speeds
- Limited access and exits (no intersections, crossings)
- Separate roadways with two or more lanes moving in the same direction
- Gentle, banked curves
- Graded hills
- Minimum and maximum speed limits
- Uninterrupted flow of traffic
- Highway hypnosis

Advantages of expressway driving and limited access roadways include:
- they carry a larger volume of traffic;
- collisions and fatality rates are lower than other types of roadways;
- cross traffic is not present because of interchanges;
- opposing traffic is separated by some barrier (guardrail, cement, median);
- pedestrians, bicyclists, and slow-moving vehicles are not permitted on expressways; and also
- they are designed to help drivers anticipate conditions ahead.

INTERCHANGES

Freeways are designed for traffic moving at higher speeds. As such, the normal intersections with stop signs or traffic lights have been eliminated.

Access is provided by special entry ramps and drivers exit by special exit ramps. Cross traffic passes under or over the freeway. This permits traffic to merge or to exit with a minimum of disruption of speed or movement. These are, in reality, still intersections; however, because of their special design, they are normally referred to as interchanges.

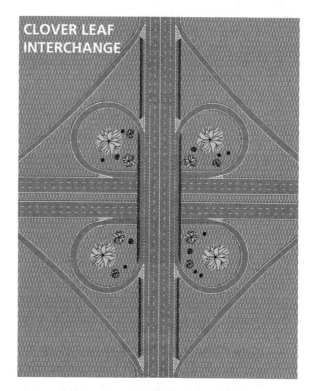

CLOVER LEAF INTERCHANGE

CLOVER LEAF INTERCHANGE

Allows for the intersection of two expressways with minimal disruption of speed or of movement. It is characterized by an entrance and exit ramp with a sharp curve to replace any left turn maneuvers. The problem with this setup is that vehicles entering (instead of a left turn) and vehicles exiting (instead of a left turn) must share the same extra lane, called a weave lane.

The curved ramps may have banked or flat exits which lead to braking and steering problems as drivers adjust from high speed to the speed of the curve. The curves often are noted by reflector poles which are knocked down due to loss of traction by drivers that did not adapt.

DIAMOND INTERCHANGE

Allows for interchange of a major expressway with secondary dual or multi-lane roadway. It has intersections with traffic control devices on the smaller of the two roadways to permit left turn maneuvers (and often right turns, as well). Access to the expressway is provided by entrance ramps that begin at these intersections.

TRUMPET INTERCHANGE

Allows for the interchange of secondary two-way roads to a multiple lane roadway with minimal traffic mix. It is used instead of a T-intersection with no weave lane situations. These intersections are often found when interstate feeder roads stop at the interstate or loop.

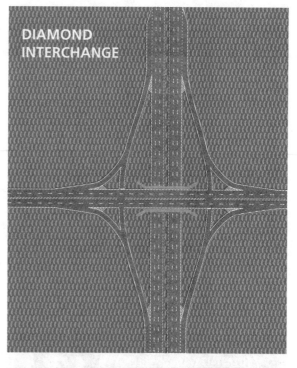

DIAMOND INTERCHANGE

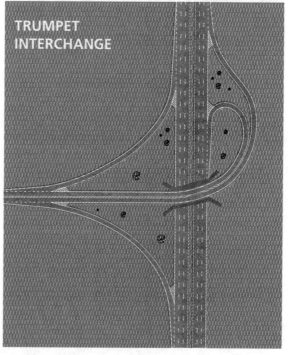

TRUMPET INTERCHANGE

16

FRONTAGE ROAD INTERCHANGE

Allows for the interchange of vehicles using parallel secondary two-way or one-way roadways and a major multiple lane roadway. It permits dense city traffic flows to mix efficiently with higher speed traffic of the multi-lane roadway. Frontage road turnarounds allow drivers to exit the high speed roadway in one direction and then use the the opposing frontage road to re-enter the multi-lane roadway in the opposite direction.

Yield rules and roadway markers may vary based on the direction of the flow of traffic on the frontage road (two-way, one-way).

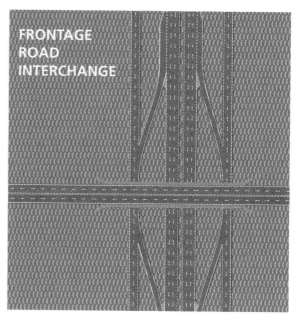

FRONTAGE ROAD INTERCHANGE

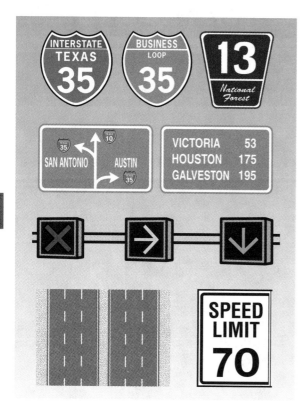

EXPRESSWAY TRAFFIC CONTROL DEVICES

The "Interstate" sign is shaped like a shield and is red, white, and blue in color. Guide signs are rectangular and may be green/white, blue/white, or brown/white, depending on where they are guiding the driver. Warning signs and regulatory signs are also posted (see Chapter 2) along expressways. These signs are located either at the side of the roadway or hanging overhead on cross posts.

Traffic signals are rare. They may be used as lane usage signals which are mounted above each lane (see Page 2.22). Lane markings are consistent with other roadways (see Pages 2.16 to 2.19).

60 to 70 mph is the usual expressway speed limit (urban, congested areas - 55 mph).

Entering an Expressway

Expressways are designed for traffic moving at higher speeds. As such, intersections with stop signs or traffic lights have been eliminated.

Access is provided by special entrances that include three areas: the entrance ramp, the acceleration lane, and the merge area. The entrance ramp allows drivers time to search traffic for flow and gaps, as well as to evaluate speed and space requirements before entering. The acceleration lane allows drivers time to adjust speed to the flow of traffic while continuing to search ahead, behind, and for the gap. The merge area allows drivers to move onto the expressway into the chosen gap at the speed of traffic.

Many collisions occur in this environment due to conflicts that result from driver errors or inexperience. Sharing the roadway at these interchanges requires applying proper procedures for entering the expressway.

ENTERING THE FREEWAY

Merging with the flow of traffic on an expressway can be a hazardous situation; to avoid unnecessary risk, apply the APE system, learn the following techniques, and practice them with a professional instructor. Once the skills have been learned, additional practice to develop the skill and the comfort required will be most valuable.

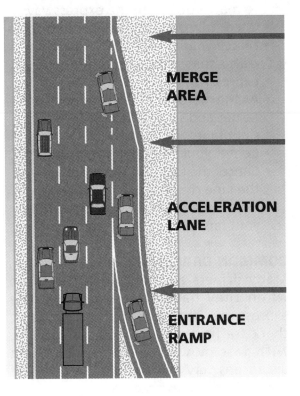

MERGE AREA

ACCELERATION LANE

ENTRANCE RAMP

ASSESS
- Check the access ramp (signs, speed, do not enter, ramp grade - uphill, downhill, level).
- Check traffic on the expressway.
- Check the flow of traffic ahead.

CAN YOU ENTER SAFELY?

PREPARE
- Adjust speed on access ramp (suggested speed, vehicles ahead and behind).
- Check for a gap on the expressway.
- Activate the left turn signal.

16

EXECUTE

- On the acceleration lane, accelerate to match traffic on the expressway.
- Check mirrors and the left blind spot.
- Match your vehicle with the gap in traffic that you selected on the expressway.
- At the merge area, look ahead, then target and steer smoothly into the right lane.
- Center your vehicle in the right lane.
- Cancel the left turn signal, or release the lane changer device.
- Adjust speed to the flow of traffic in your lane and create a space cushion.

COMMON DRIVER ERRORS

Many drivers are very uncomfortable when they have to merge onto the expressway. The need to increase speed, check traffic, signal, recheck, and merge with fast moving vehicles in a short distance is very demanding. To do all of this easily requires practice.

The most common error is to reduce speed or stop when trying to enter. This is usually caused by indecision or failure to check the flow of traffic and find a gap on the expressway as early as possible. The result is usually a collision, as the driver behind checks the traffic on the expressway in his/her mirror or blind spot and he/she plows into your trunk.

Other drivers err in judgment by merging with the traffic at speeds that are well below the flow. This results in collisions, either with vehicles bearing down upon them, or these vehicles braking suddenly or swerving into another lane, causing collisions with other vehicles.

Reducing risk on the entrance ramp

- Search for the proper entrance.
- Search ahead, behind, and on the expressway.
- Prepare to adjust speed for blocked ramp.
- Avoid stopping or backing on ramp.

Reducing risk on the acceleration lane

- Search ahead and for gap in traffic.
- Prepare to adjust speed.
- Pull ahead onto the shoulder if no merge is available.

Reducing risk in merging areas

- Search ahead and to the side.
- Blend speed with traffic.
- Search for traffic changing lanes at or near merge area.

16

SAFETY TIPS

Apply the SIPDE Space Management System when preparing to enter and while entering the expressway will help reduce risk.
Your level of experience with this complex maneuver will play an important role in your ability to adapt. Search and evaluate carefully to reduce risk!

Expressway Driving

Traveling on expressways, the posted speed limit is higher than urban or rural speed limits.

Multiple vehicle crashes occur on expressways. Drivers must adapt to the high-speed driving conditions. You must apply the SIPDE system to manage your time, space, and visibility in this controlled environment.

PLAN THE ROUTE IN ADVANCE

The high speed, the volume of traffic, boredom (highway hypnosis) from an unchanging environment and the need to remain alert place a constant strain on the driver. Whether driving for a short trip or an extended distance, you must plan a route in advance. Driving is not the time to consult a map or written directions. Know the entrances and exits, the number of the highways and all other pertinent data. On longer trips, plan rest stops and overnight accommodations.

BE FAMILIAR WITH ALTERNATE EXITS

Despite the best plan of action, you must always be ready for unforeseen situations. Construction, collisions, exit closings, or traffic congestion may require you to change your route. Prepare alternate exits and routes in advance for just such an eventuality. Listen to radio stations that announce traffic reports in the area to assist you in planning ahead. You will save a great deal of anxiety.

GUIDE SIGNS

Guide signs indicating distance/direction are posted to assist travelers to their destination. Prior to each exit, at least three signs are posted within a distance of one mile to give drivers plenty of time to prepare to exit. Signs may indicate that a lane must exit. Choose a lane of travel appropriate to your intentions. An exit sign (gore sign) designates the exact location.

PLAN TIME OF TRAVEL

To avoid unfamiliar or congested traffic situations, plan the time that you are on the road to arrive in a given area while it is still daylight, and not during rush hour traffic. Planning a rest or sight seeing stop so that you enter or cross an urban area after the peak rush hour traffic period may end up saving you time and a great deal of frustration.

DRIVING ON THE FREEWAY

Adjust your speed to the traffic, the speed limit, the road and weather conditions. Search 20 seconds ahead, the full width of the roadway. Identify potential hazards. Keep space around your vehicle; increase your following distance to at least three or preferably four seconds. Maintain an open space area on at least one side of your vehicle. Avoid driving in "packs". Adjust your speed and space early and gently. Avoid large vehicles that block your visibility.

16

POTENTIAL DANGERS ARE:

- the effect of high speed on your braking distance;
- the effect of high speed on your field of vision;
- the hypnotizing effect of expressway driving (highway hypnosis);
- the velocitization effect of extended high speed driving;
- the presence of slower moving vehicles;
- entrance and exit ramps on the right and sometimes on the left;
- vehicles on the shoulder re-entering the roadway; and also
- windy sections of the roadway.

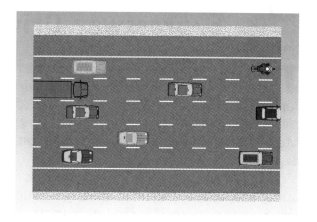

LANE SELECTION

Drive in the right lane (two lane) or the second lane (three or more lanes) as much as possible. Leave the left lane for passing. Adjust your speed to the traffic, the speed limit, the road and weather conditions. (Minimum and maximum speed limits no longer apply in adverse driving conditions.) Driving at the common speed of traffic, without exceeding the speed limit, is the best way to establish and maintain a safe space around your vehicle.

CHANGING LANES

The need to change lanes on the expressway occurs often. It can be more dangerous when there are more than two lanes going in the same direction. When you change lanes, check the blind spot across the entire roadway, as other vehicles may be changing to the same lane you intend to occupy. **Always change one lane at a time.**

PASSING

Passing is one of the most dangerous maneuvers a driver can attempt. On the expressway, passing can occur on the left or the right. It is much more similar to a couple of lane changes than passing maneuvers in other driving environments (no oncoming vehicles). However, because of the higher speeds of most of the vehicles and the volume of traffic, extreme care in evaluating the situation prior to deciding, and also when preparing to pass, must be exercised.

It is very easy to misjudge the speed of a vehicle approaching you from the rear, or the vehicle ahead that you are approaching (maybe faster than you realize). Evaluate speed carefully and allow an extra margin of space in this environment that seems safe. Remember, it is illegal to exceed the speed limit, even when passing.

See Chapter 15-E for the correct passing procedures and don't forget to sound the horn (to communicate).

If you apply the SIPDE system and get the big picture of the traffic scene around you, you can manage to minimize lane changes and passing situations while following the flow of traffic safely.

BEING PASSED

When another vehicle is passing you, you must apply the following risk reducing strategies:

- check the position of the passing vehicle;
- move away from it if too close (change position in your lane);
- do not increase speed; and also
- once passed, adjust speed to regain your correct following distance.

APPROACHING AN ENTRANCE RAMP

When driving in the right lane, you approach an entrance ramp and you notice a vehicle trying to enter the expressway. Cooperate by changing lanes to the left if the traffic situation permits. If traffic does not permit you to change lanes safely, be prepared to adjust your speed to assist the driver to merge with the flow of traffic.

When you approach an entrance ramp that is not clearly visible - closed line of sight (curve or overpass), avoid a potential conflict by changing lanes to the left immediately, even though you are not sure that vehicles may be entering. Moreover, on any approach to an entrance, a lane change to the left would eliminate the possibility of a conflict situation arising. (See vehicle A below, a lane change would have eliminated this situation.) Expect the unexpected and stay out of trouble.

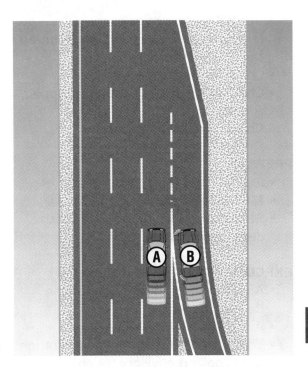

SAFETY TIPS

Applying the SIPDE Space Management System to the freeway environment will help reduce risk. Remember to increase your following distance (3 to 4 seconds) due to the higher speed.

Your level of experience with this environment will play an important role in your ability to adapt. Stay alert. Search far ahead to reduce risk!

16

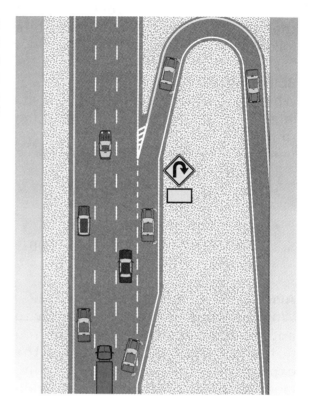 Exiting the Expressway

Plan your route ahead of time; make sure you know the highways and the exits you will be using. At least three signs will be posted to advise you of each exit. Prepare to exit by changing into the right lane (exit at right) about one-half mile (20 to 30 seconds) prior to the exit.

ASSESS
- Verify the type of exit (entrance and exit combined, curved ramp, clover leaf).
- Check for traffic entering.
- Check the exit ramp (advisory speed, curve).
- Check mirrors / blind spot.

PREPARE
- Activate the right turn signal.
- Maintain speed.
- Recheck mirrors / blind spot (at the deceleration lane).

EXECUTE
- Aim and steer smoothly onto the deceleration lane.
- Apply the brakes firmly.
- Verify the speedometer (velocitization, check posted advisory speed).
- Reduce speed to or below posted speed.
- Check for traffic stopped ahead.
- Steer along the center of the exit ramp (level, uphill, downhill, sharply curved, straight).
- Cancel the turn signal.
- Keep a space cushion ahead and behind.

After exiting the freeway, the extended driving at high speed will have created a false impression of speed (velocitization). Check your speed frequently by glancing at the speedometer for several minutes after you exit, this will assist you in readjusting to the slower speed.

If you miss your exit, continue straight ahead and proceed to the next exit. Then return to your intended exit on the other side of the freeway. Never reverse on the expressway, the entrance and exit ramps, or on the shoulder. This is highly dangerous, as well as illegal!

Special Expressway Situations

Although expressways are designed by traffic safety specialists and engineers with the intention of reducing risk and potential injuries, the existing roadways in the HTS may present a variety of special or unusual situations.

Whether the road was designed and built many years ago or was upgraded in recent years and utilizes the newest in highway construction technology, the driver must be capable of maneuvering in complete safety.

EXPRESSWAYS THROUGH CITIES

When an expressway is located in an urban environment, the volume of traffic may increase dramatically. Speeds may slow to a crawl. Drive in the left or center lane to avoid merging conflicts, especially during rush hour. Search for exits early and adjust position for exits as soon as possible.

DISABLED VEHICLES

When you see a disabled vehicle ahead, you must reduce speed and increase the space between your vehicle and the disabled vehicle. This may require that you change lanes. Be alert for tow trucks, pedestrians, and/or police vehicles.

If your vehicle becomes disabled:
- pull off as far as possible onto the shoulder or median;
- activate the emergency flashers;
- raise the hood to signal for assistance;
- stay in the vehicle and lock the doors;
- ask anyone who stops to go to a phone and call for assistance; and
- do not get into a stranger's vehicle.

CONSTRUCTION AREAS

When you see signs warning of a construction area ahead, reduce speed. Search for other warning signs informing of road conditions ahead. Adjust your lane position to maintain space around your vehicle. Be prepared to further adjust your speed to the unusual situation that construction sites present.

TOLL BOOTHS

Some expressways have toll booths that require road users to pay a fee for driving on the roadway. They may have toll areas every so many miles with a set fee, at entrances to bridges, or at each entrance and exit (a ticket is issued as you enter and you pay the fee when you exit). These can create special problems.

As you approach, begin reducing speed early as traffic may be backed up at the booth. Search for signs indicating the distance ahead, a reduced speed, green lights indicating open booths, exact change automated booths, special I-Pass lanes (electronic payment system), attendants issuing change and

16

designated lanes for special vehicles. Check for other vehicles making sudden lane changes or stopping unexpectedly.

REDUCED SPEED LIMITS

Reduce speed to the posted limit and check your speedometer (velocitization).

DISTANCE AHEAD

When signs indicate the distance to the toll area, check for correct change (ideally, you should have it prepared ahead of time). As soon as possible, position your vehicle in the correct lane.

DESIGNATED LANES - SPECIAL VEHICLES

Multi-axle vehicles and vehicles towing a trailer are usually required to use designated lanes and booths. Drivers with correct change or tokens may use the automated booths. Cooperate with other drivers who may have to change lanes as they approach because they realize they are in the wrong lane.

As you exit the toll booth, check for drivers on either side of your vehicle because they may wish to enter the same lane as you intend to use. Cooperate and yield to more aggressive drivers. Accelerate smoothly and re-establish your space cushion.

ENTRANCE RAMP ON LEFT

In some cases, an entrance ramp may be to the left of the freeway. The potential for conflict problems is greater. To enter, you must check traffic on your right and to the right rear and then merge with the far left lane which is used by the highest speed traffic. Once on the expressway, you must change lanes to the right. You may have to change more than one lane if your planned speed is less than traffic on the expressway.

If you are driving on the expressway in the left lane, apply the same concepts as when in the right lane near an entrance. That is, be prepared to change lanes or adjust your speed to facilitate entry.

WEAVE LANES

If an entrance and an exit use a common extra lane (acceleration/deceleration) as shown below, this is called a weave lane. This can cause conflicts for both drivers using a weave lane. Avoid problems by adjusting speed to plan your arrival so that you arrive and exit (or enter) when there are no other vehicles approaching to enter (or exit) the expressway.

The driver entering from the entrance ramp should yield the right-of-way to the driver leaving the expressway.

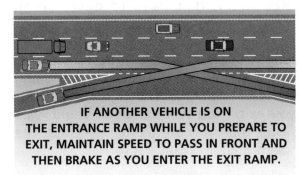

IF ANOTHER VEHICLE IS ON THE ENTRANCE RAMP WHILE YOU PREPARE TO EXIT, MAINTAIN SPEED TO PASS IN FRONT AND THEN BRAKE AS YOU ENTER THE EXIT RAMP.

ENTERING DIRECTLY ONTO THE FREEWAY

Some expressway entrances do not have an acceleration lane, or it is shorter than usual, and this creates a more difficult situation. You must use the access ramp to check the traffic as well as to adjust speed. You must find a longer gap than usual in order to merge with expressway traffic. You must accelerate more quickly

than usual (use the kickdown) in order to match speed and blend into traffic. Not all vehicles can do this easily.

DIAMOND LANES

A white diamond painted on the road indicates a reserved lane (HOVs, taxi). Signs supplement these symbols and designate which vehicles may use the lane. Double yellow lines mark the lane and may restrict access to specific entrances and exits.

Do not drive in these lanes unless your vehicle qualifies, nor cross double yellow lines to enter or exit the designated lane.

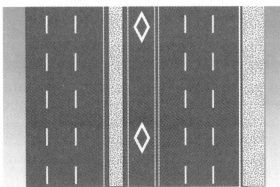

RAMP METERING

At the beginning of the acceleration lane, timed signal lights, one red and one green, are posted to control access and to space the vehicles that are entering. Usually, a sign indicates that only one vehicle is permitted to enter on the green signal. On the green light, you must accelerate quickly to blend with the flow of traffic.

16

High Speed Considerations

When you drive in any high speed and multiple lane environment (which includes the expressway), there are many problems that may arise that can create high risk scenarios. You must apply the SIPDE system to reduce risk.

POTENTIAL EXITING PROBLEMS

Consider each of the following and decide how you could reduce the potential risk that they present:
- weave lane conflicts;
- traffic stopped on an exit ramp;
- a short deceleration lane; and
- a very slow ramp speed.

ON THE ROADWAY ... DO NOT

In any high speed environment, here are a few maneuvers that are very dangerous and also, in most cases, illegal:
- driving over the median, a yellow solid line, or a raised dividing section;
- making a left turn or a U-turn;
- using the left lane except for passing;
- changing lanes without signaling, checking for an open gap, or checking the blind spot across the full width of the roadway;
- driving onto the expressway without using an on-ramp;
- parking on the expressway, except at areas provided;
- parking on the shoulder, except in case of emergency; and also,
- backing up on the expressway.

MULTIPLE LANE ROADWAY DANGERS

Higher speed affects your braking distance; the faster you travel, the longer the braking distance becomes. For this reason, you must keep a longer following distance. A 3 or 4 second interval will help reduce the risk.

Your vision is also affected by the higher speed. As your speed increases, your field of vision narrows. At high speeds, tunnel vision can result.

VELOCITIZATION
Though you will not find this word in the dictionary, it it used to describe an incorrect sensation of vehicle speed after driving at expressway speed for any length of time. You will be fooled into thinking your vehicle is not really going fast. An even greater danger occurs after you exit. You will think you could walk faster than you are traveling - check the speedometer. What a surprise!

When driving on the expressway, check the speedometer regularly to prevent yourself from continuing to increase speed. When exiting, check it before the exit ramp to ensure that you match the posted ramp speed.

After exiting, check your speedometer more often than usual for several minutes until your system has a chance to readjust to the slower speed of the rural or urban area in which you are driving.

On long trips, it is a good idea to pull into a service station as soon as you exit the expressway. This short rest will allow your system time to readjust to the slower speeds while you are stopped.

HIGHWAY HYPNOSIS

Driving mile after mile at a steady speed lulls most drivers into a relaxed then progressively more inattentive state of mind. Some drivers have even fallen asleep. This problem is even more acute at night.

To help avoid drowsiness

- Ventilate your vehicle (set the air conditioner at a lower temperature).
- Rest prior to starting out and at regular intervals (walk around the car).
- Force your eyes to scan; move your eyes and head more than normally.
- Change your seating position slightly from time to time.
- Converse with passengers, chew gum, change the radio station, etc.
- Avoid eating heavy meals before or during the trip.

The only real solutions are to **stop and rest** as long as is necessary or **change drivers** to someone who is more alert.

RE-ENTERING THE EXPRESSWAY

To re-enter the expressway when stopped on the shoulder, you must realize that you are starting from a stopped position. Cancel the hazard signals and activate the left turn signal (right turn signal if you are on the median shoulder). Check the shoulder ahead of you for hazards. Check the traffic approaching from the rear and find a large gap in the lane beside you.

If the shoulder ahead of your vehicle is clear, accelerate on the shoulder until you match the speed of the traffic on the freeway in order to blend easily with the flow of traffic.

When another road user ahead is parked on the shoulder and signals to re-enter the roadway, check around your vehicle and make a lane change to the left, if possible. Help create a gap to allow him/her to re-enter. If you cannot change lanes, adjust your speed to create a gap.

LONG TRIPS ON MULTI-LANE ROADWAYS

- Check your vehicle for maintenance problems.
- Plan your route and time of travel to avoid congestion.
- Check with police for construction delays or detours.
- When packing your vehicle consider weight distribution (center of gravity), as well as access to the spare tire.
- Plan stops for food, rest, and fuel.
- Take a map with the planned route clearly marked and ask a passenger to serve as navigator.
- Carry money, travelers checks, or credit cards in case of unforeseen expenses.
- If anyone takes medication, make sure you carry a sufficient supply.
- Carry a spare set of keys.

16

Review

VOCABULARY - WRITE A SHORT DEFINITION FOR EACH OF THE FOLLOWING :

- Controlled access
- Clover leaf interchange
- Diamond interchange
- Trumpet interchange
- Frontage road

- Access ramp
- Acceleration lane
- Merge area
- Time interval
- Highway hypnosis

- Velocitization
- Deceleration lane
- Exit ramp
- Toll booths
- Weave lanes

SUMMARY

Apply the SIPDE system to the freeway environment so that you can make reduced-risk decisions and actions.

Entering, driving on, and exiting the freeway require adapting to the higher speed and special conditions.

WRITE A SHORT PARAGRAPH ANSWERING / EXPLAINING THE FOLLOWING.

1. A) Describe the characteristics of the freeway environment.
   B) What is the purpose of an interchange?

2. A) What are the procedures for entering an expressway?
   B) What special considerations are required to drive on the freeway safely?
   C) How should you exit the freeway?

3 A) How should you proceed on the approach to a toll booth?
   B) What are the procedures for using a weave lane?

4. A) What should you avoid in any high speed environment?
   B) How can you counteract the danger of velocitization?

TODAY'S HANDBOOK PLUS WORKBOOK

Check your comprehension and mastery of the contents of this chapter by completing the corresponding exercise that is found in the complement to the TODAY'S HANDBOOK PLUS:

TODAY'S HANDBOOK PLUS WORKBOOK

Complete the exercise on Pages 94 to 97. If necessary, review the chapter when uncertain of an answer and refer to your instructor for further guidance.

Adverse Conditions

Foresight is a characteristic of good drivers. Each season presents specific hazards to vehicle control. Assuring your vehicle is adequately prepared to overcome these potential dangers is essential. From small details, such as windshield wiper blades and fluid to match the weather conditions, to major details, such as a tune-up and proper tires, there are many items to be considered. Anything less is unacceptable!

Foresight also relates to mental preparation. Fleet operators, who prepare their drivers for changing driving conditions with meetings, videos or memoranda, have cut vehicle "downtime" due to collisions and mechanical mishaps. You can achieve the same results. Prepare yourself mentally for the hazards of the ever-changing seasons.

Don't leave it to chance, your safety depends on proper preparation of your vehicle and yourself.

AFTER COMPLETING THIS CHAPTER, THE STUDENT MUST BE ABLE TO RECOGNIZE POTENTIAL HAZARDS AND ADAPT DRIVING STRATEGIES TO:

- **road conditions.**
- **visual conditions.**
- **changes in traction due to unusual environmental conditions.**

ADVERSE CONDITIONS

The good driver knows how to adapt his or her driving to the driving conditions in order to drive safely. This ability comes with experience and practice.

As a beginning driver, you must learn to recognize variables in road conditions, traction, visual conditions, etc. that require you to adapt your driving. Although techniques do not change, you must learn to be cautious. It is better to approach a maneuver too cautiously rather than too aggressively.

Road Conditions

Besides the slope and the banking of the road surface (Chapter 9), other road conditions require special adaptations.

SAND or GRAVEL on the pavement acts like tiny ball bearings between the tires and the road. Avoid turning, braking or accelerating while crossing the sand or gravel. Reduce your speed before this hazard and coast over it. Resume speed once you are safely past the danger.

FALLEN LEAVES on the pavement reduce traction (especially when wet). Maneuver gently. Increase your following distance and, if you must brake, use a gentle pumping action to counteract the layers of leaves that slip against each other.

HEAVY VEHICLE or **TRUCK CROSSINGS**, and the immediate vicinity, may have the pavement coated with mud, earth, sand or gravel. Anticipate this possibility and reduce your speed.

POTHOLES or bumps in the pavement occur more frequently during the spring thaw season.

It is advisable to avoid them by driving around them whenever safety permits. They can prove disastrous to rims, tires, suspension and steering components. In order to maintain control of your vehicle and minimize damage, when you cannot avoid the hazard, you should:

- Check your rear-view mirror.
- Activate the hazard lights.
- Slow down as much as possible.
- Release the brakes just prior to the hazard (allow the suspension system to stabilize).
- Roll over the hazard (clutch depressed in standard transmission).
- Return to normal speed.
- Deactivate the hazard lights.

If you were unable to slow sufficiently to roll over the hazard at a safe speed (the impact felt severe), leave the hazard lights operating and look for a place to park. Check for damage before proceeding.

APPROACHING UNPAVED ROADWAYS,
two hazards are usually present; gravel on the paved portion of the roadway near the end of the pavement; as well as potholes on the gravel side, just after the end of the pavement.

Think ahead, reduce your speed while approaching the end of the pavement. You will avoid sliding on the gravel as you try to reduce speed and you will reach the potholes at a reduced speed.

DRIVING ON UNPAVED ROADWAYS,
traction is reduced (Chapter 11) and even lost on wet or oil sprayed surfaces. The posted speed limit is reduced. Following any vehicle creates danger from the cloud of dust obscuring vision and flying rocks damaging the windshield or headlights.

To drive safely, you should:
- Drive at a much slower speed in keeping with the reduced traction.
- Lengthen your following distance, especially when clouds of dust or large vehicles block your vision.
- Avoid the ruts in the road, especially when raining.

17

- Dive well over to the right.
- Allow a larger safety margin if you must pass (the space needed to pass and advance further than normal before returning in front of the vehicle you passed).
- Cooperate with other road users.
- Move over or stop to assist others in passing you.

When you return to normal pavement, you should take a few moments to stop and check your vehicle as well as clean the headlights and windshield.

HILLS

On hills, gravity affects the movement of your vehicle - uphill reduces speed and shortens the braking distance, downhill increases speed and lengthens the braking distance. When the hill is quite steep, a warning sign may be posted.

SHIFTING GEARS

Uphill, shift to a lower gear (even with an automatic transmission) to make the engine turn faster and develop more power to climb more easily. Downhill, shift to a lower gear as well (without pressing the accelerator) and the engine compression will help control the speed so that you will not have to press the brake pedal firmly and continuously.

VISIBILITY AND SPEED

As you approach the crest of the hill, your visibility will be reduced. Keep your vehicle positioned to the right in your lane and ease off the accelerator until your line of sight allows you to see the other side (your lane and oncoming traffic). Expect the unexpected! Reduce speed in relation to your line of sight.

BRAKE FAILURE OR OVERHEATING

Check the brakes by tapping on the pedal prior to downgrades. If they were to malfunction, you will have time to perform an emergency stop before gravity will increase your speed and thus the danger.

Moreover, continuous braking on steep slopes (if you don't downshift) causes the brakes to heat up and brake "fade" may occur. As a result of brake "fade", a normal pressure on the brake pedal will not result in normal speed reduction.

Uphill, the transmission and the engine are both working harder than normal, especially if you don't downshift. (On shorter hills in an automatic, the transmission "kickdown" may suffice to climb without over-straining.) If you don't downshift, the excessive straining that results will cause both the engine and the transmission to overheat and can lead to a breakdown.

MOUNTAIN DRIVING

Driving in the mountains affects both the driver and the vehicle. High altitude can cause drowsiness, shortness of breath and headache. Plan rest stops or change drivers regularly.

VEHICLE CONDITION

The carburetor (if you still have one of these) and the cooling system may require adjustment. Otherwise you might get poor response from them. Computer controlled systems adjust automatically to the change in altitude. In either case, have your vehicle checked.

SPEED

Use the techniques (downshifting) just mentioned in the "Hills" driving section to control your vehicle's speed.

ALLOWING OTHER VEHICLES TO PASS

Whenever you notice vehicles behind that want to pass, look for pull-out areas or use a wide shoulder rather than impede their progress. If you meet an oncoming vehicle and the road is too narrow for both to get by, the vehicle on the downgrade should back up the hill to a wider area. Co-operate!

PASSING SLOWER VEHICLES

Be patient and careful. Make sure you can see far enough to ensure the maneuver is safe or wait for the vehicle to reach a pull-out area. The thin air and lower atmospheric pressure reduce vehicle acceleration. It will take longer to pass than you would normally expect.

SPECIAL PROBLEMS IN HIGH ALTITUDES

Driving in the mountains often presents very sharp curves called switchbacks (see illustration for warning signs). These curves are similar to U-turns and require a very slow speed to negotiate them safely. Be prepared to reduce speed to the (suggested) posted limit and look out for any oncoming vehicles that may inadvertently cross the center line.

OVERHEATING

The engine might overheat; check the temperature gauge frequently. Stop to allow it to cool. (Activate the heater in the HOT position with the fan on HIGH and some of the engine heat will enter the passenger compartment.)

VAPOR LOCK

This raised operating temperature can also lead to a condition called "vapor lock". The fuel can vaporize in the gas lines near the engine (especially when you turn the engine off) and the system cannot pump this vaporized fuel into the engine. The vehicle will not restart. Let the engine cool and then try again.

17

DESERTS

Desert areas are also stressful for drivers and vehicles; they are larger and hotter than most people realize. Prepare your vehicle. Put heavier oil in the engine: at least S.A.E. 50 grade. Have the engine cooling system double checked.

Drive at night, when it is cooler, if at all possible. If not, plan rest stops every few hours or change drivers frequently. Check all fluid levels every time you stop. Never open the radiator cap when the engine is hot. Carry a water supply for the occupants as well as for the vehicle, just in case. Check the tire pressure every morning when the tires are cool.

Wear a good quality pair of sunglasses to protect your eyes from the glare. If they forecast strong winds, delay your departure, since dust or sand storms could cause a lot of problems in addition to damaging the paint of your vehicle.

Storms, though rare, cause flash floods. If a storm occurs, drive to higher ground and avoid stopping in natural drainage areas. Wait for the water level to return to normal before continuing on your way

RAIN

Rainfall reduces traction (Chapter 11) as well as visibility (visual conditions later in this chapter). Roads become especially slippery during the beginning of a rainfall (even more so after a hot dry spell). The water causes the oil and dust on the pavement to float creating an oily film that will wash away as the rain continues. The lighter the rain the longer the washing-away process takes. As the rain continues, water may accumulate on the road. Puddles, sheets of water and, in extreme cases, flooded pavement become possible hazards. (Wet snow and slush also reduce traction, hide potholes, and clog the tire treads.)

DRIVING IN THE RAIN

To counteract these hazards:
- Reduce your speed.
- Lengthen your following distance.
- Drive in the tracks of other vehicles.
- Brake sooner and more gently (if tires skid, ease up, re-apply gently).
- Accelerate more gradually.
- Steer with smooth gentle motions.
- Use windshield wipers (blades in good condition; full fluid reservoir).
- Activate the defroster and rear window defogger to prevent fogging or condensation (keep a window slightly open as usual).
- Make sure the tires have good tread and are properly inflated.

17

When approaching puddles and sheets of water, they may be deeper than they seem or they may hide potholes. Avoid them if possible. Be aware of and try to minimize the splashing that will ensue for your vehicle and also for pedestrians.

When you cannot avoid the situation:
- Check traffic behind you.
- Reduce speed as much as possible.
- Activate the hazard lights.
- Grip the steering wheel firmly (water resistance varies with depth and may pull the wheels off course).
- Release the brakes and coast through the water slowly (in deep water, accelerate gently to maintain the slow speed).

CROSSING DEEP PUDDLES

After crossing, apply the brakes gently (check the rear-view mirror first). If the brakes respond normally, turn off the hazard lights and proceed on your way.

If the brakes are wet, the vehicle will not reduce speed. If this is the case, continue (right foot on the accelerator) and apply the brakes simultaneously (using your left foot). The friction produced by braking steadily will dry the brakes. As soon as they respond normally, release the brakes and turn off the hazard lights.

When you approach a stop (stop, light, blockage in traffic), begin braking earlier than normal and check the rear view mirror. The driver behind you may not have checked his/her brakes and is only now discovering that the brakes are wet. By anticipating this problem, you can avoid a rear-end collision (Chapter 18) before you come to a complete stop.

HYDROPLANING can occur when a combination of speed, tire wear, tire inflation, or the depth of the water on the pavement causes the tires to lose traction. In wet weather (water, wet snow, slush), the tires cut through and maintain contact with the pavement at speeds of less than 30 mph.

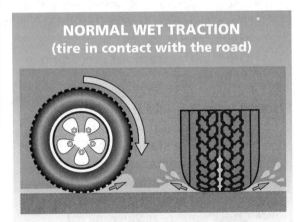

NORMAL WET TRACTION
(tire in contact with the road)

Unless the tires are excessively worn (bald tires) or underinflated, or the water is very deep; in any of these cases, you may still hydroplane at slow speeds.

17

At higher speeds (40 mph and higher), the wedge of water in front of the tires may pass under the tires and the tires will ride on the cushion of water. Traction will be lost completely.

HYDROPLANING
(cushion of water - loss of contact)

To prevent hydroplaning:
- Check your tires and tire inflation regularly.
- Reduce your speed even more than normal, when facing standing water and puddles.
- Drive in the tracks of preceding vehicles.

Should your vehicle hydroplane:
- Shift to neutral (depress the clutch for a standard).
- Activate the hazard lights.
- Grip the steering wheel firmly.
- Avoid braking or accelerating.
- Check your rear view mirror.

The water resistance will slow your vehicle. As soon as the tires regain contact, brake gently to reduce your speed, re-engage the transmission, resume driving at a slower speed and turn off the hazard lights.

WIND by itself does not affect the road conditions; however, in combination with rain or wet snow and cold temperatures, the wind can create icy patches. Handle this hazard in the same fashion as sand or gravel on the roadway. Slow before the danger, coast over the icy area and proceed. Scan the pavement ahead for other patches especially when nearing or driving on raised expressways, bridges, tunnels, wide open areas, or between tall buildings.

AIR TURBULENCE
ONCOMING LARGE VEHICLES

Gusty or high winds can push at your vehicle making it difficult to remain in your lane. This effect is even greater on large boxy vehicles, vehicles towing trailers, and vehicles with luggage on the roof.

To maintain control, you should:
- Reduce your speed.
- Grip the steering wheel firmly.
- Compensate gently for the wind

gusts as soon as the vehicle moves off course even slightly.
- Avoid passing.
- Increase your following distance.
- Keep away from other vehicles on either side (multi-lane road).
- Position your vehicle close to the right in your lane (on roads with one lane in each direction).

Besides the wind, large heavy vehicles generate air turbulence as they drive at high speeds. Passing or meeting an oncoming vehicle of this type can affect your vehicle control. Compensate by reducing speed and changing your position within the lane to leave as much space as possible from these vehicles.

Visual Conditions

Anything that reduces your ability to see; reduces your ability to control your vehicle. Automotive engineers have done their utmost to design vehicles and accessories to assist your vision. You must learn to use them to your advantage and to minimize any other obstructions.

The headlights should be turned on whenever you drive (Chapter 8). Daytime automatic headlight laws (like Canada) are being considered. If they become law, check your owner's manual. The parking, side marker and taillights may not come on automatically. The intensity of the headlights may be reduced. Drive with your normal headlights on at all times to make your vehicle more visible.

PASSENGERS or **CARGO** in your vehicle can become visual obstructions if not seated or stored properly. Try to minimize the blockage. When driving, if your view is not clear, double check and maneuver more gradually.

17

A FILM OF DIRT on the windows reduces vision, reflects light and causes glare. Keep windows clean (inside and out) to eliminate this danger and realize that the lights and taillights also require cleaning so that you can see and be seen to full advantage.

NIGHT VISION

Reduced lighting at night makes driving more difficult and dangerous. The effects on your vision are:

- Reduced visual acuity.
- Distance and depth perception decrease.
- Colors and contrasts are less distinct.
- Eyes must constantly adjust to changes in light intensity (oncoming lights, trailing vehicles, area lighting, etc.).
- Visual fatigue and cranial fatigue, and its affects on vision.

Your field of vision is more or less restricted to the narrow beam of light provided by the headlights.

HEADLIGHTS AT NIGHT

The most dangerous time to drive is at dusk. The eyes are subjected to a bright horizon (and sky) and a dark road and sky. The partial light condition reduces the effectiveness of headlights as an aid to your vision.

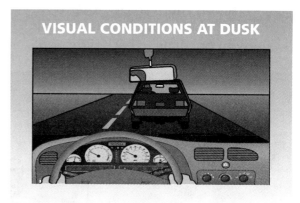
VISUAL CONDITIONS AT DUSK

To drive safely at night:
- Reduce your speed in accordance with the range of your headlights (about 200 feet for low beams).
- Increase your following distance.
- Allow a larger safety margin as all maneuvers take longer and your ability to judge distance is diminished.
- Use your high beams on unlit roads (dim to low beams when meeting or following another vehicle).
- Scan beyond the range of the headlights to identify hazards as early as possible.
- Adjust the dash lights to the exterior lighting conditions.
- Clean windows and lights.
- Avoid interior glare (lighter, matches, dome light).
- Communicate to make sure you are

seen (flash the high beams, flash the brake lights then brake, use the hazard lights, turn signals).
- Activate the defroster and the defogger as needed.

Eyes that are exposed to glare over an extended period of time develop a diminished capacity to adjust to the dark and to recover from exposure to glare. You must protect your eyes by wearing sunglasses during the day in order to retain the ability to adapt to night driving.

When driving at night, if your speed requires a total stopping distance that exceeds the range of your headlights, **you are over-driving your headlights**. You will not be able to stop your vehicle before reaching the hazard; you will have to perform an emergency evasive maneuver to avoid the danger. Instead of creating this situation, reduce your speed so that you can stop comfortably within the range of your headlights.

In curves and turns, the headlights are aimed straight ahead. You must scan into the curve or turn beyond the path that is illuminated by the lights and reduce speed more than usual.

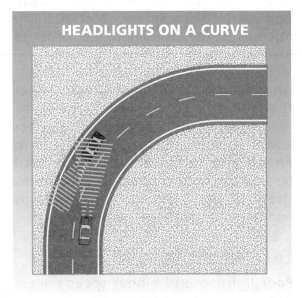

HEADLIGHTS ON A CURVE

Cooperate with other road users on right curves, dim the high beams to minimize the glare from the headlights.

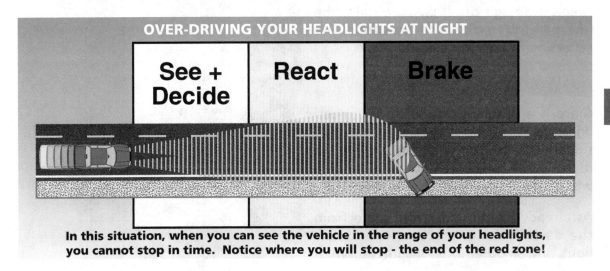

OVER-DRIVING YOUR HEADLIGHTS AT NIGHT

See + Decide   React   Brake

In this situation, when you can see the vehicle in the range of your headlights, you cannot stop in time. Notice where you will stop - the end of the red zone!

17

IN URBAN AREAS

On most major arteries, the eyes are bombarded by stimuli (neon signs, street lighting, advertisements). Utilize your selective vision to identify the data needed to drive safely. Increase the intensity of the dash lighting in order to easily see the information displayed.

On quiet dark residential streets, lower the intensity of the dash lighting to reduce glare and allow the eyes to better adapt to the exterior darkness. Scan ahead and to the sides of the road beyond the narrow beam of your lights. Use your high beams to verify hazards and communicate your presence.

IN RURAL AREAS

Poor lighting and higher speeds are a dangerous combination. Dim the dash lighting and use the high beams while maintaining a safe speed. Scan beyond the lighted zone and to the sides ahead. Take advantage of all possible data, the line of utility poles, the tree tops, the reflection of oncoming lights, etc.

GLARE

Glare is a problem caused by too much light, the reflection of bright light, or the sudden change from darkness to light. At night, glare causes temporary blindness while the eyes re-adjust to the dark.

As already mentioned, avoid glare from the dash lighting, matches, the dome light, and all other interior sources. When

the lights of a vehicle following you are blinding in the rear view mirror set the mirror to the night position. Return to the daylight position as soon as the offending headlights are gone.

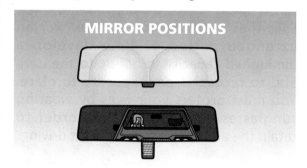

MIRROR POSITIONS

Cooperate with other road users:
- use your low beams on well-lit roads
- dim to your low beams when you approach another vehicle from the rear as soon as the range of the lights nears the rear of the other vehicle.

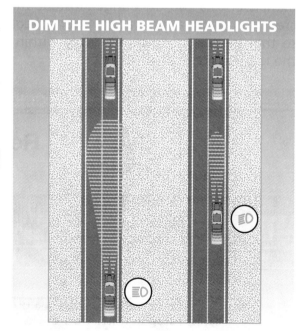

DIM THE HIGH BEAM HEADLIGHTS

- dim to your low beams when you meet an oncoming vehicle (500 feet). Don't dim your lights too soon and leave a large unlit area between the vehicles. Dim the lights before the oncoming lights become bothersome to you. Return to the high beams once you pass the oncoming vehicle.

- when passing at night, dim the high beams as you approach (200 feet). In addition, flash the high beams to warn the preceding driver and then keep using the low beams as you begin to pass. Return to the high beams when your vehicle is abreast of the vehicle you are passing.

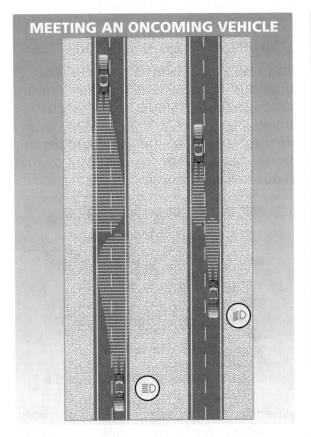

MEETING AN ONCOMING VEHICLE

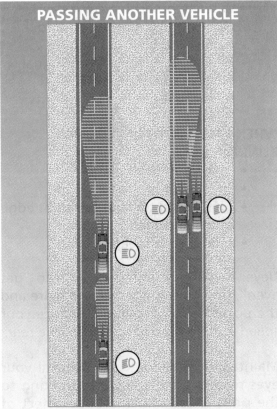

PASSING ANOTHER VEHICLE

17

SAFETY TIPS

Cooperate! If you blind other oncoming drivers with the glare of your high beams, you put yourself at greater risk of a head-on collision!

- When another vehicle is passing you, maintain the high beams to light the way for both of you until the other vehicle is abreast of yours.
Return to your high beams when the other vehicle is far enough ahead that the range of your high beams will not reach this vehicle.

- When approaching curves and climbing hills, flash to your low beams and back to the high beams. Look for a return signal from an oncoming vehicle.
Be prepared to dim your lights.

WHEN FACED WITH ONCOMING BLINDING LIGHTS:
- Flash your high beams.
- Check your rear view mirror.
- Look ahead towards the right edge of the pavement.
- Reduce your speed.

Never leave your high beams on to "get even", this merely increases the glare and the possibility of a collision. Reduce your speed if there is no danger from the rear.

Maintain your reduced speed until your eyes recover from the glare. Looking to the right ahead minimizes the effect of the glare.

WHEN FACED BY GLARE FROM BOTH SIDES:
- Flash your high beams.
- Check your rear view mirror.
- Reduce your speed considerably.

- Close one eye and look ahead to the center of your lane.

Reopen the eye once you have passed the multiple sources of glare. This eye has not been blinded and can be used to guide your vehicle at the reduced speed until the other eye recovers. Leave a longer following distance as your depth perception is not functioning.

FOG AND SMOG

Fog results from rapid condensation of humidity in the air as the temperature drops quickly. Smog includes dust or smoke particles with the fog. The density of these air masses can vary considerably from small patches to dense clouds that reduce visibility to zero.

When faced with patches of fog or smog:
- Slow your speed in relation to density.
- Drive at a steady speed.
- Use your low beam (high beams reflect back at you).
- Increase your following distance.
- Use the lane markings as a guide (following taillights may be a case

of "the blind leading the blind").
• Use the defroster, defogger, and windshield wipers as needed.
• Avoid passing.
• Be alert to faster vehicles approaching from the rear.
• Use hazard lights or flash brake lights to warn of imminent danger.

Special fog lights which penetrate the fog should be installed if you drive in foggy areas consistently. They should be mounted as low as possible so they will be most effective and should be used only in the fog.

In very dense fog (zero visibility):
• Safely move as far off the road as possible and stop your vehicle.
• Activate the hazard lights and the dome light. Turn off the driving lights.
• Do not return to the roadway until there is a marked improvement in the visibility conditions.

Rain and snow create similar visual problems and require the same adaptation as fog.

SUN GLARE

When the sun is low on the horizon, the glare from the sun and the reflection off the roadway reduces visibility. The cleanliness of the windshield can further deteriorate the visual situation.

If you are driving into the sun, wear polarized sunglasses and adjust the sun visor to block the glare without restricting your view ahead. Oncoming vehicles will be difficult to identify especially if driving without using their headlights. Reduce your speed.
The brake lights and turn signals of preceding vehicles will be less visible. Increase your following distance.

If you are driving with the sun behind you, oncoming vehicles have the glare problem and will have difficulty seeing you. Your headlights should be turned on whenever you are driving and, in this situation, it is essential in order to be seen properly. Communicate your intentions early and monitor traffic ahead and behind to ensure that you have been understood.

Winter Conditions

Winter can be very harsh in most parts of the country. This exacts a heavy toll on a vehicle. It is intelligent to make sure that your vehicle is well prepared and ready to cope with all of its rigors. Protocol requires the following precautions and they may save you a great deal of trouble and inconvenience.

•**ENGINE TUNE-UP** to ensure that the fuel and ignition systems will perform in all conditions. The engine oil should be replaced with an engine oil of the correct viscosity for cold-weather. A block heater is a good investment to ensure starting in extreme cold.

•**THE FUEL SYSTEM** should be protected from gas line freezing by keeping the fuel level as full as possible. Allow at least fifteen minutes of driving time to elapse after a fill-up before turning off the engine. This ensures moisture will pass through the system rather than collect at the bottom of the tank and in the fuel lines and freeze. In extreme cold, add gas line antifreeze at each fill-up.

•**THE ELECTRICAL SYSTEM** should be checked to make sure that the battery is charged and operates at maximum strength.The terminals should be cleaned. The alternator should be tested and the V-belt adjusted to ensure maximum efficiency.

•**THE TIRES** should be of the correct type for the winter conditions in your area. Snow tires are recommended and should be installed before the onset of winter. The inflation pressure must conform to manufacturer's specifications and should be checked regularly.

•**THE COOLING/HEATING SYSTEM** should be tested and the coolant anti-freeze level and concentration added to as needed. The system should be flushed every third year. The air ducts and fan should perform properly. Keep the outlets clear.

•**THE BRAKE SYSTEM** should be verified, adjusted and repaired as needed. It must respond effectively and precisely to pedal pressure to ensure control in critical winter driving conditions. The parking brake is part of the system and must also function properly.

•**THE WINDSHIELD WIPER/WASHER SYSTEM** should have special winter wiper blades installed. The wiper arms should be checked to make sure they will last the season. Make sure that the washer fluid in the reservoir and in your trunk is appropriate for winter temperatures.

•**THE EXHAUST SYSTEM** should be checked for leaks and looseness all the way to the tailpipe. Winter conditions test the system severely.

•**THE LOCKS AND SEALS** should be prepared for the rigors of winter. The locks should be lubricated with a product recommended by the manufacturer. The rubber seals around the doors and the trunk (hatchback) should also be treated with an appropriate product to prevent sticking and freezing.

INDISPENSABLE ACCESSORIES

- Brush and scraper
- Snow shovel
- Traction aids (anti-skid grids or mats)
- Sand or salt
- Lock de-icer fluid (carry it with you)

17

INDISPENSABLE ACCESSORIES

IN CASE OF A MECHANICAL FAILURE

Booster cables; flares or reflectors; a flashlight; a small tool kit; and spare fuses and bulbs. It is a good idea to have these on hand at all times; however, winter requires a few extra items.

SURVIVAL KIT

In case of an out of town trip, a long stop will necessitate the following items to combat the cold:

- Candles, matches and/or lighter, and a metal candle holder. A lit candle will provide light and heat thus reducing the need of operating the engine.
- Non-perishable food with a high caloric content.
- A thermos of hot, sweet, non-alcoholic beverage.
- Space saver blankets, warm clothes gloves and plastic bags.
- A first aid kit.

APPROACH TO THE VEHICLE

Besides the normal procedures, start the engine and activate the defroster and defogger. Then clear the snow from your vehicle - windows, roof, hood and trunk lid, all lights, and license plate. scrape all the windows to remove ice accumulation, If necessary. Unstick and clean the wiper blades. Remove any packed snow or ice in the wheel wells that may inhibit the normal movement of the wheels. This will also permit the engine to warm up before putting your vehicle in motion.

REMOVING SNOW AND ICE

When re-entering, kick the snow from your footwear to ensure that your soles will make firm contact with the pedals.

After performing the preliminaries, tap the accelerator pedal to disengage the automatic choke before moving the selector lever (automatic) or gearshift lever (standard). Remember to drive slowly for the first few minutes to allow the entire power train to become lubricated and warm up.

17

WINTER DRIVING

To get your vehicle moving follow the normal steps; however:

- Straighten the front wheels
- AUTOMATIC - release the brake pedal and apply a gentle pressure (if needed) on the accelerator pedal. STANDARD - raise the clutch to the friction point and gently engage, add a slight pressure on the accelerator, if necessary.
- Once in motion, press more firmly on the accelerator as needed to gradually increase your speed and steer in the desired direction. Should your vehicle get stuck, reverse in the path already created and try again. Avoid spinning your tires - they sink in the snow and melt the snow forming a layer of ice under the wheels.

While driving test the traction from time to time by lightly applying the brake pedal. On slippery surfaces, drive more slowly. Look further ahead and to the rear more often and keep a longer safety margin both in front and to the rear. Be gentle with the accelerator, the brakes and the steering. Sudden or quick maneuvers are the most common cause of loss of control on slippery surfaces.

Plan your maneuvers sooner so that you may reduce your speed more than usual in "good time". When turning, start at a much slower speed and accelerate later than usual and more gently. While driving, activate the windshield wipers (if not already operating) before you meet oncoming vehicles, a vehicle passes you or you pass another vehicle. Avoid passing unless it is absolutely necessary; make sure that the driver ahead is in no danger of steering off course and the space available for passing is much longer than normal.

In snow or blowing snow, travel in the lane with the least snow or ice. In fact, follow the path of the preceding vehicles even though it may not coincide with the center of a lane. Avoid driving in ruts; do not attempt to get out of them at high speeds.

Wet roadways are especially slippery as the temperature nears the freezing point (32 degrees Fahrenheit). Extra caution should be exercised on bridges, elevated expressways and shaded areas as these surfaces freeze more quickly.

SLOWING OR STOPPING

- Allow a longer braking distance.
- Ease off the accelerator gradually. A sudden release of the gas may cause an un-balancing effect - drive wheels and differential. Should the vehicle deviate from its course, shift to neutral (automatic) or depress the clutch pedal (standard) and steer where you wish to go. Normally, the engine compression, while still in gear, will assist you to slow your vehicle.
- Apply the brake pedal gently. If one or more of the wheels skid, release the brakes and re-apply more gently. If they still skid, shift to neutral and pump the brakes.

PARKING

In heavy snow, create a path for your tires by driving past the parking space and then reversing. Leave your vehicle in the middle of the tire tracks thus facilitating your departure.

It is always preferable and safer to park your vehicle (parking lots, driveways, etc.) so that you can leave the parking space by driving forward. In winter, this is even more important.

The parking brake can stick in freezing temperatures. To disengage when this occurs, reverse slowly while releasing the lock mechanism.

WHEN STUCK ON ICE OR SNOW

- Make sure the front tires are straight
- Drive slowly. Spinning tires dig deeper and create ice.
- Limit your movement forward and backward to the range attainable without spinning the tires.
- Accelerate gently when the tires grip, then shift to neutral and coast. Brake when you reach the limit of travel even if it is only a few inches. Repeat in the opposite direction. You will slowly rock your way out without damaging the power train.

WHEN ONE TIRE SPINS

Rear wheel drive vehicles, if the tires are straight and one of the rear tires is spinning, apply the parking brake (keeping it unlocked) while accelerating

gently. Release the parking brake slowly and you will move forward.

THE PRINCIPLE

The differential reacts to the resistance of the drive wheels. It transfers power to the wheel with the least resistance.

SPINNING TIRE (REAR WHEEL DRIVE)

EXAMPLE

If one wheel rests on a dry surface and the other on ice, the one on ice will spin while the other doesn't turn. The parking brake intervenes by mechanically giving both wheels the same resistance.

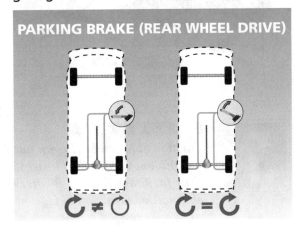

PARKING BRAKE (REAR WHEEL DRIVE)

17

RESULT

The differential transfers the same amount of power to both wheels. The resulting traction will get your vehicle moving forward.

USING TRACTION AIDS

- Place the mats or grids against the traction wheels with the spikes downward. To move forward, place in front of wheels & vice versa.
- Advance or reverse cautiously onto the grids. Once in motion, maintain momentum (don't spin the wheels).
- Make sure no one is standing near the vehicle as the grids may be thrown out from under the wheels.

TRACTION GRID (REAR WHEEL DRIVE)

WHEN STALLED OR SNOWBOUND

- If possible, drive onto the shoulder
- Use your hazard lights.
- Keep a window slightly open for air circulation.
- Get your survival kit from the trunk.
- Turn off the engine to conserve fuel. Do not use any electrical accessories while the engine is not operating.
- Run the engine for ten minutes every hour to charge the battery and warm the interior; check that the exhaust pipe is clear (Carbon monoxide gas).
- Use the plastic bags to encase your feet and legs to retain body heat.
- Use the blankets and clothing to further insulate against the cold.
- Keep awake. If accompanied, take turns sleeping for short periods.
- Unless you are CERTAIN that you can reach help nearby; do not leave your vehicle. It provides shelter and is more visible.
- Use the candles, food and beverage sparingly.

Following these procedures, you and your passengers can wait out any situation until help arrives.

SAFETY TIPS

Traction aids can be thrown out from under the wheels, with violent force. Make sure no one is standing nearby. Also note the red ribbon in the illustration, this is to facilitate finding it afterwards. Kitty litter or sand could be used as an alternative to traction aids.

17

Review

TERMS TO REMEMBER - WRITE A SHORT DEFINITION FOR THE FOLLOWING :

- Foresight
- Adverse conditions
- Potholes
- Hydroplaning
- Air turbulence

- Over-driving your headlights
- Dash lighting
- Night mirror
- Glare

- Smog
- Fog lights
- Booster cables
- Survival kit
- Traction aids

SUMMARY

Proper preparation of your vehicle and attention to small details will permit you to drive safely in adverse conditions. Adapting to road, weather and visual conditions will diminish the risks.

Learning to handle poor driving situations is part of the learning to drive process. Until you gain experience, choosing not to drive may be the correct choice in some situations.

TEST A - WRITE "T" BESIDE STATEMENTS THAT ARE TRUE AND "F" BESIDE THOSE THAT ARE FALSE.

_____ 1. When driving on a slippery roadway, your minimum following distance should be increased.

_____ 2. If your vehicle hydroplanes, you should shift to neutral.

_____ 3. To start off in deep snow, the tires should be turned as much as possible.

_____ 4. Ice on the pavement is most slippery when the temperature is near the freezing point.

_____ 5. In foggy weather, you should drive with the high beam headlights.

_____ 6. On a windy day, you should reduce speed, keep extra space and be prepared to correct the steering.

_____ 7. On a gravel road, you should decrease your following distance so that you can see the preceding vehicle better.

_____ 8. When a vehicle passes you at night (from the rear), you should dim your high beams when the other vehicle is abreast of your vehicle.

_____ 9. Near the crest of a hill at night, you should flash your high beams, then proceed more slowly with low beams until you can see over the hill.

_____ 10. Approaching a curve at night, you should activate the high beam headlights to see further into the curve.

Student notes

_____
_____
_____
_____
_____
_____
_____
_____
_____
_____
_____
_____
_____

TODAY'S HANDBOOK PLUS WORKBOOK

*Check your comprehension and mastery of the contents of this chapter by completing the corresponding exercise that is found in the complement to the **TODAY'S HANDBOOK PLUS**:*

TODAY'S HANDBOOK PLUS WORKBOOK

Complete the exercise on Pages 98 to 103. If necessary, review the chapter when uncertain of an answer and refer to your instructor for further guidance.

TODAY'S DRIVERS IN-CAR MANUAL

*Before any in-car session, prepare yourself and facilitate the development of proper driving skills and habits by reading the corresponding lesson in the complement to the **TODAY'S HANDBOOK PLUS**:*

TODAY'S DRIVERS IN-CAR MANUAL

Your instructor will evaluate your progress in the manual. Licensed parents or guardians should supplement your practice by following the manual procedures and coordinating with your in-car instructor.

Emergency Situations

Driving in normal weather and road conditions is a challenge of itself.

There are times when driving becomes even more difficult. The hood may FLY OPEN! A tire may suddenly BLOW OUT! Another vehicle may approach HEAD-ON in your lane.

Foresight in the proper maintenance of your vehicle can prevent many possible emergency situations. Applying the SIPDE system and active visual habits while driving can evade many others.

Despite the best of intentions and precautions, you are most likely to face at least one critical situation at one time or another during your driving career.

Avoid panic! Easier said than done!

18

AFTER COMPLETING THIS CHAPTER, THE STUDENT MUST BE ABLE TO RECOGNIZE PROBLEMS AND PERFORM LOSS CONTROL TECHNIQUES IN RELATION TO:

- vehicle failures and the value of preventive maintenance.
- driver and road sharing errors.
- emergency vehicles and unusual occurrences.

W hat is panic? When the brain receives input from the senses either too quickly to assimilate or concerning a totally unknown situation; it is incapable of reaching a decision. A weighty, telling pause ensues... !

A decision will then be rendered which has no factual basis. It is highly likely to be an incorrect response.

This chapter is intended to mentally prepare you for the possible emergency situations which might arise. Then the brain will have the necessary information. You will not panic. The correct response will be readily available and the situation can be resolved safely.

Vehicle Failures

BLOW OUT

A blow out is a rapid loss of tire inflation (explosion or reaction to driving over an object on the roadway). A flat while driving produces a similar effect.

The result: the vehicle pulls to the side where the front tire has deflated. If a rear tire deflates, the rear of the vehicle swerves back and forth.

WHAT TO DO
- Maintain speed - DO NOT BRAKE!
- Grip the steering firmly and steer to keep the vehicle in a straight line.
- Activate the hazard lights
- When under control, ease off the accelerator
- Check traffic and select a safe path
- Change lanes to move off the roadway as far as possible to change the tire.

PREVENTION
Check tire inflation regularly. Check the tire tread and sidewall each time you approach the vehicle (have a more thorough examination performed when the vehicle is being serviced - oil change). Replace tires when worn, bulging, or cracked. Avoid driving over objects on the roadway

ACCELERATOR PEDAL STICKS

If the gas pedal is released and the vehicle maintains speed or continues accelerating, the accelerator control is stuck. A broken spring or engine mount, a sticking linkage, a crumpled floor mat or ice around the pedal could cause this problem.

WHAT TO DO

If you must stop quickly:
- Apply and maintain pressure on the brakes (until you are stopped).
- Shift to Neutral (depress the clutch).
- Turn off the ignition switch.
- Activate the hazard lights.

If you do not have to stop:
- Without looking, try to free the pedal with your right foot - if no success...
- Activate the hazard lights.
- Shift to neutral.
- Check traffic, choose a safe path, and steer off the roadway.
- Apply the brakes in a continuous manner until the vehicle is stopped.
- Turn off the ignition switch (on today's modern vehicles, the Electronic Control Module [ECM] will prevent over-reving).

Have the problem corrected before restarting the engine.

PREVENTION

Check the floor mat and foot pedals. Lubricate the accelerator cable. Have the accelerator control checked at the first sign of any abnormality.

HEADLIGHT FAILURE

Usually one light will burn out; however, both headlights can fail due to dimmer switch failure, a blown fusible link, a relay failure or a short circuit. Your ability to see and be seen is compromised.

WHAT TO DO
- Activate the hazard lights.
- Reduce speed.
- Maintain your lane position using the image of the roadway that you have imprinted in your brain.
- Turn the headlight and dimmer switches on and off several times.
- If the lights function, proceed to the nearest service center. Be careful to dim the high beams (even to no lights) for oncoming traffic.
- If the lights do not function, check traffic and select a safe path.
- Change lanes to move off the roadway as far as possible.
- Install flares, a flashing lantern, or reflectors if you cannot stop in a lit area.

SAFETY TIPS

If you must stop at the side of an expressway or major highway, where possible, stop your vehicle beyond the end of a guardrail, back up to the outboard side of the guardrail, and then stop your vehicle. The guardrail will be between your vehicle and the traffic.

HOOD FLIES UP

While driving, the hood pops open. Stop the vehicle in a safe place, open the hood and re-close it, making sure that it is securely latched. If it flies up blocking your forward vision, depending on your speed, it may fold against the roof and/or crack the windshield. An improperly closed hood or faulty hood locks are the usual causes. Engineers design vehicles with a double lock to prevent this possibility.

I CAN SEE!

WHAT TO DO
- Maintain your forward vision - look through the space between the hood and the dash, or lean to your left to look past the side of the hood.
- Activate your hazard lights.
- Reduce your speed while maintaining your lane position.
- Check traffic, choose a safe path, and steer off the roadway.

- Park in a safe location.
- Close or tie down the hood firmly.
- Drive slowly, checking the temporary fastener frequently, to the nearest service center.

PREVENTION
Lubricate the hood lock and hood release mechanism when washing the vehicle. Check that the hood is securely latched whenever you close it.

DEFECTIVE WINDSHIELD WIPERS

While driving, the wipers stop working or don't start working when the switch is activated. The cause could be a defective switch, burnt fuse, or the wiper linkage.

WHAT TO DO
- Activate the hazard lights.
- Reduce your speed.
- Turn the switch on and off several times.
- Check traffic, choose a safe path, and steer off the roadway.
- Park in a safe location.
- If the problem cannot be corrected on the spot, and if the rain or snow continues, have your vehicle towed.

PREVENTION
Never use the wipers to clear the windshield after a snowfall, freezing rain or when it is dry. Have the wipers checked and repaired as soon as they operate abnormally.

SAFETY TIPS

Activating the hazard signal is not a priority in emergency situations; however, communication is. If you practiced your driving compartment drill, activating the hazard lights should be second nature and require a fraction of a second.

THE ENGINE STALLS

The engine of your vehicle stops suddenly while driving. Mechanical failure, empty fuel tank, water or cold are the normal causes of this situation.

SHIFT TO NEUTRAL AND MOVE OVER

WHAT TO DO
- Shift to neutral (depress the clutch).
- Activate the hazard lights.
- Activate the starter using the ignition switch several times.
- If the engine restarts, shift to the appropriate gear, accelerate and turn off the hazard lights.
- If the engine does not restart, check traffic, choose a safe path, and steer off the roadway or near the curb.
- Apply the brakes with continuous pressure until you stop.
- Park in a safe location.

Power steering becomes more difficult to turn when the engine stalls. Grip the steering firmly and you can control your vehicle. (Low power steering fluid level, a broken V-belt or a defective pump may also cause power steering failure.)

Power brakes work normally for one more application when the engine stalls. Apply the brakes in one continuous application, modulating the pressure, without releasing. If you brake then release the brakes completely, the brakes will require a much greater pressure to work.

PREVENTION
Follow the recommended service intervals in your owner's manual. Check the fuel gauge every time you start your engine. Check the fluid levels every time you refuel. Allow the engine extra time to warm-up in extreme cold conditions before driving in heavy traffic. Avoid, when possible, puddles and splashing.

BREAKDOWN ON RAILROAD TRACKS

Should the engine stall, try to coast over the tracks, or perform an emergency stop before the tracks.

WHAT TO DO
- Check if a train **is** or **is not** approaching.
- IF A TRAIN IS APPROACHING, get all occupants out of the vehicle.
- Move at least 100 feet away from the vehicle in the direction from which the train is approaching.
- **IF A TRAIN IS NOT APPROACHING**, try to restart the engine.
- Shift to neutral and then push the vehicle off the tracks.

18

ENGINE OVERHEATS

The gauge or indicator light shows the engine temperature is rising above the normal level. This may occur in slow-moving traffic during hot weather or due to a mechanical defect in the cooling system. Lengthen your stopped distance from the preceding vehicle, activate the heater in the hot position with the fan on high, shift to neutral while stopped and rev the engine slightly. The temperature should return to the normal range, if not...

WHAT TO DO
- Check traffic, select a safe path and steer onto the shoulder or near the curb.
- Park in a safe place; turn off the engine.
- Activate the hazard lights.
- Open the hood to allow heat to escape (cover your hand with a glove or cloth).
- Visually check hoses, belt, etc. while the engine cools.
- If the coolant level (overflow tank) is low or empty, get a container of water.
- Unlock the radiator cap (1/4 turn), and step back from the front of the vehicle.

- After the pressure has been released, push down and turn the radiator cap to remove completely.
- Add some water slowly.
- Restart the engine and fill the radiator as needed.
- Close the cap and proceed to the nearest service center to have the cooling system verified.

PREVENTION
Proper maintenance of the cooling system as outlined in Chapter 19.

TOTAL STEERING FAILURE

Though a very rare occurrence, if you lose steering control completely, a breakdown in the front suspension or steering is the reason.

WHAT TO DO
- Activate the hazard lights.
- Shift to neutral (depress the clutch).
- Hold the parking brake release mechanism and pump the parking brake firmly to reduce speed quickly.
- Be prepared for a collision as you cannot control the direction in which the vehicle will move.

PREVENTION
The steering and suspension will not breakdown without warning. Any abnormal looseness, shimmy, wandering or noises should be verified by a service technician immediately. Following the recommended service intervals in your owner's manual will permit early diagnosis and repair.

BRAKE FAILURE

Complete service brake failure is rare in modern vehicles as they have a dual braking system (Chapter 20). Should one fail, the other will stop your vehicle and a warning light will advise you of the problem. Partial or temporary brake failure can occur due to lack of brake fluid, overheating, wet brakes, V-belt failure (on some models only), etc.

WHAT TO DO
- Downshift to use the engine compression (taking advantage of engine braking).
- Pump the brake pedal several times (to restore braking power).
- Activate the hazard lights if possible.
- Pump the parking brake while releasing the lock mechanism (to use the rear [mechanical] brakes to stop).
- Select a safe path while slowing (steer around obstacles).

If none of these permit you to stop, look for an uphill slope, guard rail, or curb to further reduce your speed. As a last resort, select objects that will give on impact (Chapter 11) to bring you to a complete stop.

PREVENTION
Check the brake fluid level monthly. In wet weather (Chapter 17) and on steep hills (Chapter 2 and 9), follow the aforementioned procedures. Have the brakes verified by a service technician at recommended intervals - owner's manual. Verify the proper operation of the parking brake by using it every time you park.

POWER BRAKE FAILURE

When the engine stalls, the power brake unit will be affected. However, the power brake will function normally for one more application of the brake pedal. Apply the brake in one continuous motion, modulating the pressure without releasing, and your vehicle will stop normally.

SAFETY TIPS

Practice performing emergency stops using the parking brake in a safe, off-road environment, then you'll be able to stop easily if this situation occurs.

If the power brakes fail and you release the brake pedal, you'll have to press much harder to achieve the desired result, but you will stop.

18

FIRE

Vehicle fires rarely occur, but when they do, you must act quickly to minimize danger to people and property. While driving, if you see or smell smoke in the passenger compartment, the ashtray, under the dash or under the hood, your vehicle has a fire.

WHAT TO DO
- Activate the hazard lights.
- Select a safe path and move your vehicle out of the traffic flow.
- Park away from crowds, vehicles and buildings (especially service stations).
- Turn off the ignition.
- All occupants should move at least 100 feet away from the vehicle.

A CIGARETTE OR MATCH
Don't over-react, the materials used in the passenger compartment are non-flammable. When stopped, locate the cigarette or match and put it out. Make sure that any smoldering embers are out as well. Proceed on your way.

AN ASHTRAY FIRE
Close the ashtray while driving, this will cut off the oxygen supply somewhat. When parked, remove the ashtray and extinguish the fire outside the vehicle.

UNDER THE HOOD
Once the vehicle is safely stopped, have someone call the fire department. Decide how serious the fire is: high heat and flames - wait for the fire department.

If you have a fire extinguisher (ABC type) and the fire appears to be minor, cover your hands with cloth or gloves. Release the hood latch. Approach the front with your head below the hood line, pull the hood release and raise the hood slightly. Aim at the base of the fire through the narrow opening and smother the flames. Open the hood and smother the area completely.

A fire extinguisher should be mounted in the passenger compartment within reach of the driver.

UNDER THE DASH
This is an electrical fire and can be very difficult to extinguish. Call and wait for the fire department.

Driver Error

TIRES DROP OFF THE PAVEMENT

Due to fatigue, lack of concentration, or to avoid an oncoming vehicle, the right tires of your vehicle have dropped off the pavement onto the shoulder.

WHAT TO DO
- Grip the steering firmly.
- Stabilize your vehicle parallel to the pavement.
- Ease off the accelerator and allow the vehicle to reduce speed (*do not brake - traction is unequal*).
- Check traffic, mirrors, and blind spot.
- Activate the left turn signal.

- Turn the steering wheel a quarter turn towards the roadway.
- When the right front wheel climbs the edge, countersteer towards the center of the lane to stabilize the vehicle.
- Accelerate and turn off the signal.

AVOIDING AN OBSTACLE

When driving at such a speed that an obstacle which appears in the road cannot be avoided by stopping, the only alternative is to steer around the object.

WHAT TO DO
- Apply the brake to perform an emergency stop.
- Activate the hazard lights.
- Select a safe path around the obstacle (avoid crossing the center line as you may encounter oncoming traffic).
- Look and steer in the desired direction.
- Ease up on the brake to allow full steering input to direct your vehicle in the chosen direction (vehicles with ABS brakes will steer during hard braking).
- Stabilize your vehicle.
- Check traffic and return to your lane.

SAFETY TIPS

Should you choose to leave the pavement completely and drive on the shoulder, whether to avoid an oncoming vehicle, in a passing emergency situation, or some other conflict, follow the same procedures described under TIRES DROP OFF THE PAVEMENT above.

SKIDS

When a wheel or wheels slide against the roadway due to insufficient traction, the vehicle is skidding. A vehicle can lose traction in the front or rear when the driver steers, brakes, or accelerates improperly for the situation. The resulting traction loss will be to either the front or the rear tires.

FRONT WHEEL SKIDS

The front wheels slide and your vehicle continues straight ahead.

Braking skid (no ABS)

Excessive brake pressure locks the front wheels. The front wheels are sliding and your vehicle will not respond to the steering. It continues straight.

WHAT TO DO

- Release the brake pedal.
- Look and steer in the desired direction.
- Reapply the brake more gently to continue reducing speed.

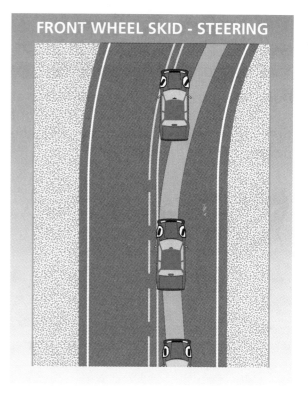

FRONT WHEEL SKID - STEERING

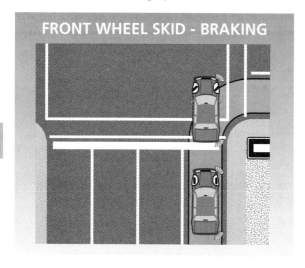

FRONT WHEEL SKID - BRAKING

Steering skid (understeer)

1) A sharp turn of the steering wheel and your vehicle continues straight. (Tires tend to roll under.)

WHAT TO DO

- Unwind the steering wheel slightly to regain steering control.
- Re-establish front wheel rolling traction. Jab the brake pedal to shift vehicle weight towards the front, encouraging rolling traction.
- Look and steer in the desired direction.

2) With a front wheel drive vehicle, while accelerating, you turn the steering wheel and your vehicle continues straight ahead.

WHAT TO DO

- Shift to neutral (depress the clutch).
- Reestablish rolling traction. (With ABS, applying the brake is a helpful tool to regain steering, while slowing.)
- Look and steer in the desired direction.
- Reduce your speed after the turn.
- Re-engage the transmission and proceed at a slower speed.

REAR WHEEL SKIDS (oversteer)

The rear wheels slide and the rear of your vehicle moves to the right or left.

1) While turning, the rear of your vehicle slides towards the outside of the curve.

2) While driving in reduced-traction conditions, you downshift, release the accelerator quickly, or accelerate sharply, and the rear of your vehicle begins to skid to the side.

WHAT TO DO

- Ease off the pedal (brake or accelerator).
- Look and steer in the desired direction. (Light progressive acceleration will help return rolling traction to rear wheels, if the vehicle is Traction Control System [TCS] equipped.)

As you straighten from the skid, the rear of your vehicle may begin to slide in the opposite direction (fishtail, lateral force).

- Keep targeting your path of travel.
- Steer quickly and smoothly to direct your vehicle where you are looking.
- When under control, reduce speed.
- Proceed at a slower speed.

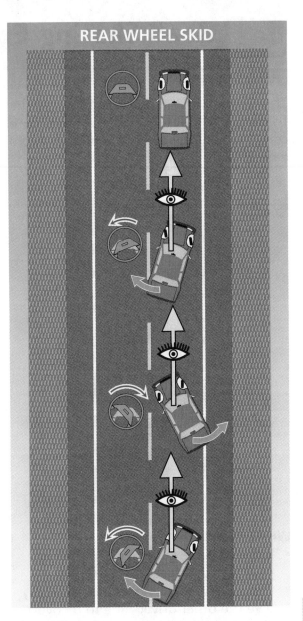

REAR WHEEL SKID

ABORT - RETRY

*As in all driving maneuvers, if at first you don't succeed, **don't give up**. Keep trying to correct the situation, and you will succeed. A course in skid control would be well advised.*

18

Road Sharing Errors

HEAD-ON COLLISION

This is the worst type of collision as the force of impact is the highest (the combined energy of both vehicles). Avoid a head-on collision at all costs.

WHAT TO DO

- Begin an emergency stop (reducing your speed reduces the force of impact, gives you more time, and may give the other driver time to recover).
- Signal with your horn and headlights.
- Select the safest path of travel (the shoulder, off the road completely).
- Ease off the brake pedal.
- Target and steer toward your open path of travel.

If a collision is inevitable, choose objects that will "give" on impact or sideswipe rather than hit directly (Chapter 11).

REAR-END COLLISION

While stopped at an intersection, you notice a vehicle approaching from the rear. It does not seem to be able to stop in time.

WHAT TO DO

- Check traffic and select an **"out"** (turn right, cross the intersection, climb the curb - whichever is safest).

If there is no safe "out"

- Ease up on the brakes to allow a little forward movement on impact.
- Brace your head and body against the head restraint and seat by pushing against the dead pedal.
- On impact, re-apply the brakes fully.

SIDE-IMPACT COLLISION

While crossing an intersection, another vehicle approaches in the transverse lane (on the cross street) at high speed.

WHAT TO DO

- Accelerate quickly to free the intersection.

Side-impact collisions require a rapid decision to brake or accelerate quickly; whichever seems more likely to avoid the collision. If a collision cannot be avoided, try to receive the impact towards the rear of your vehicle thus protecting the passenger compartment.

Emergency Vehicles

Any emergency vehicle (police, fire, ambulance) that has its siren operating and its lights flashing, must be given the right-of-way.

APPROACHED FROM THE REAR

While driving on a two-way roadway or a multilane highway, an emergency vehicle requesting passage approaches from the rear.

WHAT TO DO
- Check traffic, and select a safe path.
- Change lanes to the right side of the road.
- Stop your vehicle safely.
- Wait for the emergency vehicle to pass.
- Safely proceed on your way.
- Follow at least 500 feet behind.

If an emergency vehicle should approach from the rear WITHOUT a siren operating or lights flashing, still move to the right (if possible) and slow down to facilitate its passage in traffic.

MEETING AN ONCOMING VEHICLE

While driving, an emergency vehicle requesting passage approaches in an oncoming direction.

WHAT TO DO
- Check traffic, and select a safe path.
- Change lanes to the right.
- Slow your vehicle.
- Wait for the emergency vehicle to pass.
- Proceed safely.

STOPPED AT AN INTERSECTION

While stopped at an intersection, an emergency vehicle approaches from the rear with its siren and lights operating

WHAT TO DO
- Check the position of the emergency vehicle in your rear-view mirror.
- Remain stationary until it passes.

If the emergency vehicle nears your vehicle in your lane, check traffic and proceed in a safe manner to clear its path.

Unusual Occurrences

ELECTRICAL WIRES CONTACT YOUR VEHICLE

Due to an accident or a storm, live electrical wires are in contact with your vehicle.

WHAT TO DO
- Remain in your vehicle
  (the tires insulate you from danger)
- Activate the hazard lights
- Turn off the ignition
- Advise people not to touch the vehicle
- Request that someone call for help
- Wait for qualified assistance

If you must leave the vehicle (a fire breaks out), be sure to jump out, as far as possible with both feet simultaneously. Make sure you are not in contact with the vehicle and the ground at the same time. Do not touch any of the wires lying on the ground.

IMMERSION IN WATER

If you drive or plunge into water, the vehicle will float for several minutes before sinking. Act quickly.

WHAT TO DO
- Occupants should unfasten seat belts
- Open the window farthest out of water
- Leave the vehicle while it is floating
- Swim away from the vehicle to avoid being pulled down by the wake of the sinking vehicle

If the vehicle sinks, air will be trapped in the highest part of the vehicle. Float in the vehicle, get a couple of deep breaths, open the door nearest the air pocket and leave the vehicle.

WASPS, BEES OR OTHER INSECTS

If a bug threatens to sting you or is buzzing around in your vehicle, remain calm.

WHAT TO DO
- Roll down your window
  (All windows, if power windows)
- Select a safe path and park
  (if the bug does not fly out)
- Shoo the bug out of the vehicle.

Review

TERMS TO REMEMBER - WRITE A SHORT DEFINITION FOR THE FOLLOWING :

- Panic
- Blow out
- Fusible link
- Short circuit
- Hood latch

- Engine stalls
- Breakdown
- Engine overheats
- Power steering failure
- Power brake failure

- ABC fire extinguisher
- Emergency stop
- Skid
- Head-on collision
- Side-impact

SUMMARY

A wide variety of emergency situations could arise while you are driving. The first concept is prevention. Maintain your vehicle properly to prevent most of these occurrences. Should a situation arise despite the best of precautions, do not panic. Study the outlined procedures carefully now and, when the situation occurs, you will be capable of responding quickly and easily. Thus, avoiding the potentially dangerous results.

TEST A - WRITE A "T" FOR TRUE OR AN "F" FOR FALSE IN THE SPACES PROVIDED

_____ **1.** When a blowout occurs, you should immediately pump the brake.

_____ **2.** When the right front wheels of your vehicle drop off the pavement onto the shoulder, you should brake firmly then re-enter the roadway.

_____ **3.** If the hood of your vehicle flies open while driving, swerve towards the shoulder immediately.

_____ **4.** If the brake system fails, fully apply the parking brake immediately.

_____ **5.** If the engine stalls while driving, shift to neutral and try to restart while your vehicle continues to roll forward.

_____ **6.** If your vehicle is equipped with power steering and the engine stalls while driving, the steering will not turn.

_____ **7.** When the engine stalls, the power brakes will function normally for one more application of the brake pedal.

_____ **8.** Approaching a railroad crossing and the engine stalls, coast over the tracks or make an emergency stop before reaching the tracks.

_____ **9.** The rear wheels slide and the rear of the vehicle moves to the left, you should release the accelerator pedal and steer towards the right.

_____ **10.** You notice an approaching vehicle in your lane (head-on); brake sharply to reduce speed, then release the brake and steer onto the shoulder.

Student notes

_____

_____

_____

_____

_____

_____

_____

_____

_____

_____

_____

_____

_____

_____

_____

_____

_____

_____

_____

_____

_____

TODAY'S HANDBOOK PLUS WORKBOOK

Check your comprehension and mastery of the contents of this chapter by completing the corresponding exercise that is found in the complement to the **TODAY'S HANDBOOK PLUS:**

TODAY'S HANDBOOK PLUS WORKBOOK

Complete the exercise on Pages 104 to 110. If necessary, review the chapter when uncertain of an answer and refer to your instructor for further guidance.

The Engine and Power Train

As a vehicle owner, you are responsible for keeping it in proper operating condition and ensuring that it is equipped to handle the different seasons and driving conditions.

An engine that is properly maintained will operate at maximum efficiency. It is less likely to break down and cause inconveniences. In this chapter, we will review the components and support systems of the automobile engine as well as the maintenance that each may require.

Far from intending that you become a mechanic the intention is to remove the mystery that surrounds the automobile. The owner's manual should also be consulted for specific information related to your make and model and its maintenance schedule.

A well maintained vehicle is safer and cheaper to drive as well as producing less pollution!

AFTER COMPLETING THIS CHAPTER, THE STUDENT MUST BE ABLE TO LOCATE THE COMPONENTS, DESCRIBE THE GENERAL FUNCTION OF AND TAKE RESPONSIBILITY FOR:

- the internal combustion engine and proper maintenance thereof.
- the engine support and power train systems.
- basic maintenance procedures as well as owner manual requirements.

Internal Combustion Engine

The engine in your automobile is an internal combustion engine; that means it burns fuel in a combustion chamber inside the engine. The energy produced is converted into mechanical energy. Let's begin by examining the major components.

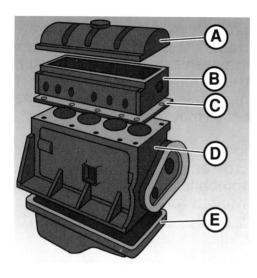

THE MAIN (NON-MOVING) COMPONENTS:

A) **VALVE COVER**: prevents oil leakage and permits adding oil through the filler cap.

B) **HEAD**: forms the combustion chambers, conducts the fuel mixture to and exhaust gases from the engine and supports the valve train.

C) **HEAD GASKET**: seals the head to the block to prevent any leakage.

D) **CYLINDER BLOCK**: contains the four cylinders and the major moving parts.

E) **OIL PAN**: acts as a collector and reservoir for the engine oil.

THE MAIN MOVING ENGINE COMPONENTS:

1) **PISTON**: moves in the cylinder using piston rings to seal against the cylinder wall.

2) **CONNECTING ROD**: converts the reciprocal piston motion to crankshaft rotary motion.

3) **CRANKSHAFT**: transmits the power to the support systems and power train.

4) **CAMSHAFT**: opens the valves at the correct time. An overhead camshaft (OHC) is mounted on the head above the valves.

5) **VALVES**: open and close to control the flow of gases into and out of the engine.

6) **FLYWHEEL**: balances engine operation; engaged by starter to crank engine and transmits power to the transmission.

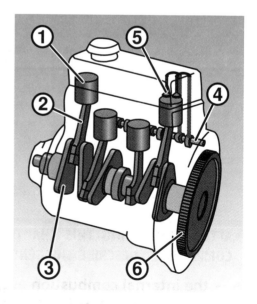

THE FOUR STROKE CYCLE

Most motorized vehicles are equipped with engines that operate on a four stroke cycle. Some motorcycles and a few diesel engines are the exception; they use a two stroke cycle.

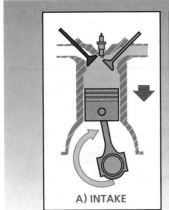 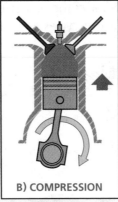 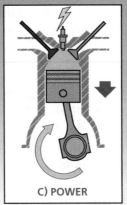 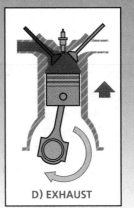

| A) INTAKE | B) COMPRESSION | C) POWER | D) EXHAUST |

A) INTAKE STROKE: The intake valve opens. The piston is descending in the cylinder and the air fuel mixture enters the cylinder.

B) COMPRESSION STROKE: Both valves are closed and the piston ascends in the cylinder. The fuel-air mixture is forced into the space at the top of the cylinder and compressed (combustion chamber).

C) POWER STROKE: A spark from the spark plug ignites the highly explosive air-fuel mixture initiating combustion, thereby pushing the piston down in the cylinder.

D) EXHAUST STROKE: The exhaust valve opens and the fumes begin to escape. The piston rises forcing the burned air-fuel mixture out of the cylinder.

This sequence repeats thousands of times per minute in each cylinder. Each cylinder operates on a different stroke of the cycle in order to smooth out the engine operation. The more cylinders an engine has; the more power it produces (it also uses more fuel). Engines may have 2, 3, 4, 5, 6, 7, 8, 10, 12, or 16 cylinders.

MAINTENANCE TIPS

Keep the exterior of the engine clean in order to spot any leaks as soon as they appear on the clean engine.

Check your owner's manual for service intervals for the engine components - valves, tune ups, timing chain, etc.

Whenever engine performance or noise are abnormal, have your vehicle verified. This will prevent costly breakdowns and higher repair costs.

19

The Cooling System

The cooling system brings the engine to its most efficient operating temperature as quickly as possible and maintains that temperature in all operating conditions. Some of the heat absorbed is used to provide heat for the passenger compartment in inclement weather. The majority of vehicles use a liquid cooling system. Motorcycles are usually air-cooled.

THE BASIC COMPONENTS

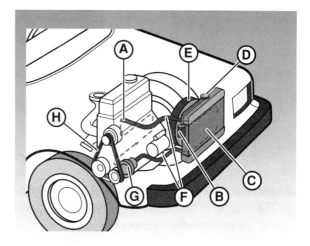

A) **THERMOSTAT**: a temperature-sensitive valve regulates coolant flow.

B) **EXPANSION TANK**: connected to the radiator neck, helps maintain coolant level. Marks to verify coolant level.

C) **RADIATOR**: reservoir, transfers heat to the air passing through the core. The coolant returns to the engine when needed to absorb heat.

D) **RADIATOR CAP**: seals the radiator, pressurizing the cooling system, to increase the coolant boiling point and thereby improve the ability of the system to perform efficiently. **Remove only when the engine temperature is cold!**

E) **COOLING FAN**: provides a draft of air through the radiator fins. It may be driven by a belt (rear wheel drive) or an electric motor with a control switch (front wheel drive).

F) **RADIATOR HOSES**: reinforced rubber hoses that conduct the coolant to the radiator and, after cooling, back to the engine. Two smaller hoses for the heater radiator.

G) **WATER PUMP**: circulates the coolant (a mixture of water and anti-freeze) through the engine, and radiator (when the thermostat opens).

H) **DRIVE BELT**: drives the water pump and the fan (rear wheel drive).

GAUGE / INDICATOR LIGHT: mounted in the instrument panel (not shown), informs the driver of the operating temperature of the engine.

ENVIRONMENTAL TIPS
Anti-freeze is a poisonous liquid , children and pets are attracted by the sweet taste. Though biodegradable, it can contaminate water and soil temporarily. Take care in storage and disposal.

MAINTENANCE TIPS

Check coolant level regularly, add to the expansion tank if necessary. Should this occur frequently, check system for leaks.

Check the condition and tension of the drive belt at the same time. The operation of the entire system relies heavily on the proper action of the belt.

Check the hoses as well. Softness and swelling or brittleness and cracking are all signs that replacement is required.

When washing your vehicle, take the time to wash the radiator by spraying water from the fan side towards the exterior. This will clean the radiator core removing dust, insects, etc.

Test the anti-freeze every year prior to winter. Every third season, have the system flushed (cleaned) and new anti-freeze installed. The anti-corrosive additives lose effectiveness with time.

The Lubrication System

The engine lubrication system circulates oil, a liquid lubricant, under pressure to all the moving engine components. The oil must: reduce friction, cool and clean moving parts, cushion shocks, seal the rings against the cylinder walls and prevent rust.

THE BASIC COMPONENTS

A) GAUGE/INDICATOR LIGHT: (not shown), informs the driver of the pressure of oil in the lubrication system.

B) OIL FILLER CAP: (removable) on the valve cover permitting access to the crankcase to add engine oil.

C) DIPSTICK: an oil level indicator to check the level in the oil pan.

D) OIL PAN: reservoir, encloses the bottom of engine block to collect oil dripping from the components.

E) OIL PUMP: draws oil from the pan and circulates the oil (under pressure) to the filter, then to all moving components through the galleries (lines or passageways in the parts).

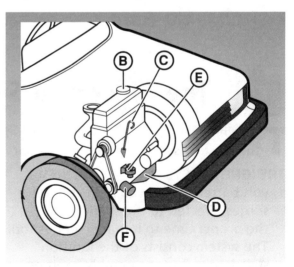

F) OIL FILTER: removes impurities from the oil before it circulates to all the moving components.

ENVIRONMENTAL TIPS
Engine oil contaminates soil and water, affects water in the water table and may affect water treatment facilities. Used oil may also contain particles of metal. Recycle used oil at hazardous waste collection sites.

MAINTENANCE TIPS

Check the oil level each time you gas up. The engine should be off for a few minutes and the vehicle should be on level ground to get an accurate reading.

Pull out the dipstick, wipe it, reinsert it fully, then pull it out again and check the level of the oil slick on the gauge at the lower end of the dipstick. Reinsert the dipstick. Add oil only if the gauge indicates the need for one liter.

As all oil refiners meet the American Petroleum Institute standards, you may use any brand of oil. Check your owner's manual for the grade and viscosity ratings. Verify the recommended service intervals (max. 3,00 miles [5,000 kilometers]).

The Electrical System

The electrical system of a vehicle includes the ignition system, the charging system, the starting system, and the accessory circuits and equipment.

THE IGNITION SYSTEM converts the 12 volt battery current to high voltage surges directed to the spark plug at the proper time to initiate combustion. The system consists of the ignition switch, distributor assembly, ignition coil, spark plugs, wiring and the battery. The Electronic Control Module (ECM) controls timing of the spark.

THE CHARGING SYSTEM produces electrical power while the engine is running to operate all the electrical components and recharge the battery. The system consists of a drive belt, the alternator, the voltage regulator, wiring and the battery.

19

THE STARTING SYSTEM permits the driver to turn the ignition switch to activate an electric motor to crank and usually start the engine.

The system consists of the ignition switch, the starter motor, a solenoid switch, wiring and the battery.

THE ACCESSORY CIRCUITS power the lights, safety systems, and accessories. This system includes the fuse box, wires and electrically-powered components.

BASIC COMPONENTS

1) **THE FUSE BOX**: protects the electrical equipment. Spare fuses should be stored in your vehicle.
2) **THE IGNITION COIL**: transforms the 12 volt current to a surge of current of many thousands of volts.
3) **THE SPARK PLUGS**: produce a spark to ignite the air-fuel mixture.
4) **THE BATTERY**: stores energy in chemical form so that it can supply the electricity to start the engine.
5) **THE DISTRIBUTOR**: controls the production and distribution of the surges to the spark plugs.
6) **THE STARTER**: an electric motor that cranks the engine (turns the flywheel) during starting.
7) **THE ALTERNATOR**: driven by the belt, charges the battery and provides the elctricity to operate the electrical components.

ECM/ECU (Electronic Control Module or Unit) (not shown) uses programs

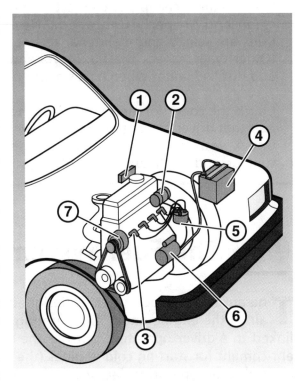

stored in memory as well as data supplied by a variety of electronic sensors to control the production and timing of the spark plugs.

ENVIRONMENTAL TIPS
Most vehicle components can be recycled. Check for a recycling center with a local environmental group. Many components can be re-manufactured - starters, alternators, etc. Batteries are especially dangerous due to the sulphuric acid in the cells. Do not dispose of in normal garbage.

19

MAINTENANCE TIPS

Spare fuses should be stored in your vehicle. If a fuse needs replacement more than once, consult a mechanic.

Check the battery regularly. Make sure the terminals, clamps, or connectors are clean and properly tightened. New units are sealed and maintenance free. (Older types - check the fluid level and add distilled water when necessary.)

Check the condition and tension of the belt that drives the alternator.
Check your owner's manual for the tune up and electrical service intervals.

Diesel engines do not have an ignition system as fuel is ignited by the heat of the compressed air. They are, however, equipped with components called GLOW plugs. These are intended to heat the combustion chamber or the air entering the combustion chamber for cold starting.

When the ignition switch is turned to the "ON" position, a light is illuminated on the dash to signify that the GLOW plugs are warming up the combustion chamber. When the light is out, you may start the engine.

The Fuel System

The automotive fuel system is designed to provide the correct amount of fuel and air to the engine under all operating conditions and power demands. It must be linked to a driver operated control - the accelerator pedal. It must also provide fuel enrichment for starting cold engines (the choke) and compensate for hot engine and high altitude operating factors. All of this must be achieved without diminishing performance in both power and economy while complying with exhaust emission standards. Many vehicles use a fuel injection system (replacing the carburetor) to deliver the fuel under pressure into the combustion chambers or into the airflow just as it enters each individual cylinder. This maximizes power and economy.

ENVIRONMENTAL TIPS
Gasoline contaminates soil and ground water and poses a risk of explosion and/or fire. Care in storage (never for an extended period of time) and try to use it up entirely. If not, bring to a hazardous waste disposal.
Conservation of fuel - a non-renewable resource - by proper driving habits and eliminating unnecessary trips (ride sharing) as well as maintenance of your vehicle will all reduce fuel consumption and pollution.

THE BASIC COMPONENTS

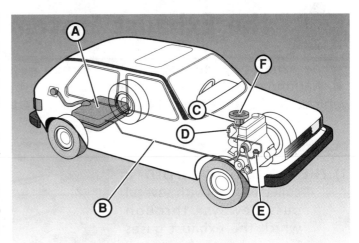

A) **FUEL TANK**: a reservoir for fuel (with an exterior pipe). A tank device controls the fuel gauge to inform the driver of the fuel available.

B) **FUEL LINE**: tubes connect the tank to the carburetor or injection system.

C) **CARBURETOR**: mixes the fuel and air and supplies it to the cylinders. Gas pedal controls the carburetor.

   or FUEL INJECTION: (most modern cars) supplies fuel to engine. Gas pedal controls air/fuel flow to the engine.

D) **FUEL FILTER**: removes dirt and other contaminants from the fuel. May also be located along fuel line between tank and engine.

E) **FUEL PUMP**: electrical or mechanical device that forces fuel from the tank to the carburetor.

F) **AIR FILTER**: removes dirt and dust particles from air entering engine.

ECM/ECU: (not shown) Electronic Control Module or Unit serves as decision-maker/controller using a micro-processor, a memory (with pre-set programs), and data from a wide variety of sensors to control the engine and fuel flow.

TURBO: (not shown) turbine to increase the air entering the cylinders.

MAINTENANCE TIPS

Check the fuel gauge every time you start your vehicle. Keep the fuel level above the one-quarter mark to avoid: • Condensation in cold weather • Fouling or clogging the system with contaminants • Running out of gas

IN WINTER, keep the fuel level above the one-half mark. Never fill-up just prior to parking your vehicle (this can lead to a frozen gas line). IN SUMMER, avoid filling the tank completely in order to leave space for gasoline expansion.

When you refuel (fill-up with gas): • Turn off the engine. • Make sure no one smokes near the vehicle. • Do not overfill as drips can damage the paint.

Check your owner's manual for recommended service intervals.

19

The Exhaust System

The exhaust system collects the burned gases from each cylinder, directs the harmful gases and heat through the exhaust pipes and releases them behind the vehicle. At the same time, the exhaust system reduces noise and exhaust pollution.

THE BASIC COMPONENTS

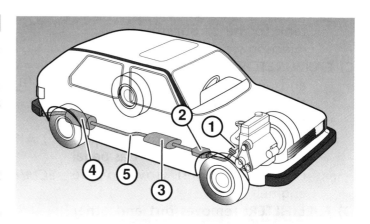

1) **THE EXHAUST MANIFOLD**: a collector pipe with several passageways through which the exhaust gases leave the engine and enter the exhaust system.

2) **THE CATALYTIC CONVERTER**: converts harmful exhaust gases by promoting a chemical reaction thus catalyzing the pollutants.

3) **THE MUFFLER**: reduces noise and produces an engine back pressure.

4) **THE RESONATOR**: auxiliary muffler on many vehicles to reduce the noise.

5) **EXHAUST PIPES**: are tubes that interconnect all of the exhaust system components and extends past the rear of the vehicle.

ENVIRONMENTAL TIPS
The exhaust system helps minimize air pollution when it meets manufacturer's specifications. Government requirements are becoming more and more demanding in this area. Do not modify the system.

MAINTENANCE TIPS

Check the exhaust system periodically to make sure that it is intact and leak-free all the way to the tailpipe. Should exhaust noise start to become louder, have the system verified. Carbon monoxide gas, one of the by-products of combustion, may seep into the passenger compartment if there are any leaks in the exhaust system.

Do not alter the exhaust system of your vehicle in any way. State laws prohibit the operation of a vehicle that does not conform to specified standards.

Power Train

19-G

The power train carries the engine power (mechanical energy) to the vehicle drive wheels. Vehicles may be rear, front or four wheel drive. Each of these types of power trains may be equipped with an automatic or a standard transmission.

BASIC COMPONENTS

A) **POWER COUPLING**: connects engine to transmission. Automatic uses a fluid coupling (torque converter). Standard uses a clutch.

B) **TRANSMISSION**: an assembly of gears that permit different ratios as well as neutral and reverse. An automatic selects the appropriate forward gear. Standard must be shifted manually.

C) **DRIVE SHAFT**: transmits rotation to the differential and permits a change in angle and length when the rear wheels move up and down.

D) **UNIVERSAL JOINTS**: change drive shaft angle while transmitting power.

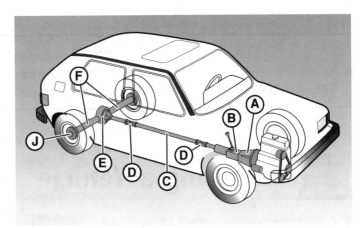

E) **DIFFERENTIAL**: permits each drive wheel to turn at different speeds.

F) **AXLE SHAFTS**: connect the differential to the wheels within a housing (rear wheel drive).

G) **TRANS AXLE**: the combination of the transmission and the differential on front drive vehicles.

H) **AXLE SHAFTS**: connect the trans-axle externally to the front wheels.

I) **C.V. JOINTS**: connect to the front wheels while sharply changing in angle so the front wheels can steer and move up and down.

J) **DRIVE WHEELS**: receive the power to push (rear wheel drive) or pull (front wheel drive) the vehicle.

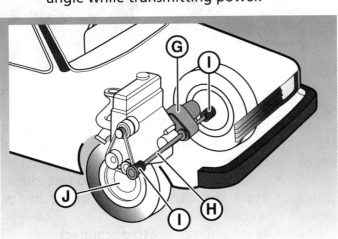

MAINTENANCE TIPS

The transmission fluid level should be checked regularly.

AUTOMATIC TRANSMISSION: The selector lever in park, parking brake engaged and the engine idling. Use the transmission dipstick (as for the engine oil). If necessary, add the appropriate oil.

STANDARD TRANSMISSION: At each oil change, ask the mechanic to verify the level and condition of the oil. (At the same time, have the clutch checked)

The differential fluid level should also be checked at every oil change.

At the first signs of slippage, clunking, abnormal noises or uneven shifting have a service technician check the power train completely.

Boosting a Vehicle

In extremely cold weather, it is not uncommon for a battery to go "dead". In order to start the vehicle, you will have to "JUMP START" or boost it using another vehicle. Make sure:

- the two vehicles are not touching
- the batteries have the same voltage
- the dead battery is not frozen
- the fluid level is not low

WHAT TO DO:

- Turn off accessories, engine and apply parking brakes
- Remove battery caps, if so equipped (Cover with a heavy cloth)
- Connect both ends of the red cable to the positive terminals (+ or marked P) of both batteries
- Connect the black cable to the negative terminal (– or marked N) of the battery being used to boost

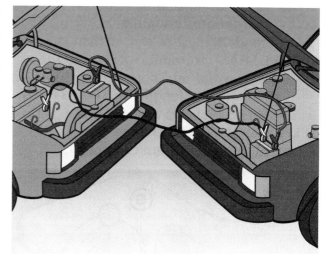

- Attach the other end to the engine block or frame of the vehicle with the "dead" battery (avoid moving parts)
- Start the booster vehicle and fast idle
- Start the other vehicle and run for several minutes
- Reverse the order to disconnect.

Review

TERMS TO REMEMBER - WRITE A SHORT DEFINITION FOR EACH OF THE FOLLOWING :

- Internal combustion
- Cylinder block
- Piston
- Flywheel
- Intake stroke

- Compression stroke
- Power stroke
- Exhaust stroke
- Radiator cap
- Starter

- Choke
- Catalytic converter
- Oil pump
- Dipstick
- Differential

SUMMARY

The operation and components of the engine and power train should be understood in at least a very basic manner to encourage the correct use and maintenance of your vehicle.

You will save money, in the long run, by maintaining and servicing your vehicle properly. A well maintained vehicle is also safer to operate.

TEST A - WRITE "T" BESIDE STATEMENTS THAT ARE TRUE AND "F" BESIDE THOSE THAT ARE FALSE.

_____ 1. Your engine may overheat if you do not check and adjust the fan belt.

_____ 2. The radiator cap should be removed only when the engine is cold.

_____ 3. The coolant, water and antifreeze, should be replaced every year.

_____ 4. Check the oil level using the dipstick while the engine is operating.

_____ 5. The oil filter should be changed as well as the oil every 3,000 to 5,000 miles.

_____ 6. If the oil light comes on and stays on while driving, you should stop and turn off the engine.

_____ 7. When filling the fuel tank the engine should be turned off.

_____ 8. The fuel system does not require service as long as it operates properly.

_____ 9. The exhaust system should be checked only if it becomes noisier than usual.

_____ 10. The differential permits the drive wheels to turn at different speeds.

Student notes

_____

_____

_____

_____

_____

_____

_____

_____

_____

_____

_____

_____

_____

_____

_____

_____

_____

_____

_____

_____

TODAY'S HANDBOOK PLUS WORKBOOK

Check your comprehension and mastery of the contents of this chapter by completing the corresponding exercise that is found in the complement to the **TODAY'S HANDBOOK PLUS:**

TODAY'S HANDBOOK PLUS WORKBOOK

Complete the exercise on Pages 111 and 112. If necessary, review the chapter when uncertain of an answer and refer to your instructor for further guidance.

The Chassis

When you own a vehicle, you are responsible for keeping it in proper operating condition.

In this chapter, we will examine the different units that are part of the chassis: the tires, the suspension system, the steering system, the brake system, and the body.

These systems are essential to the operation of your vehicle. The stability and road-worthiness of a vehicle depend on basic maintenance performed at regular intervals. Once again, if these systems are properly maintained, the cost of operation will be reduced. Check your owner's manual for specific requirements.

You also have a social responsibility to be a "GREEN" driver; one who avoids polluting the environment as much as possible. Proper maintenance procedures will reduce pollution.

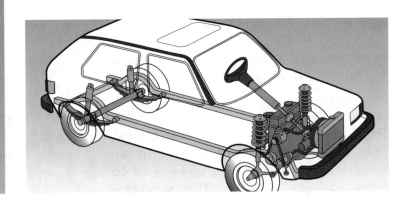

AFTER COMPLETING THIS CHAPTER, THE STUDENT MUST BE ABLE TO LOCATE THE COMPONENTS, DESCRIBE THE GENERAL FUNCTION OF AND TAKE RESPONSIBILITY FOR:

- the tires and suspension systems.
- the steering and brake systems.
- basic maintenance procedures and owner manual requirements.

Tires

Improved tire design has reduced the incidence of tire troubles on modern vehicles; yet, the tires are still one of the most neglected parts of the vehicle.

Tires have two functions. First, they are air-filled cushions that absorb most of the shocks caused by road hazards. The tires flex, or give, as they meet these irregularities. Thus they reduce the effect of the shocks on the vehicle and the passengers. Second, the tires grip the road to provide traction. This enables the driver to accelerate, brake, and steer the vehicle.

TIRE CONSTRUCTION

The tire casing is composed of plies (layers of cord impregnated with rubber) shaped on a form. The rubber treads and sidewalls are then applied to give the desired form, wear characteristics and flexibility.

There are two basic tire types: the bias ply (also belted bias ply) and the radial ply design.

THE BIAS PLY has the plies criss-crossed. This makes the casing strong in all directions; however, the plies tend to move against each other. This generates heat and tire "squirm". The tires wear more rapidly and provide less traction.

THE RADIAL PLY has the plies parallel and perpendicular to the tread. Belts (usually steel) are then attached in the same position as the tread which is then applied with the sidewall. This results in more flexibility. The tread stays in contact with the road producing greater traction. Radial tires also wear more slowly.

NEVER MIX BIAS AND RADIAL TIRES ON YOUR VEHICLE. EVEN MIXING RADIAL TIRES OF DIFFERENT MAKES AND TREAD DESIGNS IS NOT RECOMMENDED.

TIRE SPECIFICATIONS

By law, details about each tire must be molded into both sidewalls - tire size, maximum inflation pressure, load rating, construction, number of plies and manufacturer. The two most common formats are the metric and alphanumeric types (see illustrations).

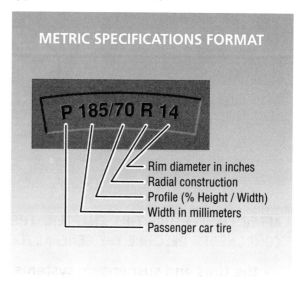

METRIC SPECIFICATIONS FORMAT

P 185/70 R 14

- Rim diameter in inches
- Radial construction
- Profile (% Height / Width)
- Width in millimeters
- Passenger car tire

ALPHANUMERIC FORMAT

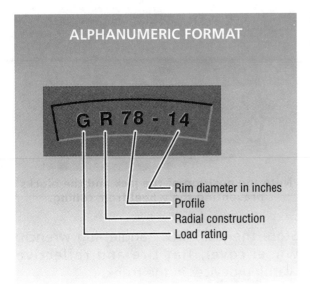

G R 78 - 14

— Rim diameter in inches
— Profile
— Radial construction
— Load rating

Most tires have wear bars or tread wear indicators, which are filled-in sections of the tread grooves. When the tread has worn down enough to reveal the wear bars as a line of rubber across the tread, the tire should be replaced.

TIRE ROTATION

The amount of wear a tire gets depends on its location on the vehicle and the type of vehicle. Turning, accelerating, braking, the slant of the road surface, etc. cause each tire to wear differently. One tire can wear out as much as twice as fast as another. To equalize wear and extend the usage of all the tires, the tires should be rotated every 12,000 miles. Check your owner's manual for the recommended interval for your vehicle.

Passenger vehicle tires can be rotated using different methods. Two patterns (no full size spare) are shown below (check your owners manual); also, check the tire inflation when rotating as the front and rear may require different tire pressures.

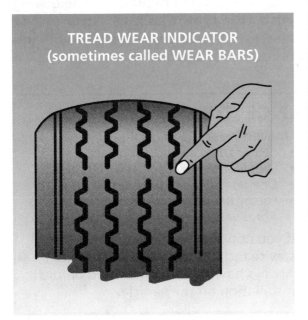

TREAD WEAR INDICATOR
(sometimes called WEAR BARS)

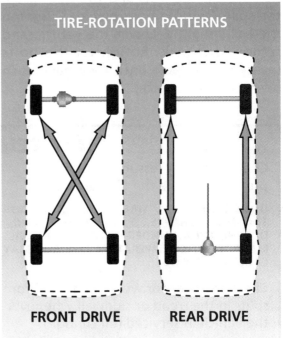

TIRE-ROTATION PATTERNS

FRONT DRIVE   REAR DRIVE

20

CHANGING A TIRE:

Too many injuries and deaths occur while changing tires every year. To proceed safely, activate the hazard lights, position the vehicle on a hard flat surface as far off the roadway as possible.and apply the parking brake. Set out reflective warning devices 100 feet in both directions.

Take the jack, jack handle, lug wrench and spare out of the trunk. Block both the front and the rear of the wheel diagonally opposite the flat using stones or blocks. Position the jack (trunk lid diagram or owner's manual) and jack up the vehicle slightly. Remove the wheel cover, use the lug wrench to loosen the bolts a couple of turns, then raise the vehicle until the flat clears the ground.

Remove the lug nuts and the flat. Install the spare and the bolts by hand. Tighten the bolts slightly. Lower the vehicle and remove the jack. Retighten the bolts (every second bolt until they have each been tightened twice).

Note the position of the jack and the blocks preventing the wheel from rolling.

Store the jack, jack handle, lug wrench, wheel cover, flat tire and reflective warning devices in the trunk.

DRIVING WITH A COMPACT SPARE:

To save space, most vehicles have an under-sized, limited mileage spare. Do not exceed 50 mph, avoid sudden change in speed or direction, and be aware of the lower ground clearance while driving with this type of spare. Stop at the nearest service station to repair and reinstall the regular tire.

MAINTENANCE TIPS

Check the tire pressure regularly preferably while the tires are cold.

UNDER-INFLATED TIRES PROVIDE POOR TRACTION. (CHAPTER 9 - LAWS OF PHYSICS) DRIVING ON AN UNDER-INFLATED TIRE WILL MAKE THE TIRE TEMPERATURE RISE AND MAY CAUSE A BLOW-OUT!

Check the tires for wear, bulges and/or splits in the tread or sidewall whenever the vehicle is serviced (oil change).

Uneven wear may signal problems:
- Center tread wear- over-inflation
- Shoulder tread wear- under-inflation
- One side wear- alignment problems
- Patchy uneven wear- shocks, brakes, etc.
- Abrasive wear- high speed cornering

If you notice abnormal wear, have a service technician correct the problem. Always have the tires balanced before installation on the vehicle.

20

20-B

The Suspension System

The suspension system supports the weight of the vehicle, holds the wheels in alignment, absorbs the shocks caused by road irregularities, and provides flexibility while ensuring vehicle stability and driveability by maintaining traction.

BASIC COMPONENTS

A) **SPRINGS**: whether leaf, coil, air (air bags), or torsion bar, support the weight of the vehicle and flex to absorb road shocks.

B) **SHOCK ABSORBERS**: one at each wheel to control the oscillating action of the springs to minimize movement and stabilize tire contact with the road.

C) **STABILIZER BARS**: (sway bar) added to the front and rear suspension to minimize body roll (lean or sway) on turns and bumps.

D) **MACPHERSON STRUT**: a suspension unit that combines the shock and the spring into one component (front and rear on small vehicles).

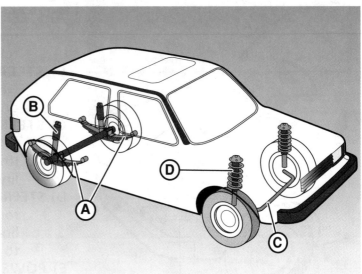

HYDRAULIC ACTUATORS: (not shown) replace shocks and can be computer or manually controlled to adjust ride and height of vehicle. They keep the tires force against the pavement constant, thereby improving traction.

MAINTENANCE TIPS

Have the shocks checked for leakage whenever your vehicle is in for service.

If your vehicle tends to bounce while driving, check your shocks by pushing down on the corners of your vehicle. The vehicle should stabilize after rebounding once. If it continues to oscillate, change the shocks.

Whenever your vehicle does not appear to be level (unloaded), have the springs checked for sag, wear and/or breakage.

20

The Steering System

The steering system controls the position of the front wheels in order to permit the driver to change the direction of the vehicle.

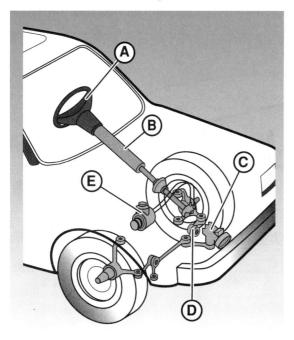

BASIC COMPONENTS

A) **STEERING WHEEL**: driver control that may be adjustable. (tilt and/or telescoping steering)

B) **STEERING COLUMN**: connects the wheel to the gearbox. Collapsible on impact to protect the driver.

C) **STEERING GEARBOX**: converts the rotary motion of the wheel into linear motion of the steering linkage: various types.

D) **STEERING LINKAGE**: a series of arms, rods and tie-rods that transmit the linear motion to the front wheels to change their position.

E) **POWER STEERING**: hydraulic pump impelled by a belt connected to the engine that facilitates steering.

ENVIRONMENTAL TIPS

Power steering fluid is toxic, contaminates soil and water, can cause eye and skin irritation and combustion produces carbon monoxide. Unused fluid can be shared with others or brought to a hazardous waste site.

MAINTENANCE TIPS

Check the power steering fluid level and the condition and adjustment of the belt regularly.

Avoid turning the steering if the vehicle is not in motion (dry steering); premature wear of steering components and tires will result.

Never force the steering at the limit of travel; back off slightly and the wheels will still be fully turned. Forcing causes early failure of power steering / steering components.

Avoid deep potholes, curbs and any other sudden or hard impacts that may damage the steering components.

Have the steering aligned at least once a year and after any serious impacts.

The Brake System

The brake system permits the driver to slow or stop the rotation of the tires. The friction of the tires against the road surface will then slow and/or stop the vehicle. Modern vehicles are equipped with two braking systems: a dual hydraulic brake system (service brakes) and a mechanical brake system (parking or emergency brake).

BASIC COMPONENTS

A) **DISC BRAKES**: superior (cool faster) brakes that utilize a pinching action on a metal disc to slow or stop rotation of the tire. Usually on the front wheels (The front does 70% of braking) but is available as an option at all four wheels.

B) **DRUM BRAKES**: brake shoes (hemispherical type) push outward on a rotating drum. (Because they are enclosed, they retain heat)

C) **DUAL MASTER CYLINDER**: brake pedal applies pressure on two pistons that pressurize the brake fluid. The fluid transmits this pressure to each wheel where it activates the disc or drum brake mechanisms. Two reservoirs supply extra fluid when needed. The dual systems each operate independently in case one should fail.

D) **BRAKE LINES**: stainless steel tubes full of brake fluid that conduct the hydraulic pressure.

E) **POWER BRAKE**: an engine-activated booster unit that reduces the effort required to apply the hydraulic brakes. Will operate one more time if the engine should stop operating.

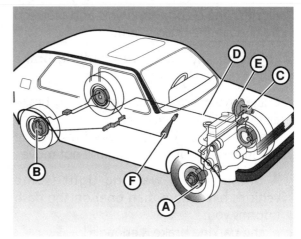

F) **PARKING BRAKE**: a lever or foot pedal that mechanically (cables and levers) activates the rear brakes only (most vehicles). Can be used for parking and if the hydraulic brakes fail.

INDICATOR LIGHT: (not shown) comes on if one of the dual hydraulic brake systems should fail or in some vehicles, if the brake fluid is low.

ABS: (Anti-Lock Braking System) (not shown) prevents wheel lockup under hard braking. A hydraulic actuator, controlled by the ABS control module which receives data from the wheel sensors, modulates pressure to each wheel. Actions combined with Traction Control by the ECM.

20

ENVIRONMENTAL TIPS

Brake fluid is toxic, (children and pets are attracted by the sweet taste), can contaminate soil and water and can contain heavy metals. Store in a safe place and recycle or dispose of at hazardous waste sites or service stations.

MAINTENANCE TIPS

Check the brake fluid level at least once a month. The second time you add (correct) fluid, have the brakes verified.

Lubricate and adjust the parking brake cables every oil change.

Check the operation of the parking brake every time you park by applying them and then EASING UP on the service brake while still in drive. Your vehicle should not move.

A brake system warning light (some vehicles have more than one) on the dash informs you:
• the parking brake is engaged
• there is a brake system malfunction
• the brake fluid level is low

Most drum brakes are self-adjusting - while reversing and braking or, in some recent models, as the parking brake is applied.

If the brake pedal feels low or "spongy" (is soft but firms up when pumped), the vehicle pulls to one side during braking, or makes any unusual noises (grinding or squealing) have the brake system checked by a service technician.

Have the brake system cleaned, verified and adjusted every spring even if it does not demonstrate any unusual symptoms.

With ABS brakes, check the owner's manual for service (brake fluid must be replaced at specified intervals).

The Body

The exterior body components, windows and interior of your vehicle also require service and maintenance on a regular basis.

• Wash your vehicle once a week. Check your owner's manual for soaps and recommended solvents.
• Wax the exterior of your vehicle once a year to protect the paint finish.
• Lubricate all hinges, locks, etc. to ensure smooth operation.
• Enquire about special rust-proofing to

protect the vehicle against rust.
• Purchase touch-up paint to repair small chips and nicks before rust has a chance to start.
• Proper maintenance will maintain the value of your vehicle as well as improving its looks while you are driving it around town.

20

Review

TERMS TO REMEMBER - WRITE A SHORT DEFINITION FOR EACH OF THE FOLLOWING :

- Tire tread
- Radial ply
- Tire specifications
- Tread wear indicator

- Tire rotation
- Springs
- Shock absorber
- Stabilizer bar

- Power steering
- Disc brakes
- Master cylinder
- Parking brake

SUMMARY

The operation and components of the chassis should be understood in a very basic manner to encourage the proper use and maintenance of your vehicle.

You will save money, in the long run, by maintaining and servicing your vehicle properly. A well maintained vehicle is also safer to operate.

TEST A - WRITE "T" BESIDE STATEMENTS THAT ARE TRUE AND "F" BESIDE THOSE THAT ARE FALSE.

_____ 1. Tires should be rotated to extend the life span of the tires.

_____ 2. When the tread wear indicator appears in the tread, you should have the tires replaced by new ones.

_____ 3. It does not matter what kind of tires you install on your vehicle as long as the tread is in good condition.

_____ 4. When the shock absorbers show signs of leakage, they must be replaced.

_____ 5. If you must add brake fluid to the master cylinder, this indicates there is a problem.

_____ 6. The parking brake applies on the front wheels only.

_____ 7. A "spongy" brake pedal is an indication of air in the brake lines.

_____ 8. The brake indicator light is illuminated when the parking brake is in the applied position.

_____ 9. It is normal for the suspension system of an older vehicle to bounce and rebound many times after passing over a bump.

_____ 10. You should align the steering system of your vehicle at least once a year.

Student notes

_____
_____
_____
_____
_____
_____
_____
_____
_____
_____
_____
_____
_____
_____
_____
_____
_____
_____
_____
_____
_____

TODAY'S HANDBOOK PLUS WORKBOOK

Check your comprehension and mastery of the contents of this chapter by completing the corresponding exercise that is found in the complement to the **TODAY'S HANDBOOK PLUS:**

TODAY'S HANDBOOK PLUS WORKBOOK

Complete the exercise on Pages 113 and 114. If necessary, review the chapter when uncertain of an answer and refer to your instructor for further guidance.

Vehicle Ownership

Driving a vehicle is a great responsibility. As you have already seen, you are accountable for your own safety, the safety of your passengers, as well as the safety of the other road users who share the HTS. Becoming the owner of a vehicle means even greater responsibilities.

Today, the purchase of a vehicle, whether new or used, is a major spending decision. It consumes a major portion of the household budget. And, for many people, the transaction is paid for with borrowed money- loan, lease, or financing.

On top of the purchase price, you must be financially capable of paying the sales taxes, the registration fees, and the insurance coverage required in most states. This coverage should be considered when deciding to purchase as it varies considerably with the type of vehicle. In addition, everyday operating expenses include the cost of fuel, tolls, parking, and maintenance.

AFTER COMPLETING THIS CHAPTER, THE STUDENT MUST UNDERSTAND ALL THE FACTORS INVOLVED IN AND BE ABLE TO ACCEPT PERSONAL RESPONSIBILITY FOR:

- deciding to buy and choosing a vehicle.
- arranging financing for the purchase.
- vehicle insurance (types and purposes for).

Deciding to Buy

When you're young, "wheels" represent liberty. The freedom to go where you want, when you want. Later on, vehicles may become status symbols or extensions of your personality with glitter and gadgets added to the basic product to create your personal "dream machine". For the more practical minded, vehicles represent transportation, nothing more. The first step is to determine whether or not you are able to afford a vehicle.

Evaluate honestly how much of your budget is available to spend on the purchase, insurance and upkeep of a vehicle. Will you have to work extra hours to pay for it? If you are a student and you intend to pay for the vehicle yourself, these extra hours will be lost from your studies and other activities. Can you afford the time?

TRANSPORTATION NEEDS

Do you need transportation for work, school, weekday and weekend activities? Is public transportation readily available at a reasonable cost? If you live in a city core, you may find a vehicle to be more of a bother than a convenience since parking can be hard to find and expensive. Public transit, taxis or biking may provide adequate "green" alternatives. The occasional rental of a vehicle can cover special requirements.

Will you transport other people and equipment regularly? A good way to establish your needs is to keep track of your transportation usage over a three to four week period. Keep a record. Is a family vehicle at your disposal? Include these trips on your list. Will the time saved balance the cost of owning your own vehicle? Remember, a personal vehicle that is not in use, still costs you money in terms of depreciation and insurance.

A mature evaluation of these needs will determine if purchasing a vehicle is really necessary and economically feasible.

Choosing a Vehicle

People are increasingly conscious of the need for quality in the vehicles they choose to drive. Quality of construction, corrosion protection, warranty protection, emission standards, and good gas mileage (carbon footprint) are important items to consider. You must also take into account the maintenance schedule, repairs, and the availability and cost of replacement parts. At today's prices, there is good reason for hoping you can keep your vehicle a long time.

21

From your transportation study, you can determine what kind of vehicle you will need to purchase. How many passengers did you usually have? What were their ages? How much baggage and equipment did you transport regularly? Will you need a two-door or a four-door vehicle?

TYPES OF VEHICLES

There are several categories of vehicles to choose from:

SUBCOMPACTS - small, easy to maneuver, economical to operate. Seating for two adults and limited trunk area. Good for short distances and light loads.

COMPACTS - good mileage, easy to handle. Seating for four adults for short periods of time. Limited trunk space.

INTERMEDIATES - more expensive to operate with seating for five or six adults comfortably. Perform well in city and highway environments. Larger trunk space.

FULL-SIZED - the largest models. Power and comfort for trips, loads and large families. More compact and fuel efficient than in previous years.

SPORTY MODELS - personality vehicles with performance and luxury features. Most expensive to purchase, operate, maintain and insure. Generally, seating for two adults.

SUVs, TRUCKS, VANS, JEEPS, RV VEHICLES - Specialty vehicles that are expensive to operate, maintain, insure, and repair.

VEHICLE PERFORMANCE RECORD

You should consult consumer information magazines or services in your area before making your choice. The "track record" for repairs, service, costs of operation, fuel mileage and safety as well as the suggested retail price can all be verified from these sources.

SAFETY EQUIPMENT

Safety is a prime consideration in deciding what to buy. Larger vehicles are safer though more expensive to operate. Is the vehicle equipped with side air bags? How did this vehicle perform in crash test and collision studies? Does the vehicle have an ABS brake system? What is the advertised braking distance?

SAFETY FEATURES
Seat belts, air bags and side air bags

You may spend a lot of time in your vehicle, so try it out. Perform the "driving compartment drill". Make sure the seats,

21

controls, and instrumentation are suitable or adjustable to suit you. Take it for a test drive. Can you check the blind spots easily? Are all the controls within easy reach? Do the seats support you comfortably? Check the road-handling and maneuverability; try parallel parking.

As you can see, there are many factors to consider when deciding to buy a vehicle. Do not rush into this purchase. Think carefully. Do your research. You will own this vehicle for some time, make sure your choice is a mature one.

NEW OR USED VEHICLES

Once you have given careful thought to the kind of vehicle you will purchase, the next step is to consider whether to buy a new or used one. A new vehicle costs more than a comparable used model; however, warranties and guaranties usually mean the new model will cost less

in maintenance. If properly maintained, it will last longer. The used model has a lower purchase price, lower depreciation per year and lower insurance cost.

BUYING A NEW VEHICLE

With the make, model and options already chosen, you must find a reputable, reliable and, if possible, conveniently located dealer. This will permit you to receive competent and courteous service at the time of purchase, during the warranty period and when routine maintenance is required. Check local consumer groups and/or ask people that you know for suggestions.

Visit a local showroom. Check out and test drive the vehicle as mentioned earlier. Get quotes on the model and the desired options. Don't be pressured into buying a vehicle in stock with extras if a base model is sufficient.

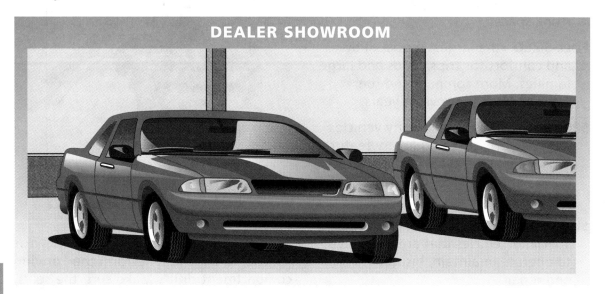

DEALER SHOWROOM

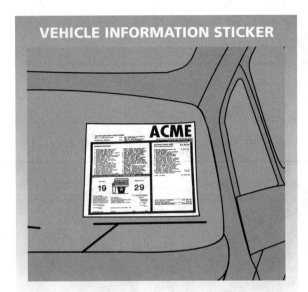

VEHICLE INFORMATION STICKER

If a low financing rate is offered, ask if you can have a rebate on the price if you pay cash. Ask to see an owner's manual and check required maintenance schedules and warranties thoroughly.

Leave the showroom and prepare to visit several others. Be prepared to negotiate the final price. The final price should be somewhere between dealer cost and the suggested (sticker) retail price. Keep in mind that you can often get a good deal at the end of the month or the end of the model year. After several quotes, negotiate the best possible price.

BUYING A USED VEHICLE

Shopping for a used vehicle can provide good service for less money, but it is a little more complicated. You can buy a used model from a dealership, a used-car dealer or a private owner. The dealers offer a warranty for a limited amount of

time which is not the case with a private owner, where the price is usually lower. The price of used vehicles will vary depending on the model year, wear and tear, mileage and general condition.

USED VEHICLE
SUGGESTED RETAIL PRICE

$1499.⁹⁹

Check the "Blue or Red Book" (dealers, banks and insurance agents) as well as the local papers for the usual price range.

Check the vehicle thoroughly for all of the following items:

• **The body**- new paint may indicate rust or a collision. Bubbles or ripples suggest rust underneath.

• **The tires**- uneven wear signals steering or suspension problems. Worn tires including the spare, are a future replacement expense.

21

CHECKING UNDER THE HOOD

- **The engine**- start it and listen for any unusual operating noises. Check all of the fluid levels, the belts, the hoses and service stickers. Check the color of the exhaust gas- blue signals major engine problems and black-grey indicates a fuel system problem.

- **The control pedals**- excessive wear may indicate stop and go driving (urban) or very high mileage.

- **The controls and accessories**- make sure they are all functioning properly.

- **The doors and windows**- should operate easily without squeaking and close tightly.

- **The transmission**- should engage smoothly without lurching or clunking.

Test drive the vehicle. It should continue straight (on level ground) when you release the steering. The brakes should work effectively (without pulling to the side) with normal pressure and the pedal should feel firm. The steering should not show any signs of looseness or shimmy.

If the vehicle passes this preliminary inspection, have the vehicle tested at a reputable diagnostic center or by your own trusted mechanic. A list of necessary repairs and their cost can then be added to or negotiated into the sale price. You will then be in a position to make an informed decision on the purchase.

Usually, you can expect an extra thousand dollars in repairs in the first year of ownership of a used vehicle.

Financing your Purchase

The least expensive way to buy a vehicle is with cash. You might put a fixed amount of money aside each month in a special savings account until you have accumulated the desired amount. For most people, some type of financing has to be arranged to buy a new or late-model vehicle. This can be obtained from banks, savings and loan associations, credit unions, finance companies, and often from the vehicle dealership.

You cannot finance the total purchase price; the limit is usually 80 percent- 20 percent is your minimum down payment. The larger the down payment, the less that needs to be financed; therefore, your purchase will cost you less. The lender will usually require **collateral** (something of value to secure the loan) in case the loan is not repaid. If the vehicle is offered as collateral, the lender retains the certificate of title until the loan is paid in full.

If you are a full-time student, the lender will require a responsible adult to **co-sign the loan**. Young adults who lack a sufficient credit rating may also need someone else to co-sign.

Shop around for your loan; interest and other charges vary. Get a written statement of the interest rate and other charges as well as the amount of your monthly payments and the length of the loan. Find out if it can be repaid without any penalty charges. Remember **the higher the rate, the more you borrow and the longer it takes to repay** are all factors that increase the total cost of financing your vehicle.

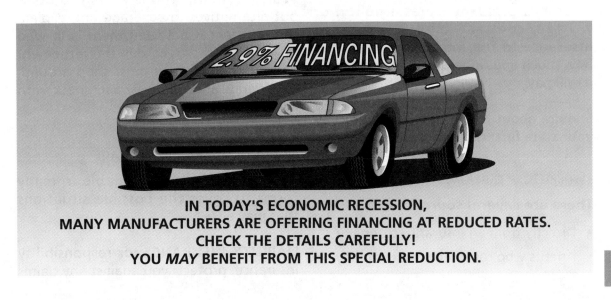

IN TODAY'S ECONOMIC RECESSION,
MANY MANUFACTURERS ARE OFFERING FINANCING AT REDUCED RATES.
CHECK THE DETAILS CAREFULLY!
YOU *MAY* BENEFIT FROM THIS SPECIAL REDUCTION.

SAFETY TIPS

If, as the owner of a vehicle, you secure a loan and use the vehicle as collateral for the said loan, the registered owner or secure party must apply to the department for a corrected certificate of title (usually within ten days).

Insuring Your Vehicle

All states require proof that an owner is capable of paying in case he/she injures a person or damages property in a collision.

Some states permit the proprietor to put up a deposit of cash, a bond, or stocks of a fixed amount. Most drivers carry auto insurance. They pay a **premium**, or fee, to provide protection from financial losses which may arise from a collision or mishap in which they are involved. The insurance company issues a **policy**, or written contract, and a proof of insurance to the individual indicating how much and under what circumstances it will pay.

Enquire about the insurance required by your state financial responsibility laws.

WHERE TO ACQUIRE INSURANCE

There are several sources:

- Directly from an insurance company
- Agents who represent one company
- Agents who represent two or more companies
- Brokers who do business with many companies
- Auto clubs which may also issue insurance
- Employers, unions or fraternal organizations offering group plans

Whatever your choice, deal with someone who takes the time to answer your questions, who is willing to point out alternatives in coverage and explain the differences between them, and who has a good track record in the settlement of claims. Again you must shop around, ask friends and relatives, and check with consumer groups.

KINDS OF INSURANCE COVERAGE

Vehicle insurance is available in many forms to cover the possible situations that may arise.

LIABILITY INSURANCE, or responsibility insurance, protects you against any claims

21

that may arise when you are held responsible for a mishap or collision. It comes in two forms: **bodily injury liability** (injuries to other people whether pedestrians or passengers) and **property damage liability** (repairing or replacing other people's property including public property).

Both of these will also pay legal fees, court costs and lost wages up to the maximum of your insurance coverage. **The minimum state requirements are insufficient as you will be held personally responsible for any claims that exceed your policy coverage.**

COLLISION INSURANCE pays for repair or replacement of your vehicle, regardless of whether you are at fault, involved in a collision with an uninsured driver or the victim of a hit and run. (Uninsured motorist insurance is more complete coverage including your bodily injury.)

Because of the increasing cost of this coverage, most insurance companies offer a **deductible** policy (the insured is required to pay the first $50 to $500). The higher this deductible; the lower the insurance premium will be.

COMPREHENSIVE INSURANCE protects you from losses due to vandalism, theft, fire, floods, or windstorms. Once again, a deductible will affect the cost of this coverage.

MEDICAL PAYMENT INSURANCE is a specific policy covering medical, hospital, or funeral costs. It covers you, your passengers, and your family in case of collisions causing injury or death.

NO FAULT INSURANCE has been adopted in many states. In this plan, you and your passengers receive payment for your adjusted claims directly from your own company regardless who is responsible. The advantages are faster settlement of claims and lower cost of insurance. **This does not, however, prevent injured parties from suing for damages.**

TOWING INSURANCE covers the cost of on-road repairs, as well as the cost of having your vehicle towed to the repair shop of your choice.

Insurance is not a simple matter. Since

SAFETY TIPS

Insurance is required by law in all states. Many states will not issue license plates for a vehicle without proof of financial responsibility. Moreover, your liability from a collision could far exceed your ability to pay. Protect yourself and your loved ones. Purchase sufficient insurance coverage. Increased coverage is less expensive than you may think. Ask your agent or broker!

21

SAFETY TIPS

Evidence of financial responsibility (usually proof of insurance) must be presented, upon request, to a law enforcement officer or to another party when involved in a collision. Make sure you carry it with you whenever you are driving a vehicle (whether you are the owner or operator).

each person's situation is unique, this means that you must arrange your coverage to meet your individual needs.

THE COST OF INSURANCE

Insurance companies use statistics to determine the cost of their insurance premiums.

The following factors are also used in determining the cost:

- **YOUR AGE**- rates change as you get older. The youngest drivers pay the highest premiums.

- **DRIVING RECORD**- traffic violations, collisions, previous claims, etc. will increase your rates.

- **VEHICLE USAGE**- if you drive to work, car pool, or use your vehicle for pleasure only; your premium will reduce accordingly. Higher mileage usually means you will pay higher premiums.

- **MARITAL STATUS**- married persons pay lower premiums.

- **GENDER**- women drive less often and shorter distances than men, and have fewer collisions. They therefore pay lower rates.

- **YOUR VEHICLE**- the more expensive the vehicle; the higher the premium will be. Sports models also cost more to insure.

- **YOUR RESIDENCE**- people residing in high density population areas pay higher rates.

- **SPECIAL DISCOUNTS**- some insurance companies offer discounts for air-bags, brake systems (ABS), alarm systems, having completed a Traffic Safety Education (TSE) program, etc.

Despite the relative high cost of insurance coverage, make sure that you have adequate protection before driving your vehicle in the HTS.

SAFETY TIPS

If an owner or operator fails to show proof of financial responsibility when required, he/she may receive a citation (in most states). The court will dismiss the charge if proof is provided that a liability insurance policy was in effect when the citation was issued.

21

NTSA
International

Review

TERMS TO REMEMBER - WRITE A SHORT DEFINITION FOR EACH OF THE FOLLOWING :

- Status symbol
- Budget
- Rental
- Depreciation
- Warranty

- Consumer groups
- Test drive
- Vehicle options
- Diagnostic center
- Financing

- Interest
- Collateral
- Insurance premium
- Insurance policy
- Insurance claims

SUMMARY

Buying a vehicle is a major decision that requires serious consideration. Finances, transportation needs, the type of vehicle and the operating costs are all factors. Safety features should also be a major consideration. Take the time to examine all the details carefully as you will own the vehicle for a long time.

TEST A- ANSWER THE FOLLOWING QUESTIONS.

1. A) What are the different types of vehicles available on the market?
   B) What are the advantages and disadvantages of each of these?

2. A) How should you proceed to purchase a new vehicle?
   B) What are the steps in purchasing a used vehicle?

3. A) What sources are available to finance a vehicle?
   B) What should you check before deciding?

4. What should you check before deciding on your insurance coverage?

TODAY'S HANDBOOK PLUS WORKBOOK

Check your comprehension and mastery of the contents of this chapter by completing the corresponding exercise that is found in the complement to the TODAY'S HANDBOOK PLUS:

TODAY'S HANDBOOK PLUS WORKBOOK

Complete the exercise on Page 115. If necessary, review the chapter when uncertain of an answer and refer to your instructor for further guidance.

Student notes

_____
_____
_____
_____
_____
_____
_____
_____
_____
_____
_____
_____
_____
_____
_____
_____
_____
_____
_____
_____
_____
_____
_____
_____
_____

22

Planning a Trip

One of the prime reasons for purchasing a vehicle is the freedom to drive where you want when you want. The ability to set your own timetable and to set out at a moments notice. The problem is that traveling on a trip, whether 20 miles or 500 miles, requires some special preparation.

The pre-driving checks and regular verifications that you perform assure the normal operation of your vehicle. High speed driving puts extra stress on all of the mechanical systems. The last thing you would want is a breakdown when you are far from home and at the mercy of unknown service technicians. Prepare your vehicle.

Extended high speed driving is also more stressful for the driver. Proper planning and foresight will avoid uncertainty and an unpleasant experience. Prepare yourself.

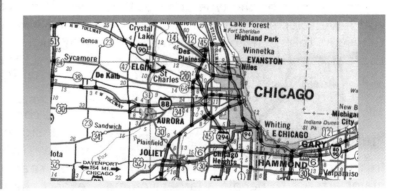

AFTER COMPLETING THIS CHAPTER, THE STUDENT MUST BE ABLE TO UNDERSTAND AND APPLY DESTINATION DRIVING TECHNIQUES WITH RESPECT TO:

- **the selection of a safe route.**
- **the preparation of the vehicle and him/her self.**
- **planning the trip.**

Choosing a Safe Route

Whenever you plan to drive a vehicle, you must consider where you are going and the safest possible route to use. A route that will present the least number of potential hazards thereby reducing the risk of a misadventure or having to cope with an unforeseen emergency situation.

Always work out the route in advance (use a map); planning the most direct route with the fewest maneuvers will usually diminish the risk. Take into account rush hour traffic, available freeways, one-way streets and problems associated with driving in an urban area. Listen to radio stations that broadcast road and weather reports.

Calculate the length of the trip in miles and calculate the average speed you can expect to travel on the type of roads that you have selected. How long should it take you to reach your destination if there are no unforeseen occurrences. Leave yourself sufficient time (with an extra margin) to reach your destination.

THROUGH STREETS VS. SIDE STREETS

In the city, engineers have designed major arteries to handle a larger volume of traffic. With this in mind, the streets are wider and usually have reserved lanes for left turns. Traffic signal lights control the major intersections. Though traffic is heavier, these streets are safer than side streets which are quieter but may present unforeseen hazards at any time.

Intersections on side streets are usually controlled by stop or yield signs and uncontrolled intersections may can be even riskier to cross.. The presence of parked vehicles may block your vision at the intersection and, at times, may make it difficult to recognize the intersection.

Side streets are residential areas and numerous other road users may be present. Children at play may enter the roadway, vehicles may back into the road, anyone of a myriad of road users may confront your path of travel.

ONE-WAY STREETS VS. TWO-WAY STREETS

One-way streets usually present less of a risk than two-way streets simply because of the absence of oncoming traffic that may turn across or swerve into your path of travel. The space available for traffic is also wider than on most two-way roads.

Traffic control devices on these streets are designed to regulate the flow of traffic. Though you must expect that some road users may not obey them (expect the unexpected), you are usually less at risk in a regulated environment. Manage space and select lane positions that require a minimum of adjustments (the lane of least resistance) and one-way streets can be a good choice.

FREEWAYS

Depending on the time of day and the density of the traffic on a particular freeway as well as the length of the journey planned, the controlled environment can offer less risk when utilized properly. Manage the entrance properly, drive in the correct lane while controlling space and then exit properly. This will permit you to use a freeway to get to your destination, possibly a little quicker, in complete safety.

PERSONAL CHOICE

Some drivers will choose to drive on a freeway whenever one is available; others avoid the freeway environment like the plague.

Though you should be competent in all driving environments, you may feel more comfortable (and thus drive more at ease) on one type of road over another. This should also be a factor taken into consideration in your choice of a safe route to your destination.

22-B Preparing the Vehicle

Your vehicle should always be in proper condition. Checks should be performed every time you drive. (See Chapter 7 - Preliminaries and Chapter 9-A - Starting the Engine)

On a short trip, 50 miles or less, these will normally ensure a trouble-free excursion. However, before a longer journey, take the vehicle to your service station to be checked and serviced more completely.

This should include the following:
- Brakes- condition / adjustment
- Tires- condition / inflation (the spare)
- Fluid levels- battery, cooling system, power steering, brake fluid,engine , transmission,and differential
- Belts and hoses
- Front-end- steering and alignment
- Shock absorbers
- Exhaust system
- Lights and electrical system

When leaving, make sure that the fuel tank and windshield washer reservoir are full and you have plenty of windshield washer fluid in reserve. Check your emergency supplies and tool kit. (Chapter 17 - Adverse Conditions) Make sure that you have an extra set of keys on you at all times.

LOADING YOUR VEHICLE

Check the owner's manual for maximum load and recommended tire pressure; adjust the pressure to the specifications. Pack luggage carefully to distribute the weight as evenly as possible. Make sure the load is secure so that it will not move under hard braking or sudden maneuvers. (This is especially important in vans and hatchbacks as luggage is stored in the passenger compartment). Don't block your view to the rear or to the blind spots. Heavy articles should be at the bottom; emergency equipment and spare should be accessible.

Only light luggage should be stored in a car-top carrier and secured using straps. Check the tightness of these after one-half hour and again every time you stop. Be aware that the center of gravity/wind resistance of the vehicle changes with a roof-top carrier and adjust your driving.

TOWING A TRAILER

Towing requires major adjustments by the driver. Quick swerving maneuvers are not possible; stopping distances are increased. Acceleration is slower. Passing maneuvers take longer and need more space. Adjust following distance to a minimum of 4 seconds and scan further ahead. Control speed on downhills and assist the transmission on grades by shifting to the appropriate gear. Practice

reversing with an empty trailer until you are confident in your ability to park.

To tow a trailer consistently, the vehicle requires a tow package. (Suspension, shocks, radiator, differential, etc.) Check the engine oil and transmission fluid frequently. Use an appropriate trailer hitch and attach the safety chains. Install special side-view mirrors and a hook-up for the trailer lights. You may need extra emergency equipment for breakdowns. Check the trailer manual for additional information and the vehicle manual for the maximum towing load.

When packing, load heavy items at the bottom over the axle. Distribute the weight evenly from side to side and secure the load firmly. Check the trailer and vehicle are level when finished. After one-half hour of driving, stop and check the hitch connections, straps, etc. Repeat this verification each time you stop.

Preparing Yourself

Get plenty of rest prior to the journey. Plan your route and rest stops. Avoid rush hour and congested roadways. Be certain to bring extra money or credit cards to cover unforeseen expenses.

Never start out at the time when you would go to sleep. Your alertness is at it lowest at this time. If, while driving, you find yourself becoming fatigued, stop

and rest or change drivers. On long trips, travel with at least one companion who has a valid license and split the driving. Every two hours stop for a break. Make sure you have all necessary documents in a safe and easily accessible place. If you take medication, take along sufficient medicine to last the trip. Make sure your vehicle insurance and medical coverage is proper to the area you will be visiting.

SAFETY TIPS

Be aware of your down time between one and five p.m. and plan to take a break during that period of the day. Since two out of three traffic fatalities occur at night, avoid driving after dark when visibility is limited, and particularly after 11 p.m., when you are more apt to fall asleep.

Planning the Route

On short trips, work out the route in advance especially when traveling to places you have not driven to previously. Take into account rush hour traffic. Use a map to locate the route, highways, streets, etc. that you must use.

Contact road information services to verify the route you have chosen; have alternate routes already planned, just in case something unexpected develops. While driving, listen to a local radio station that carries road and weather reports. Leave yourself plenty of time for the journey.

For longer trips, consult your local auto club or tourist agency. They can supply maps (strip maps) as well as assist you to plan a route that will permit visiting interesting areas along the way, scenic routes or the shortest, quickest possible trip. Recommended service stations and hotels can also be supplied.

Plan your schedule with rest stops and overnight accommodations in advance. Reserve your facilities ahead of time;

make sure you ask about rates and the availability of parking. If you are going to be late, call ahead and cancel if necessary. Don't speed up to make up for lost time or stay on the road longer as this will put you and your passengers in danger. Allow extra time for unexpected stops or delays. Calculate your budget for the entire journey and add an extra amount for unforeseen expenses.

Acquire the necessary maps that will direct you all the way to your destination. Familiarize yourself with these road maps. Get to know the legend (the map key that explains the symbols) that appears as an insert on the map. Study the distance scale and work out the distances to be traveled daily.

When traveling alone, never try to check a road map while driving; pull off the roadway to a rest area or onto the shoulder when this can be done safely.

While on the road, try to start out early each day, eat lightly to avoid drowsiness and allow time to stretch your legs at each stop. Keep your radio tuned to local stations that transmit regular road and weather bulletins (these are often posted on roadside signs). Often they will warn of unforeseen circumstances that you may be able to avoid by a slight detour.

An unplanned scenic stop to avoid being caught in rush hour traffic may get you to your final destination at about the same time without the aggravation. Keep alert. Adapt the SIPDE system to your driving environment and you will enjoy your journey without any mishaps.

ROAD MAP SKILLS

Using road maps is a basic skill that you should master. Acquire a state and local road maps, and complete these exercises.

A) **On the local map**, locate where you live. Determine the map co-ordinates for your home. (Map co-ordinates are located on two sides of the map. One side uses numbers and the other uses letters.)

Place your finger on where you live and then move across the map

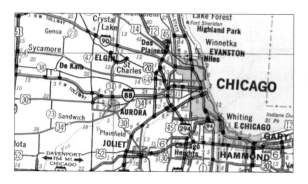

horizontally to locate the letter co-ordinate. Repeat moving vertically to find the number. Put these two together (example D4) and these are the map co-ordinates for your home.

Repeat this exercise for your school, the city hall and the local court house.

B) **Find the map scale.** (This informs you of distance in miles as related to this particular map) Measure the distance, using a ruler, as the "crow flies" from your home to the city hall. That is a straight line measurement. Compare this distance to the scale and convert it to miles.

How far is it? Repeat for your school and the local court house.

C) **Plan the route** that you would use to get from your home to school, the city hall and the court house. Be careful to include the possibility of one-way streets, recent construction, as well as the safest route possible. Notice that the driving distance is much longer than your previous measurement.

Calculate the amount of time required. Allow for the posted speed limit and some extra time for unforeseen delays.

D) **On the state map**, find your community in the map index. It is listed alphabetically. Beside the name, you will find the map co-ordinates for your community. Locate your community on the map. Choose another community where a friend or relative lives outside your local area. Look it up on the index, and locate it on the map.

Are the names written in the same size type? The larger the type , the greater the population. Are the symbols used the same? Check the map insert for the legend as to the meaning of the different symbols.

E) **Measure the distance** between them (as the "crow flies") using the map scale. Check the map mileage chart. If both are listed, the driving distance will be listed. How do they compare?

F) **Plan a route** to travel from your home to the other community. Follow this route on the map. As you move from one place to another, the distance in miles will be printed over the roadway. Mark them down.
When you reach your destination, add them up. This is your traveling distance. How long should this trip take? Allow for unexpected delays, construction, traffic jams, etc.

G) **As you move along your route**, notice that all roadways do not have the same symbols. Check the legend to find the meaning of the different symbols. List the roads that you will use to travel to the other community. What speed limits will be posted on these roadways? What type of traffic can you expect? Plan rest stops.

H) **As a project**, choose an out-of-state city or town. Plan a trip to this locale. Visit a local auto club to obtain a strip map to that location. Create a budget to travel and visit including overnight stops, gas, food, etc. Plan the route. Include some sight-seeing and the necessary rest stops. Compare notes.

I) **Using the internet**; many websites offer helpful trip planning aids; http://maps.google.com/ and http://www.mapquest.com/ are two examples. By entering your starting location and your final destination a route is chosen and listed in a step by step manner describing distances and travel time.

J) **GPS (Global Positioning System)** enables a GPS receiver to determine its location, speed, direction, and time. GPS receivers are now available factory installed or "after market" and give the user immediate access to the vehicles current position. With the vehicle parked enter a destination into the device; a route is planned and the directions are verbally presented.

SAFETY TIPS

Map skills are essential to planning a trip. Remember, you must never consult a map while driving - this will distract you. Ask a passenger to act as navigator. If this is not possible, stop in a safe place before consulting the map.

Review

22-E

- Maximum load
- Tire load
- Trailer
- Tow package

- Trailer hitch
- Safety chain
- Trailer axle
- Roof top carrier

- Auto club
- Map insert
- Map legend
- Map scale

SUMMARY

Choosing a safe route, even on short urban trips, will save frustration as well as diminish the risk. Planning a trip requires preparation to ensure an enjoyable, trouble-free journey.

Your vehicle, how to transport baggage, choosing the route, rest periods or alternate drivers, the finances, as well as the number of hours of driving must be considered carefully.

TEST A- ANSWER THE FOLLOWING QUESTIONS.

1. A) What are the factors that you should consider when planning the route?

2. A) What should you have checked on your vehicle prior to a long trip?
   B) When stowing luggage, name the basic guidelines to follow.
   C) If you intend to tow a trailer, what extra preparations should you make?

3. A) How should you prepare yourself for a long trip?

4. What steps should you follow in planning your route?

TODAY'S HANDBOOK PLUS WORKBOOK

Check your comprehension and mastery of the contents of this chapter by completing the corresponding exercise that is found in the complement to the **TODAY'S HANDBOOK PLUS:**

TODAY'S HANDBOOK PLUS WORKBOOK

Complete the exercise on Page 116. If necessary, review the chapter when uncertain of an answer and refer to your instructor for further guidance.

ABS An anti-lock computerized brake system.

Acceleration lane A highway merging lane to allow drivers to increase speed to blend with traffic.

Air bag A passive restraint device that inflates with air to cushion the occupants in the event of collision.

Antifreeze A chemical mixed with water to prevent freezing and corrosion in the cooling system.

Automatic transmission A system that shifts through the forward gears as the vehicle speed increases.

BAC (blood alcohol concentration) The percentage of alcohol in a person's blood,

Back-up lights The white lights on the rear of a vehicle that come on when transmission is in reverse.

Banked curve The roadway slopes down toward the inside of the curve to help overcome inertia.

Basic speed limit The speed, below the absolute limit, that is adequate to existing driving conditions.

Blind spots Areas neither visible in the driver's forward field of vision nor in the rear-view mirrors.

Blow out A rapid loss of air pressure in a tire.

Blue book A price guide to the average value of used vehicles.

Brake fade Temporary brake failure due to overheating of pads/shoes caused by hard continuous braking.

Brake system An hydraulic and mechanical system to slow or stop a moving vehicle.

Carbon monoxide A colorless, odorless, tasteless and toxic gas that is a byproduct of combustion.

Center of gravity The point where vehicle weight is balanced.

Clutch A driver control that permits dis-engaging the engine from the transmission (to shift or stop).

Collateral An object of value given as security for a loan.

Collision insurance Protection against damage to one's own vehicle in a crash.

Comprehensive insurance Protection against damage or loss due to theft, vandalism, storms, or fire.

Compromising hazards Low risk involvement with a less serious hazard to avoid involvement with a more serious one.

Cooling system A system to remove excess heat and maintain engine operating temperature.

Countersteering Steering in the opposite direction after an initial steering motion.

Crowned road A road higher in the middle than at the sides.

Deceleration lane An extra lane at exits to allow drivers exiting the highway to reduce speed.

Deductible The sum the insured must pay before the insurance company pays in the event of a claim.

Defogger Electric wires to heat / clear the rear window.

Demerit point system A system to track driver violations and penalize drivers at predetermined limits.

Depreciation The value a vehicle loses due to age and wear and tear.

Diagonal parking Parking spaces arranged at an angle to the curb or other boundary.

Disc brakes Brakes that slow/stop the wheels by squeezing a rotating disc.

Drive train Components that send the engine power to the wheels.

Driving while intoxicated (DWI) Operating a vehicle while the blood alcohol concentration (BAC) is above the legal limit.

Drum brakes Brakes that slow/stop wheel rotation by rubbing curved shoes (pads) against a drum.

Edge lines White lines on the road marking the limit of the roadway.

Emergency brake The parking brake system.

Emergency flashers Hazard lights activate all four turn signals at once to warn of danger or breakdown.

Entrance ramp A roadway leading to an expressway (freeway).

Exhaust system Collects the burnt cylinder gases, directs and releases them behind the vehicle.

Exit ramp A roadway leaving an expressway (freeway).

Expressway A controlled-access, divided highway with multiple lanes in each direction intended for high speed driving (freeway).

Fan belt A rubber band driven by the crankshaft that powers the water pump and the alternator.

Fatigue Temporary physical or mental exhaustion due to lack of rest or sleep.

Field of vision The area the eyes can perceive without moving the eyes or head; approximately 180°.

Financial responsibility laws A law requiring proof of the ability to pay damages resulting from collisions before issuing registration/plates for a vehicle.

First aid Emergency treatment given to an injured person before medical professionals arrive.

Following distance The space that a driver maintains from preceding vehicles (2 or more seconds).

Force of impact The energy that a moving vehicle collides with another.

Friction The resistance to motion between two objects in contact.

Friction point The clutch position when the engine power begins to move the transmission.

Fuel system Stores fuel and supplies the fuel-air mixture to the engine.

Fuse Opena a circuit when current is excessive, to protect equipment. A "burned" fuse must be replaced.

Gear A toothed wheel that meshes with others of varying sizes to transmit (the same, increased or decreased) rotation (speed/power).

Glow Plug A unit to preheat the combustion chamber on diesels.

Ground viewing habit Scanning near the pavement to determine the position of vehicle's wheels and to notice any signs of potential vehicle movement.

Guide signs Signs that inform about location, services, or pts. of interest.

Hallucinogen Affects the senses and distorts vision and perception.

Hazard lights A signaling device that activates all four turn signals to warn of danger or breakdowns.

Headlights White lights mounted on the front of the vehicle that should be illuminated when driving.

Headrest A restraint device attached to the top of the seat back to cushion the head in collisions.

High beams Brighter white lights on the front of the vehicle to see further than low beams.

Highway hypnosis Reduced attention to the driving task caused by long periods of high speed driving.

Hydraulic pressure Pressure exerted on a fluid is transmitted by fluid.

Hydroplaning A layer of water between the tires and the road eliminating traction.

Idle The engine speed when operating without any pressure on the accelerator.

Ignition switch The switch to activate the electrical systems and start the engine.

Ignition system Components that produce, control and distribute the spark that initiates combustion.

Implied consent law A legal requirement that all drivers submit to a blood alcohol concentration (BAC) test when requested.

Inertia The tendency of an object in motion to move in a straight line and one at rest to remain at rest.

International signs Symbolic road signs used in many countries.

In-vehicle exam The DMV practical driving test.

Jaywalking The pedestrian practice of crossing a roadway without regard for rules or signals.
Junction See intersection

Kinetic energy The energy of motion.
Knowledge test A test on signs, signals, road markings and rules of the road at the DMV to acquire an instruction permit (written test).

Lane use signals Lights mounted above lanes to control the flow and direction of traffic.
Legend A key (insert) explaining the symbols / markings used on a map.
Liability insurance Protection from financial loss due to a collision when the you are responsible.
Lubrication system The components that supply oil to the moving parts to prevent damage/overheating.

Margin of safety See safety cushion
Master cylinder Brake system unit where the fluid is stored and pressurized to activate the brakes.
Medical payments insurance Insurance that covers the cost of hospitalization and treatments for injuries incurred during a collision.
Merging The blending of traffic.
Minimizing hazards Reducing risk of a collision from a hazard by adjusting speed and/or lane position.

Neutral The gears are not engaged and cannot transmit power.
Night vision The ability to see clearly, judge depth perception and recover from glare in the dark.
No fault insurance Insurance that pays claims to the insured regardless of responsibility.

Odometer A device indicating the total distance a vehicle has been driven.
Oil filter Device that removes dirt and particles from the oil.
Oil pressure gauge Light/indicator shows the pressure at which the oil is circulating through the engine.
Oil pump A device that forces oil to the moving parts.
Overdriving your headlights Driving at such a high speed at night that you would be unable to stop in the distance illuminated by the headlights.
Owner's manual Manufacturer's booklet giving detailed information about the vehicle, its operation and recommended maintenance.

Parking brake A mechanical unit that acts on the rear wheels to keep them from moving when parked. Also used to slow /stop if the brake system fails.
Passive restraints Safety devices that act without requiring any action by the user.

Peripheral vision Portion of the field of vision outside the central 3o conic vision . Vision to the sides.
Perpendicular parking Parking at a 90o angle to the curb or boundary.
Power train Components transmit the engine power to the wheels.
Premium The sum an individual pays the insurance company for insurance coverage - the policy fee.
Pumping the brake Applying pressure on the brake pedal, releasing the pressure sufficiently to allow the tires to roll and then re-applying the pressure.

Radial tires Tires with the plies straight across the tire parallel to each other encircled by a steel belt.
Radiator A heat exchange unit that stores and cools the engine coolant before it circulates in the engine.
Regulatory sign A sign that controls the flow of traffic at a location.
Reversible lane A lane on which the direction of the traffic flow changes at specific times.
Revocation The cancellation of a driver's license.
Right-of-way Traffic rules determine who should yield to other road users in given situations.
Risk The danger of involvement in a collision.

Safety belt A restraint device to restrain occupants from striking the vehicle interior - seat belts.
Scanning The visual searching of the area around and ahead you.
Separating hazards The technique of dealing with hazards one at a time.
Shock absorbers Devices that limit and stop the bouncing action of the vehicle springs.
Shoulder The strip along the sides of a roadway, paved or unpaved, intended for emergency use only.
SIPDE system A five step driving strategy (scan, identify, predict, decide and execute) to process information and evade potential danger in an organized manner.
Space cushion A traffic free area around the vehicle maintained to have room to maneuver.
Stimulants Drugs speed up the central nervous system.
Suspension The withdrawal of a driver's license for a period of 30 to 90 days due to traffic violations.
Suspension system Components to support the vehicle in a flexible manner absorbing road shocks.
Switchbacks Sharp turns on mountain roads, similar to U-turns, that allow the road to climb a steep slope.

Tailgate Driving too closely behind

another vehicle.
Temperature gauge An indicator light or gauge that displays the engine operating temperature.
Thermostat A device that regulates engine temperature by controlling the flow of coolant to the radiator.
Threshold braking A technique in which the driver applies the brakes just short of locking up.
Title Legal proof of vehicle ownership - certificate of title.
Towing insurance Optional coverage that protects against the cost of on-the-road repairs and towing.
Traction The friction between the tires and the road.
Tread Patterns on the outer surface of tires that contact the road.
Tread wear indicator Bars that appear in tire treads when they are less than 1/16 of an inch deep.
Trip odometer An indicator that registers vehicle mileage since the last time it was reset to zero.
Turnabout A turning maneuver to travel in the opposite direction.
Turn signal Lights activated by the driver to warn of his/her intentions. Also hand signals.
Two second rule Technique for calculating / keeping a minimum following distance in ideal conditions.
Uninsured motorist insurance Protection from financial loss due to a collision caused by a driver who does not have insurance.

U-turn A turnabout maneuver performed by turning left.

Vapor lock Fuel vaporizes in the lines and the system cannot pump it into the carburetor or injectors.
Velocitization The improper sensation of vehicle speed.
Visual acuity The ability to see details up close and from afar.
Visual eye lead time The time and distance that a driver's vision precedes the vehicle.
Visual Tracking Aiming and steering in the desired path of travel.

Warning lights and gauges Dashboard indicators to inform the driver of vehicle condition.
Warning signs Traffic signs that warn of danger ahead.
Water pump A device that circulates the engine coolant.
Wheel alignment Mechanical adjustment of the steering to proprer vehicle specifications.

Yield To give another road user the right-of-way.